Roger Blaney (Ruairí Ó Bléine), son of Mary Ellen and William Patrick Blaney of Lurgan, Co. Armagh, was educated in Lurgan, Armagh and Queen's University, Belfast where he qualified in medicine in 1957. After a number of hospital appointments, including three years in Guy's Hospital, London, he specialised in public health medicine and was head of the Department of Community Medicine at Queen's, Belfast before he took early retirement in 1988. His publications include papers in the medical press, co-authorship of books on public health and he is author of *Belfast: 100 Years of Public Health* (1988). He has written on the history of the Irish Language and has contributed to *An tUltach* and the newspaper *LÁ*. He is married to Brenda Quinn, has two sons and three daughters and lives in Holywood, Co. Down.

D1492873

Robert MacAdam
1808–1895

PRESBYTERIANS
AND THE
IRISH LANGUAGE

ROGER BLANEY

ULSTER HISTORICAL FOUNDATION
and
ULTACH TRUST

Published 1996, reprinted 1997 and 2012
by Ulster Historical Foundation,
49 Malone Road, Belfast BT9 6RY
www.ancestryireland.com
www.booksireland.org.uk

in association with
the ULTACH Trust
6–10 Sráid Liam/William Street
Ceathrú na hArdeaglaise/Cathedral Quarter
Béal Feirste/Belfast BT1 1PR
www.ultach.org

© Roger Blaney
ISBN: 978-1-908448-55-2

This book has received support from the Cultural Traditions Programme of
the Community Relations Council which aims to encourage acceptance
and understanding of cultural diversity.

Typeset by FPM Publishing
Cover and Design by Dunbar Design
Printed by Berforts Group Ltd

CONTENTS

LIST OF ILLUSTRATIONS

FRONTISPIECE

1 Robert MacAdam (1808–1895)

SECTION A

2 John Abernethy 1680–1740
3 James Bryson 1730–1796
4 William Neilson 1774–1821
5 William H. Drummond 1778–1865
6 John Edgar D.D. 1798–1866
7 Norman McLeod D.D. 1783–1862
8 Dr Reuben J. Bryce 1797–1888
9 James MacAdam 1801–1861
10 Billy Parish Church
11 *Cleas an Chopáin* (Cop Tossing), engraving, dated 1842, by C.W. Sharpe based on the original painting by N.J. Crowley. Mary Ann McCracken is said to have sat for the gypsy.

SECTION B

12 Postcard from Aden written in Irish by William MacArthur to his son
13 Sir William P. MacArthur (1884–1964) as a young officer
14 The Health Caravan, organised by Lady Aberdeen, inscribed in English on one side and Irish on the other. *c.* 1907
15 The prize-winning *seanchaí*, Bridget Costello, at the 1910 Oireachtas captured by Robert Lynd

SECTION C

16 Rose Young (Róis Ní Ógáin) 1865–1947
17 Robert Lynd 1879–1949
18 Aoidhmín Mac Gréagóir (1884–1950) in Ranafast, Co. Donegal, 1936.
19 Seán Pasker taking an Irish class at the Y.M.C.A
20 Unveiling a plaque to Róis Ní Ógáin at Galgorm Castle
21 Rev. Patricia McBride, Irish-speaking Presbyterian, and Mr Risteard Ó Glaisne, Methodist preacher, 17 November 1995

PREFACE
to the
THIRD PRINTING

The reader is reminded that this book is a reprint of the initial publication of 1996 and not a new edition. With regard to the final sections on present day events, new details have become available and many events have occurred which would suggest that a new edition is desirable. One has seen Presbyterian church services in Irish grow up and flourish. Presbyterians are taking a greater part than ever in the promotion and use of the language, in learning it and taking part in Irish language activities. For example, the 'Tor ar Lasadh' (The Burning Bush) holds regular monthly services in Irish which are very well attended. It is significant that the Cultúrlann, set up in a Presbyterian Church in West Belfast, has been named after Robert MacAdam representing Irish speaking Presbyterians, jointly with Cardinal Ó Fiaich who similarly supported the language.

The decision to publish a reprint at this time is due to the steady and sustained demand for this book which has resulted in it now being out of print. However, the opportunity has been taken to rectify some typographical errors and generally to improve the graphical presentations, including a newly designed cover.

PREFACE AND ACKNOWLEDGMENTS

THE ASSOCIATION OF PRESBYTERIANS with the Irish language is a relatively unpublicised subject. The impression of the majority of people would be that there is so little connection between the two that the material could be dealt with adequately in a short article. It is hoped that the present work will help to correct this impression. The truth is that a considerable amount has been written on the subject; yet most of the material is, for the most part, inaccessible to an English-speaking readership, partly because it has been written in Irish. One of the greatest published sources, Ó Buachalla's book, *Béal Feirste Cois Cuain* has never been translated.[1]

In addition much information is available only in the form of articles in historical journals, making it difficult to unearth. Ó Snodaigh's pamphlet, *Hidden Ulster*, is a very useful summary, but it deals with Protestants generally.[2] Perhaps the most useful source of all, the thesis of the Rev. Jim Stothers appears, from its lack of citation, to have been sitting unopened on the library shelf for a number of years now.[3] An added difficulty is the problem of identifying individuals as Presbyterian. What Hempton and Hill had to say could be applied even more to Presbyterians. 'Indeed the concern of some Methodists and Evangelicals for the preservation of the Irish language, not only on grounds of missionary expediency, is a forgotten aspect of Irish cultural history.'[4]

In just over 70 years, the effect of the division of Ireland by the Government of Ireland Act (1920) has been to give a sense of distorted perspective to history. Particularly among younger people, there is a feeling that Ireland has always been sharply divided into Protestant/Unionist/British/Northern Ireland, on one side, and on the other, a Catholic/Nationalist/Gaelic/South of Ireland. This has made it easier for many commentators to sound credible while they interpret the history of Ireland through present-day eyes.

The Stalinist British and Irish Communist Organisation once promulgated the theory that there are two nations in Ireland.[5] However, it might be just as plausible to argue that there are at least three nations in terms of class distinction; that Ireland is also divided deeply from east to west and that, socially, there are numerous divisions in terms of urban/rural contrasts. The 'two nations' theory was also expounded by Heslinga.[6] Yet it is hard to escape the conclusion that the fact that there are two distinct states in Ireland and that these resulted from deep political disagreements, have confounded the discussion. The cultural differences may not be regarded as significant and do not coincide with political boundaries.

From prehistoric times Ireland has been something of a 'melting' pot of races, classes, cultures, languages, religions and beliefs. So there is nothing new about having differences. At the same time groups who live together for centuries inevitably develop great similarities and a sense of common identity. This should also be recognised.

The choice of Presbyterians for the present analysis is not intended to suggest that they were more active or interested than any other denomination. The topic was chosen because of the particular experience of the author. During my time as a student at Queen's University, my own awareness was sharpened by meeting and becoming close friends of Irish-speaking Presbyterian students, both in the University Gaelic Society and in the Y.M.C.A. Gaelic Fellowship.

It is intended that this book will help to inform those who have no knowledge of Irish and its history and that it will hearten and encourage those who still use and love the language. It is hoped that the information revealed will show that, contrary to the belief of some, the language is a bond between different denominations.

*****

In the course of researching and writing this book I have been assisted and encouraged by many people, to whom I am most grateful.

For help on the Bryson family and others I am much indebted to Joseph Clint of the Department of Epidemiology and Public Health, Queen's University, Belfast, to Dr Paul Darragh of the same Department who directed me to many references, and to Professor Alun Evans who gave help on the Aberdeens.

I am grateful to Bertha Geddes and to Barry Kinghan for details about the Y.M.C.A. Gaelic Fellowship.

I also wish to thank Rev. Mr Clarke, Presbyterian Minister Dundalk; Mr A.B. Swan, Ravensdale; Rev. Ian Hart of Ballyhenry Presbyterian Church; Rev. John Barkley; Maolcholaim Scott.

My brother, James Blaney, provided me with innumerable references, mainly from newspapers including the *Belfast News Letter*, and the *Down Recorder*.

Dr Brian Trainor of the Ulster Historical Foundation has been most patient and understanding.

I owe a debt of great gratitude to Rev. James Stothers who generously gave permission to me to copy his most valuable unpublished thesis and for allowing me to use it and quote from it. I have relied very heavily on his excellent work.

It was Rev. John Ross of Holywood High Street Church who first alerted me to the existence of Rev. Stothers' thesis.

My grateful thanks are due to the following who helped in various ways: Hal MacMaster of Holywood; Robert Bonar of the Presbyterian Historical Society; Noel Nesbitt, formerly of the Ulster Museum; Irene Whelan; Ian Mac G. Binnie; Diarmaid Ó Doibhlin; Eileen Black; Rev. Robert F. Jackson; Fionnuala Nic Shuibhne for advice on Robert MacAdam; Dr Kieran Devine for extensive information on Aoidhmín Mac Gréagóir and his help with computing; Rev. J.W. Nelson of Larne for details on William Hamilton Drummond; Dr Eamon Phoenix for data on Rev. Lyttle etc.; Colán MacArthur for details of his father; Dr Jan Duncan and Patrick Scott for help on Robert Lynd; my son, Garrett Blaney, for practical assistance and advice on computing; Professor Ronnie Buchanan; and Doreen McDowell in the Gamble Library.

Lastly I am deeply appreciative of the support and tolerance of my family. In addition my wife, Brenda, read every word of the manuscript, corrected many errors and gave most helpful advice.

I

INTRODUCTION

THERE ARE TWO INDIGENOUS LANGUAGES spoken in Ireland, north and south. These are Irish and English, both of which are recognised as official languages in the Republic of Ireland.[1] Although the Presbyterian Church is a national church of Ireland, only a small minority belong to the 'Southern' Presbyteries of Donegal, Monaghan, Dublin and Munster.[2] In other words Presbyterianism is weakest where Irish is more likely to be strong. On the positive side Stothers points out:

> Yet, as is well known, most of the Presbyterians would trace their ancestry to Scotland where on any Sunday there can be found Presbyterian congregations where the service is in Gaelic from start to finish, and where there is nothing unusual about a Gaelic-speaking Presbyterian. Indeed, the strongholds of the language are the Protestant Churches in the Highlands and Islands with their Gaelic Bible, Catechism, metrical psalms (1694), and sermon. When we learn that the Lecturer in Irish and Acting Head of the Department of Irish and Celtic Languages in Trinity College, Dublin is a Presbyterian minister, the Rev. T.P. McCaughey, we begin to see that adherence to Presbyterianism and the use of Irish are not incompatible.[3]

To set the present day scene, it may be useful to examine the contemporary status of the Irish language in Ireland.

The Irish language has been spoken here for the last 2,000 years. Like any living language it has been used by all kinds of people for every type of purpose: for prayer and for cursing; by rich and by poor; by unionists and by nationalists; for folklore and for science. It is eminently suitable for expressing emotions and sensitive feelings, as it is for communicating in scientific terminology. An appreciation, even partly or indirectly, of the great manuscript and printed material in Irish is essential for a full understanding of the history, development and character of all of the people of this island.

Detailed figures of the extent of present day Irish-speaking are given in the Appendix. In summary, over one million persons in the Republic declare themselves as Irish-speakers, but only a proportion of them speak the language on a day to day basis, perhaps about 60,000. As returned in the 1991 census for Northern Ireland the number of persons with knowledge of Irish totals 142,000. Of these, 79,000 can read, write and speak the language. There had been no question on an individuals' ability to understand Irish since the 1911 census when a total of 30,000 Irish-speakers was returned.

Four hundred years ago Irish was the universal language of Ulster. Prior to the Plantation of Ulster, the Irish language was stronger in Ulster than in any other part of Ireland. Ulster chiefs who visited the English court either used an interpreter or spoke in Latin. Since the foundation of the Kingdom of Dál Riata in 500, Ulster shared a common language and culture with Gaelic Scotland, a relationship which still survives.

The language in the North lost its patronage when the Ulster Chiefs, who had been defeated at the Battle of Kinsale, set sail from Lough Swilly on 4 September 1607, never again to return ('The Flight of the Earls'). Their lands were confiscated and given to planters from England and Scotland who brought with them the English, Gaelic and Scots languages. Other parts of Ireland had previously been planted but on a smaller scale, and the majority of newcomers assimilated so that they were '... more Irish than the Irish themselves.' For example, Gerald fitz Maurice Fitzgerald, 3rd Earl of Desmond (d. 1398), was a Norman Baron, but was known in Irish as Gearóid Iarla and was a noted poet in Irish.[4]

In the year 1600, about 90 per cent of the population of Ireland were Irish-speaking. So, of a total population in the region of 600,000[5] the Irish-speakers would have numbered approximately 540,000. Using various sources[6, 7] and extrapolations based on a graph devised by Stothers[8] it is possible to show that, despite the Irish-speaking proportion continuing to fall from 90 per cent, around 1600, to about 53 per cent in 1800, the actual number of Irish-speakers grew substantially. This was because of the great increase of the Irish population. Thus, between 1600 and 1800 Irish-speakers grew from

0.5 million to 2.6 million. By the eve of the Great Famine in 1845, the number of Irish-speakers had reached an all-time peak of at least 3.5 million. Although the actual figures can be open to question, there is no doubt about the trends. The Great Famine was a major blow to the language and reduced the speakers by one million.[9] After the Famine the continuous decline in total population, along with a sustained fall in the Irish-speaking fraction, caused the number of speakers of Irish to fall rapidly until in 1911, the census showed a figure of 0.58 million (13.3 per cent of the population). It should be remembered, however, that this was still larger than the number of 0.54 million in 1600, when 90 per cent of Ireland was Irish-speaking.

FORTUNES OF THE PRESBYTERIANS

The Presbyterian population of Ireland grew from under 10,000 in the early seventeenth century to over 420,000 in the late twentieth century. Growth was not smooth, however, and there were two major troughs. The first was a result of the 1641 Uprising when the native Irish, under the leadership of Sir Felim O'Neill, attacked the settlers. At first the Scots were immune, but later were treated as part of the enemy. Modern historians consider that there was considerable bloodshed and suffering on both sides and have revised downwards the estimated number of casualties among settlers as some 4,000 killed and 8,000 dying of exposure and disease following the rising.[10] Between a third and a half of these would have been Presbyterians, representing what Holmes reports as, '… a horrific experience which etched itself upon the folk memories of the Ulster Scots.'[11]

The other fall in Presbyterian numbers occurred in the seventeenth century. They suffered, as did Catholics, under a penal code. For example, the Test Act of 1704 required the holders of all public offices to take the Sacrament of the Lord's Supper according to the rights of the Episcopal Church.[12] It was not until 1780 that the Protestant Dissenter Relief Act was passed, repealing the sacramental test.[13] Landlords and bishops used their influence in the Irish Parliament to prevent any improvement in the legal position of Presbyterians.[14] Difficulties were put in the way of building meeting-houses. For example, leases of episcopal lands in Derry had a clause prohibiting leases to, '... any mass or popish priest, or to any minister or teacher dissenting from the Church of Ireland.'[15] Episcopalians tried to deprive Presbyterian ministers of the right to solemnise marriage. Such marriages were stigmatised as invalid, the partners described as living in sin, and the children classified as illegitimate.[16] It was not until 1842 that an Act was passed confirming the validity of marriages celebrated by dissenting ministers.[17] In addition to these disabilities and restrictions of liberty, economic conditions were unfavourable. These included tithes which by law had to be paid to the Established Church by persons of all religions. For these reasons emigration among Presbyterians in the eighteenth century was significant. One calculation is that at least 100,000, and possibly as many as 250,000, left Ulster to settle in North America in the period leading up to the American War of Independence. By the end of the century about one sixth of the white U.S. population claimed to be of Scotch-Irish descent.[18]

From these experiences, suffered by both the Catholic and Presbyterian peoples of Ireland, it might have been concluded that they would have been brought closer together. For a while this was true, and their common grievances were expressed in the formation of the United Irishmen in the 1790s. Both denominations, and also some Episcopalians, took part in the 1798 Rebellion. However, the conduct of the uprising reputedly took on a sectarian aspect, especially in Wexford and, after the Act of Union of 1800, Presbyterians grew away from Catholics and closer to Episcopalians, through institutions such as the Orange Order. Nevertheless, for most of the nineteenth century Protestants generally in Ireland, while favouring the Union with Great Britain, had no doubts about their Irishness. Catholic Emancipation (1829), followed by agitation for repeal of the Union, the Home Rule movement, and finally the 1916 Rebellion were followed by the partition of Ireland in 1920.

However, the Presbyterian Church in Ireland is a national church and knows no border in its work.[19] The official policy of the Church to the Irish language was stated in 1965:

It has always been the policy of the Irish Mission to provide the Scriptures for people in the Gaelic where they are required. Colporteurs are provided with these in Gaelic. The Mission has always endeavoured to have on the staff at least one versed in the Irish language. The Presbyterian Church co-operates with the governments of Northern and Southern Ireland in anything which will preserve the art, culture and literature of the country, and which will instill in people a pride in, and love for, their land ... .[20]

METHOD

Having looked briefly at the separate fortunes of the Irish language and the Presbyterians in Ireland, this book aims to show how the two impinged on each other over a period of nearly four hundred years. Sources have been already mentioned including census records. The very many printed Presbyterian histories often make oblique references to Irish; but it is a subject which is usually dealt with indirectly. The historian's problem is that contemporary accounts tend not to inform about the language used.

John Wesley did not explain how he could, in the 1760s, address the monoglot Irish-speakers of the West, as he himself had no Irish. He did sometimes mention a person standing beside him as he preached, who we must conclude to have been an interpreter.

Every attempt will be made in this work to weigh up the evidence, on the understanding that there are so little data available that the task is often difficult and, sometimes, impossible.

II
ARRIVAL AND SETTLEMENT
SEVENTEENTH CENTURY

PRE 1642

Before the year 1642 Presbyterians were not formally organised as a separate and distinctive church in Ireland. This fluidity had originated from Scotland where the various phases of religious change had blurred the edges between episcopalianism and presbyterianism. Indeed, for a while in Scotland, one could find Presbyterian bishops. It was, therefore, not unusual to find Anglican clergymen in Ireland with clear Presbyterian leanings and, on the other hand, Presbyterian ministers who acted as Established Church clergy with the approval of the bishops. Stothers points out that some of the latter were English, such as Walter Travers, Henry Avey and William Temple, who were Provosts of Trinity College and, at the same time, Puritan divines.[1]

All of this flexibility came to an end with the advent of the first presbytery at Carrickfergus on 10 June 1642. Before that date, under the system of 'Prescopalianism',[2] it would be difficult to separate the Anglican involvement with Irish from that of the Presbyterians. Reid, the Presbyterian historian, praised the Reformed Church for, at last, making attempts in 1571 to communicate with the native Irish in their own language, when Nicholas Walsh and John Kearney, dignitaries of St Patrick's Cathedral, Dublin, brought into Ireland a printing press with a set of Irish types, the first ever cast. The plan was to print the liturgy in Irish and to designate a special church in the chief town of every diocese where Divine service would be conducted in Irish.[3] This information he had taken from Ware's *Annals of Ireland*,[4] but the outcome of the plan was not reported on. Apparently it was Queen Elizabeth herself who sent over the font of Irish types '... in hope that God in mercy would raise up some to translate the New Testament into their mother tongue'.[5] However, the first book to use the Queen Elizabeth Irish type was *Aibidil Gaoidheilge agus Caiticiosma*, i.e.

The Irish alphabet and catechism, published in 1571. The New Testament in Irish was not published until 1602, but it was printed in the Queen Elizabeth Irish type, as was the Book of Common Prayer in Irish when it appeared in 1608.[6]

Whatever was accomplished through publications by the Established Church, relatively little was done in the way of preaching and Reid is only one of countless authorities who attributed the failure of the Reformation in Ireland to the lack of use of the native tongue to communicate with the people.[7] In his commentary on this period Stothers has identified more than the previously recognised number of Gaelic preachers from the Highlands of Scotland who were active in Ireland. Christopher Anderson had mentioned only one, Donald McFeig, but Stothers discovered that there were at least four ministers in Ulster who knew Irish, with 14 incumbencies having assistants or reading-ministers who knew Irish. The diocese with the biggest concentration of parishes with Irish-speaking clergy and assistants was Raphoe in Co. Donegal. Here was Andrew Knox, a Scottish bishop who had been appointed to Raphoe in 1610. He, in turn, encouraged other Scots ministers to come over.[8] Three of these were also Irish-speakers and, through their use of the vernacular, both priests and lay persons were converted. Two of the clerical assistants in the Diocese of Raphoe were priests who had turned Presbyterian.

One of the Irish-speaking Scots was Dugald Campbell of Letterkenny. The congregation was also known as Conwall.[9] He seemed to move backwards and forwards between Ireland and Scotland and to be equally happy to preach to the Gaelic Scots or the Irish-speaking Irish.[10] He was a minister of Presbyterian convictions who, from 1622, was able to preach in Irish.[11] John Ross, another Scotsman, was in the year 1622 a reading-minister in Irish in Gartan, Co. Donegal, birthplace of St. Colm Cille. His superior was William Cunningham of Gartan and Ramelton, who had more than usual Presbyterian leanings. We do not know if Cunningham knew Irish,[12] but it is clear that he was very keen to employ an Irish-reader. However, Stothers has shown from the Ulster Visitation Book[13] that between 35 per cent and 50 per cent of parishes in the Diocese of Raphoe had Irish-speaking ministers or assistants.[14] He also showed that Armagh and Derry had Irish-speaking clergy. He was of the opinion that the actual use of Irish in services was underestimated, because many converted priests with totally Irish names, then synonymous with Irish-speaking, were not listed.[15]

Although the exact number of Ulster parishes in which Irish was employed in the early seventeeth century cannot be known for certain, we can be sure that Irish was less likely to be used in the heavily planted and settled areas. Conversely, those ministers of Presbyterian leanings working in mainly Irish-speaking areas were willing to provide services and preach in Irish whenever possible. Scots-speaking congregations would often have a Gaelic-speaking minority. Linguistic pressures on them would mean that in time they or their children would learn Scots or English. The Irish-speaking congregations would include a significant proportion of Gaelic-speakers from Scotland. In conclusion therefore, before the year 1642 it is clear that 'there was a certain amount of preaching in Irish both by and to Presbyterians.'[16]

POST 1642

As observed earlier, the year 1642 saw a radical change in the position of Presbyterianism in Ireland, because on 10 June the Army Presbytery was constituted in Carrickfergus. This had been formed by the chaplains and officer-elders of General Robert Munro's army who had come to Ireland to put down the 1641 Rebellion and protect the Irish protestants.[17] From then onwards the number of congregations and of ministers grew consistently in number until by the end of the century there were 130 congregations overseen by six presbyteries: Down, Antrim, Belfast, Laggan, Route and Tyrone.[18]

Many converts were made among the native Irish, many by default, because the struggling Presbyterian Church had neither the ability nor the inclination to have a positive policy of conversion. Much of the recruitment from the native Irish came because of the weakness of the Roman Catholic Church and its inability to provide sufficient clergy or services to meet the needs of the native Irish. The first native Irish speaker to become a Presbyterian minister was Jeremiah O'Quinn (Diarmaid Ó Cuinn), whose role is outlined in closer detail later in this chapter. It is significant that, although he was often in conflict with his Presbytery, the fact that he was native Irish was never held against him. In his day, he was one of a small band of thirty Presbyterian ministers permanently settled in Ulster.[19] He was acclaimed by the Synod as being very successful in communicating effectively with his fellow Irish-speakers. When O'Quinn died in 1657, he was succeeded in the parish of Billy, Co. Antrim, by another Irish-speaker, Gabriel Cornwall, suggesting that there was Irish-speaking in the Bushmills area at this time on a significant scale.

In the year 1661 there were seventy Presbyterian ministers in Ulster and there were signs that the Church now felt confident enough to make some evangelistic approaches through the Irish language. The main participants were O'Quinn, Cornwall, and probably Wallace. However, many other names were mentioned in relation to preaching in places such as Tipperary, Connaught and elsewhere in the south and west. The individual ministers mentioned included Archibald Hamilton, Samuel Hallyday, William Henry, Robert Kelso, Duncan Campbell, John Hamilton, William Hampton. They were missionaries in Irish-speaking areas and it can be safely assumed that they too spoke Irish. Of course, the possibility of interpreters being used cannot be ruled out: in later years, as has been already noted, John Wesley used an interpreter standing beside him when addressing people of the Irish-speaking west. There is, however, no hint of this device being used elsewhere so it seems highly probable that the ministers mentioned were Irish-speakers.

It can be taken as certain that very few native Irish would have known any English up until 1700. But, before this time, the Session-books are full of Irish names, indicating that the Presbyterian Church would have been able to deal capably with Irish-language communication. An analysis by Stothers[20] of Presbytery and Kirk Session minute books from 1646 to 1735, for eight different areas, shows substantial numbers of Presbyterians with native Irish names. It would appear, therefore, that the Church had been able to enlist a large number of Irish-speakers for whom becoming Presbyterian brought no political advantage.[21] Of these, the most influential were Gabriel Cornwall, Jeremiah O'Quinn and James Wallace.

The next sections give further details about these three Irish-speaking ministers.

GABRIEL CORNWALL (d. 1690)

This Irish-speaking Presbyterian minister was a member of a family which owned extensive lands in the Dungannon area.[22] He was educated at St Andrews. His parents, John and Grace Cornwall, who then appeared to be resident in Scotland, made representations that their son might go to Ireland to preach. Their request was granted on 28 September 1653.[23] In 1655 he was ordained to Ballywillan, Co. Antrim and received a stipend of £50 *per annum* from the Protectorate. This was increased to £100 in the following year. When Jeremiah O'Quinn died in 1657, Cornwall succeeded him at Billy (Bushmills) and was responsible for both congregations. So the first two ministers to Bushmills, covering the first 44 years of its history, i.e. from 1646 to 1690, were both fluent Irish-speakers. Without doubt many members of their congregations would have had Irish as their first language.

As well as speaking Irish, Cornwall could also preach in the language and did so from time to time. He was sent out, now and then, by the Presbytery to propagate the Gospel in that vernacular. In the succeeding century his 'remarkable success' in his Irish preaching was referred to in the records of the General Synod.[24] One of his preaching tours, which took place in Connaught, lasted three months. He was deposed for non-conformity in 1661, but continued to preach at Ballywillan and Billy. He lived at Maddybenny near Coleraine, and it appears that he took services in his own home before the congregation were able to build a church.[25] He died in 1690 and his will was proved in July 1691. He had two sons who were ministers, Josias Cornwall of Cavanleck (Fivemiletown), and William Cornwall of Clogher and St Johnston.[26, 27]

JEREMIAH O'QUINN (d. 1657)

The first native Irishman to become a Presbyterian minister was Jeremiah O'Quinn (also written O'Queen, which is a phonetic rendering of the original Ó Cuinn). Born in Templepatrick, he was accepted into the Presbyterian community as a person of '... great reputation and zeal'.[28]

O'Quinn was taught by a Mr Upton as a scholar, although he was older than the average student.[29] He was awarded M.A. from the University of Glasgow in 1644. Licensed at 'Army Presbytery' in 1646, he was ordained at Billy, also called Ballintoy, or sometimes Dunluce, now called Bushmills.

In 1649, he was suspended for refusing to read in public the 'Representation', a denunciation of the recent execution of King Charles I by the Cromwellians. Both O'Quinn and another minister, James Ker of Ballymoney, were a source of much embarrassment among their colleagues, because the Presbyterians had aligned themselves with the Royalists against Cromwell.[30]

O'Quinn was in continual trouble with the Presbytery and government.[31] In November 1651 he was directed to be removed from Ulster. In May 1654 he was ordered to Athy in Co. Kildare and to preach in Irish to the people of Clare and Connaught. Later in that year he was still engaged in preaching in Irish to the people of Connaught. At last he returned to Billy and remained there until he died in 1657.[32] In the following century, the Synod of Ulster (1710) referred to the success of O'Quinn's preaching in Irish, when they resolved to recommence this work.[33]

He died on the last day of January 1657.[34] His gravestone in Billy cemetery can still be read because it was re-cut in 1823 when a rector of Billy, Thomas Babington, was interred in the same grave.[35]

JAMES WALLACE

He is mentioned by Stothers as assisting O'Quinn on his preaching tour of Connaught, and it is therefore very likely that he too was an Irish-speaker.[36] He was educated at Edinburgh where he graduated M.A. in 1643. In 1654 he was ordained to Urney, Co Tyrone, with the instruction 'to preach the Gospel where ordered by the Commander-in Chief.'[37, 38] It seems he may have been in Urney before he was ordained, because Adair has him settling there in the period 1646–47. If so, it would help to explain the gap of eleven years between his graduation and ordination.

From 1655 onwards he received £80 a year from the Protectorate. It was in that same year that he accompanied Jeremiah O'Quinn on a missionary tour of Connaught. In 1661 he was deposed for non-conformity, but continued to minister.[39] He died towards the end of 1674, and his will was proved in 1675.[40]

LANGUAGE OF THE EARLY PRESBYTERIANS

Irish Presbyterianism began with the immigrants who arrived in Ulster from Scotland in the seventeenth century. Although there were earlier Scottish settlements in Antrim and Down, the main movement started with the Plantation scheme and continued throughout the century. There have been frequent discussions about the language spoken by these early settlers. Many of them spoke Lowland Scots (Lallans), but an assessment of the proportion who spoke Irish/Scottish Gaelic is more problematic. Stothers has pointed out that, in the absence of comprehensive statistical information, it is very difficult to be absolutely certain.[41] It can be taken that, from the early seventeenth century, apart from the significant numbers of Irish who became Presbyterian, the terms 'Presbyterian' and 'Scottish' are essentially synonymous. Since the incoming Presbyterians originated mainly in Scotland, it would be useful to examine the position of the Gaelic language in Scotland at the time of the Plantation.

Beginning as early as the third century, a movement of population from Co. Antrim across the North Channel to Argyll culminated in the foundation of the kingdom of Dál Riata about the year 500 AD by Fergus Mór mac Eirc.[42] Thus began the spread of the Gaelic language through Scotland. The Irish people at that time were called *Scotti* in Latin, and it is from them that Scotland is named. Argyll (Earra Ghàidheal) which means 'coastland of the Gaels', also takes its name from the same people who came from Ireland. Around 843 Kenneth MacAlpín, King of Dál Riata united the Scots and the Picts.[43] Ecclesiastical evangelisation by Colm Cille from Derry added to the Gaelicisation movement, so that at its height the Gaelic language was probaby spread over the entire area of Scotland. The strongest evidence for this is the language of place names. A search of Gaelic elements in place names, such as baile (a townland) and achadh (a field), shows clearly that Gaelic settlement, at one time or another, has included the whole of Scotland.[44] As Thomson has stated:

> It is worth emphasizing this point, as propaganda to the contrary has been for long been part of the stock in trade of popular, and sometimes of academic writers.[45]

Following the Battle of Carham (1018) the Gaelic Scots had achieved pre-eminence throughout the area which we know today as Scotland and, for a time, the hegemony stretched as far as Cumbria and Northumberland.[46] The turn of the tide did not begin until the Anglian linguistic invasion in the twelfth century, culminating in the change of language from Gaelic to English in the King's Court in the thirteenth century.

The earliest information about the extent of the Gaidhealtachd (Gaelic-speaking area) in Scotland relevant to the Plantation of Ulster dates from1689.[47] The area included the Islands and the Highlands (Sutherland, Ross and Cromarty, Inverness, Argyll), and the greater part of Caithness, Nairn and Perth, and parts of Moray, Banff, Aberdeen, Stirling and Dunbarton. By 1755 there were 289,798 persons in these areas, 22.9 per cent of the population of Scotland. If the place of origin of the settlers in Ireland was known it would be possible to extrapolate the language distribution. Barkley identified the areas of origin as Renfrewshire, Ayrshire, Argyllshire, Galloway, Wigton, Lanarkshire and Kirkcudbright,[48] places which on the whole had been settled by the Irish, centuries previously.

Athough we cannot be fully sure about these origins, there is still much information surviving about the language of the settlers. For example, some Gaelic-speaking members of the MacNeill family from Kintyre emigrated to Ireland around 1688.[49, 50, 51] Archibald and Malcolm, who were half-brothers, settled at Ballymascanlon, near Dundalk, Co. Louth. Another brother, Niall Buidhe MacNeill, made his home in Killquin in Co. Antrim, and the eldest brother, John, bought land in Ballymascanlon.

This was the origin of the Ballymascanlon Presbyterian community, which from the beginning was Gaelic-speaking (at that time the same as Irish-speaking). The MacNeill family of Mount Pleasant near

Dundalk brought clergy over from the Gaelic-speaking areas of Scotland, particularly the island of Islay, because very little English was understood in this district until well into the nineteenth century. From 1700 until 1818 every minister was Gaelic/Irish-speaking, and the congregation likewise.

For the period from 1700 to 1785 the Ballymascanlon ministers were Gaelic-speakers from Argyll: John Wilson 1700–1702; Patrick Simpson 1713–1761; Robert Drummond 1762–1778; Colin Lindsay 1779–1785. The ministers who followed, Andrew Bryson 1786–1796 and William Neilson 1796–1818, were Irish- rather than Gaelic-speaking and were firmly fixed in the Presbyterian East Ulster tradition of Irish-speaking. There was nothing doctrinaire about the position of these ministers and to them their use of the language was perfectly natural. The early ones had moved from one Gaelic-speaking area (Kintyre), which was on the borders with lowland culture, to another which bordered on the English Pale.[52] They were very used to dealing with bi-lingualism.

Another group of Irish-speaking Presbyterians was recorded in north Antrim. This was documented by Richardson (1664–1747), in his pamphlet of 1711.[53] He pointed out that it was futile to try to communicate with the native Irish in a language (English) which they did not understand. So, if there were to be conversions to the Established Church, Irish-speaking ministers were needed. He pointed out that the Presbyterians, by preaching to the Irish in their own tongue, were making many converts.

> They have enlisted the help of Gaelic-speaking missionaries from the Scottish Highlands. If the Established Church does not use the same methods, then there will be a great increase in converts to Presbyterianism, so harmful to the English interest.

In this pamphlet, Richardson published a letter dated 12 May 1711 from an Archibald Stewart,[54] who shared his personal knowledge about the use of the Irish language in religious affairs in north Antrim. He informed Richardson that there was a dissenting minister named Stewart, 'Who, by preaching in Irish, has brought over a considerable number of Irish to be his hearers.' This may be James Stuart, minister for Cushendall from 1708 to 1719, who is not elsewhere described as being an Irish-speaker.[55]

Richardson published another letter, dated 18 May 1711, this one from a J. Maguire, in which it is stated,

> I had been some years ago employed by the Trustees for sale of the Forfeited Estates in Ireland, on the survey of these Forfeitures, particularly in the County of Antrim, where I met many of the inhabitants, especially of the Baronies of Glenarm, Dunluce and Killconaway, who could not speak the English tongue; and asking them in Irish what religion they professed, they answered they were Presbyterians, upon which I asked them further, how they could understand their Minister preaching; to that they answered he always preached in Irish. I had the curiosity to go to their meeting on the Sunday following, where I heard their Minister ... preach to them in Irish, at which (though I think he did not do it well,) they expressed great devotion: His audience, (as I understand) was composed of native Irish and Highlanders.'[56]

This is very significant first-hand evidence of Irish-speaking among Presbyterians. Stothers has pointed out that such activities tended to be under-reported or ignored. Local preaching like this was not mentioned in the Synod.

> There must have been other places where both native Irish, and those with a Scots-Gaelic background attended regular Irish language Presbyterian Sabbath Services regardless of what plans were made in the Synod.[57]

In this discussion about the language mix, it should be clear that members of the Established Church were more likely to come from England and so, apart from the many Irish converts, most of them would, naturally, have been English-speaking. Certainly, any Scots coming to Ulster from the Highlands or the Islands of Scotland would have been Gaelic-speaking. But even among those who came from Ayr and Galloway there was a significant proportion of Gaelic-speakers. Stothers[58] finds the evidence of M.W. Heslinga convincing.

> As far as the language is concerned, there was no clear cut division between the immigrants and the 'natives'. It is fairly certain that many colonists of the first three decades of the seventeenth century who came from Galloway were Gaelic speakers. The same holds good for (later) immigrants from the Highlands whose

descendents, in some cases, remained Gaelic speaking until the first half of the nineteenth century.[59]

In view of the fact that Heslinga was arguing against a common culture between the Scots and the Irish, his testimony must be particularly influential. There is also other important evidence pointing in the same direction. T.F. O'Rahilly[60] reported that Galloway was substantially Gaelic-speaking right up to the seventeenth century. G.B. Adams,[61] reported that a certain proportion of the incoming Scots were Gaelic-speaking, coming as they did from the Highlands and also from Western Galloway, '... which at that time was still partly Gaelic speaking.'

Stothers sifted through practically all of the available evidence, weighing it up carefully, and rejected commentators such as De Blacam,[62] Ó Snodaigh[63] and D.C. Rushe,[64] who were keen to prove that most of the Scottish planters came from Gaelic or bi-lingual areas. Equally, he rejected the assertion of the British and Irish Communist Organisation that, with few exceptions, the language of the incoming Scots was almost totally Lowland Scots.[65] Stothers understood well that both sides were trying to make political points. He had more faith in authors such as Lorimer,[66] Adams[67] and Heslinga.[68] From the evidence of these authors Stothers concludes,

> that a significant number, although not nearly a majority, of the Presbyterians who settled in Ulster, spoke Gaelic.

He further concludes that they would have been reinforced during the seventeenth century by a later migration of Gaelic-speakers from the Highlands and a continuing westward drift of Highlanders into Ireland. Stothers contends that, if this is so, then these Presbyterians would have continued to use their Gaelic language at least for the first generation and possibly longer.[69]

Another significant influx into the pool of Irish-speaking Presbyterians was the substantial rate of conversions from the native Irish. The extent of this factor has been much underestimated. Latimer edited the old Session Book of Templepatrick Presbyterian Church, Co. Antrim and remarked on the number of members of the congregation who bore purely Irish names.[70] The book covered the period 1646 to 1744 and some of the names noted were Murdock O'Donnallie, Oyen McGouckin, Jein McGee, Meive O'Conalie, Patrick O'Mory, Schilie O'Donally, Shan O'Hagain, Donald O'Crilie, Rorie O'Crilie, Jenkin O'Conally. In a footnote Latimer was moved to say:

> The number of Celtic names which occur in this record is remarkable. How have these names disappeared from among the Northern Irish Presbyterians? In all probability they have become anglicised. If this has taken place even in districts where the Celts live together in large bodies, much more will it take place where they are a minority among the Scots.

Looking for the contemporary names of ministers and elders in a sample of modern congregational histories, one can note a very large number of purely Irish names, such as Grogan, McDermott, Hempsey, Callaghan, Roddy, Hegarty, Lavery, McGladdery, Shannon, Coyle, Megaw, Farley, Murphy, McBride, Drennan, etc. The most noticeable characteristic, however, is the absence of the prefix 'O', which means a descendant. Conversely, 'Mc' (Mac, son) is exceptionally common. In order to conform to the stereotype that all Presbyterians came from Scotland, a first step would be to drop the 'O'. As suggested by Latimer, there were certainly further steps towards anglicisation. Some, apparently English, surnames were used to replace the native form. Although some substitutes chosen seemed completely random, e.g. Houston for Mac an tSeachlainn (Mc an Taghlen), and Englishby for Mac an Ghallóglaigh (Gallogly), most name changes had some rationale. Mac an Rí (McAree) became King; Mac Ruairí (McRory) became Rogers; Ó Loingsigh (Lynch) became Lindsay; Ó Baoill (Boyle) became Boal; Mac Seáin (McShane) became Johnston. Many apparently English surnames can, therefore, hide the origins of their bearers, e.g. Armstrong, Baird, Smith, Cromie, Howard, Lambe, Woods, Haire, to name a few.[71]

Adams carried out a detailed study of one particular congregation, Saintfield First Presbyterian Church, which was founded in 1658 and still uses the old Irish name of Tonaghneave (from Tamhnach Naomh).[72] He found an extensive list of members of the congregation bearing old Irish surnames, such as Kelly (Ó Ceallaigh), Connolly (Ó Conghaile), Kinghan (Ó Cuinneáin), Downey (Ó Maoldomhnaigh),

Dornan (Ó Dornáin), Flynn (Ó Floinn), etc. He also pointed out that many other persons could have had their Irish surnames subsumed under more English-sounding names. This means that, to measure the extent of historic recruitment to Presbyterianism from the native Irish, one could not depend on a modern count of Irish surnames. Such a count would grossly underestimate the trend. The substantial number of early Presbyterians who spoke Irish because they were native Irish would naturally lead to increased intermarriage and to the further spread of Irish throughout congregations.

Because Irish was the prevalent tongue and because very many people did not understand English, the newcomers who were not Gaelic-speaking would, of necessity, have had to learn some in order to converse with the public, and for purposes of trade and employment. Others would look on the acquisition of the language as an added dimension to their lives and a way of making contact with a wider community. Later again, many came to place Irish literature and song in high regard and made positive efforts to save and promote the language for its own sake.

The language groups among the early Presbyterians therefore would have been:

1. Irish-speaking converts
2. Speakers of Scots Gaelic
3. Those who had learned Irish
4. Speakers of Lallans (Scots)

Not many, in any of these groups, would have had a facility with English, which at that time was quite distinct from Scots. It was only after 1603, when James VI of Scotland became James I of England, that English began to make headway in Scotland. Anglicisation of the Scots language was accelerated when the reformed churches adopted the Authorised version of the King James Bible in 1611.[73]

The Irish-speaking converts, who were so plentiful, would have continued speaking Irish early into the eighteenth century, as Adams commented, because 'One can change one's religion in a year or two, but it takes a generation or two to change a family's language.'[74]

That so many native Irish became Presbyterians indicated that the new arrivals had something to offer. The Catholic Church seems to have been at a low ebb at that time and not able to provide its flock with sufficient priests or church buildings. The law of the land had decreed that it was a crime to say Mass, punishable by being hanged, drawn and quartered. Many of the new ministers were able to preach to them in their own language. The Irish and Scots recognised each other as brethren and indeed were looked on as such by Queen Elizabeth I. It is noteworthy that for at least the early part of the 1641 Rebellion the insurgent native Irish did not attack the Presbyterian population. Ironically, it was an Irish-speaking Presbyterian, Owen O'Connolly, who hastened to Sir John Clotworthy to sound the alarm about the imminent rising.[75]

Therefore, to summarise the available evidence, it is clear that there were a number of congregations where Irish/Gaelic was, by far, the majority language. The only ones for which information has survived are North Antrim, Dundalk, and Rademon. It is reasonable to assume there must have been others. In some congregations it was the custom of having Irish-preaching every second Sunday, e.g. c.1690 at Ballybay.[76] That custom implies a congregation of at least half Irish-speaking members. However, most of the remaining congregations would have had a significant number of native Irish-speakers, as shown by counts of purely Irish surnames. As far as an overall estimate is concerned, it is not unreasonable to suggest that at least one eighth of Presbyterians had been recruited from the native Irish-speaking population; that at least one quarter of the incoming Scots were Gaelic-speaking; and that another eighth of congregations used Irish which they had learned to speak to their Irish neighbours and, even more importantly, to converse with Irish-speaking members of their own congregations. These conservative estimates suggest that at least half of all the early Presbyterians in Ulster were Irish/Gaelic-speakers.

III

CONSOLIDATION

EIGHTEENTH CENTURY

A

First Part of Century

MISSIONARY ACTIVITY

GENERAL

After the traumas of the 1641 rebellion and the turmoil of the Williamite war in Ireland, the Presbyterians were beginning to enter a period of relative stability. Their numbers were increasing steadily, augumented by Huguenots from France, a development which worried the Anglican Church and the political Establishment.[1] In spite of these troubles, the Irish Presbyterian church in the early part of the century embarked on an enterprise of missionary activity. As it happened they had an excellent pool of Irish-speakers from which to draw.

There is a list of seventeen Irish-speaking Presbyterian ministers who lived in Ulster during the period 1710–1720.[2] Confirmation of their number arises from the special effort then being made by the Synod of Ulster to initiate a preaching programme for the native Irish. It was necessary for prospective preachers not only to be fluent in Irish but also to have the additional ability to preach in the language. The minutes of the General Synod of Ulster, and other documents, frequently made this distinction. Therefore, those ministers that we know about, 17 out of a total of 128, i.e. 13 per cent, must be an underestimate of the extent of Irish-speaking among ministers. It is evident from the minutes of the Synod that it had not been necessary to set up a special programme for the teaching of Irish and clearly these ministers were mostly naturally occurring speakers; some of them had brought the language from Scotland.

The kindling of this desire to preach to the native Irish in their own tongue can be traced back to the Synod of 1699.[3] In the minutes it was recorded:

> This Morning Mr Alexr Sinclare signified that the Brethren in
> Dublin had a mind to visit ye Upper Country, by Preaching, &
> therefore judged it would be convenient that this Synod would
> appoint one or two of their number to preach in the Irish Tongue
> to go along with 'em, or any they shall appoint for this Work, so
> that, while they from Dublin are preaching to the British, the
> Person or Persons sent by this Synod may be exercised in preaching
> among the Irish; which being considered, was well approven, and
> Mr John McBride appointed to intimate so much to them by
> letter, expressing the ready and hearty concurrence of the Brethren
> here with so pious a Design, & for making this practicable, the
> Brethren in the Interloquitur appoint the Presby of Tyrone to send
> Mr Archbd McClean for some Time, when the Ministers of
> Dublin shall call him, & for making this the more easy to Mr
> McClean, the Brethren allow his Charges to be born out of R:D:*,
> & his Place to be supply'd in his Absence by the severall Meetings,
> as they shall be desir'd by the Presbytry of Tyrone. [*R:D: signifies
> the *Regium Donum*, the Royal Bounty paid to Presbyterian
> ministers].

It is noteworthy that the Presbyterians in Dublin were not able to
raise from their own number a minister who could preach in Irish, but
had to turn to the Synod of Ulster.

The tone of the minute rings with genuine enthusiasm for the
venture, yet it is remarkable that, at this period, it took an approach
from another Synod to get movement towards preaching to the Irish.
Indeed, the scheme was not developed and ultimately failed, for at the
Synod of the following year it was reported: 'Mr Archbd McClane was
not call'd by Dublin Ministers to preach among the Irish, so went not.'[4]

McClean, also spelt MacLaine, is referred to later. It was said of him
that he was '... in his day considered one of the best masters of the Irish
language'.[5] He had just arrived from Scotland, so his native Gaelic
must have been entirely intelligible in Ireland.

The question of preaching in Irish was raised again in 1710. This
time the idea seemed self-generated. It was resolved by the Synod '... to
employ some Minrs to preach to the Irish in this Kingdom'. Reference
was made to previous 'remarkable successes' by Gabriel Cornwall

(d.1690), and Jeremiah O'Quinn. The reason given for not undertaking any ambitious project before, was '... the smallness of our numbers and especially of such as understood the Irish Tongue'. However, the position had now changed radically and '... our Number is considerably augmented, chiefly seeing that we have several that understand Irish ...'[6]

Why the number of Irish-speaking ministers had increased so significantly over the previous ten years is not clear. Reading over the biographies of the seventeen ministers, one notices how few are of native Irish stock, indicating that the increase was not due to conversions of native Irish-speakers. Some had come fairly recently from Scotland, but the majority seem to be people who had been assimilated into the Irish-speaking population due to constant exposure to the language which, of course, was everywhere around them. This was particularly true for areas of high concentration of native Irish such as north Antrim, Tyrone, south Armagh, south Down and Co. Donegal.

It was at this Synod in 1710 that the first batch of ministers were named as suitable for preaching in Irish, MacLaine, McGregor, Humphrey Thompson, Samuel Dunlop, John Wilson, Archibald Boyd, in addition to the following probationers, Higginbotham, Plunket and John Dunlop, making a total of six ministers and three probationers. In his commentary on the characteristics of this group Stothers said:

> It is notable that all the ministers were settled in areas with a high proportion of Irish-speakers, being in Cos. Armagh, Londonderry, Monaghan, Donegal and Louth. Some of these ministers must have had quite a few Irish-speakers in their congregations and Thompson, for instance, is reported to have preached in English and Irish on alternate Sundays. All these nine had been born into Presbyterian families, except Plunket, who was a converted Roman Catholic. At least two came from Scotland, McClane and Wilson (and also perhaps Thompson). The others were Ulster-born; they may have picked up their Irish through study, but it is more likely that they learned it from contact with their Irish-speaking neighbours, some of whom may have been Presbyterian.[7]

This was the first proper plan for preaching in Irish organised by the

Synod of Ulster and it included detailed instructions. The preachers were to go out in pairs, a minister and a probationer together. A locum would be provided for anyone with a congregation and they would be financially supported by the Synod. Bibles, Confessions of Faith and Catechisms in the Irish language were to be made available. Each pair was to spend a period of three months among the native Irish and were to be paid 20 shillings per week per person.[8] A committee was set up to oversee the execution of the plan.

According to the Synod itself, however, the plan was not put into action for, at the meeting in 1715, it was reported:

> Little care has been taken to enquire into the State of Religion, or concert measures for reviving it; the most useful projects, and worthy of the consideration of Synods, have been either not at all entertained, or very faintly pursued. An instance of the former is the proposal for propagating the Gospel among the Irish, which was intirely and shamefully dropped ..."[9]

It was recommended that the scheme be revived and this was done in the next year.

Although this organisational plan was not implemented, normal preaching in Irish to native and planter, in various areas, continued regardless of plans made by the Synod, which never referred to local preaching,[10] presumably because it was taken for granted. These practices are described in more detail elsewhere. For example, John Richardson's publication in 1711 reported on Presbyterian congregations in north Antrim whose mother tongue was Gaelic/Irish and who had great difficulty understanding English.[11]

Much of the time of the 1716 Synod was devoted to discussing the Irish language. An effort was made to enumerate the ministers who were fluent in Irish, to the extent that they could preach in it or, failing that, could be trained up to the right standard. The result of their investigations was as follows (spelling regularised):

> Mr Robert Higginbotham, Minr. in Coleraine can speak and read Irish, but never preached in that language; Mr Saml Dunlop, Minr. in Letterkenny, is in the same circumstances; Mr Patrick Plunket at ScarnaGiroch, Mr John Wilson at Carlingford, Mr Humphrey

Thompson at Ballybay; Mr Charles Lynd, nigh to Strabane, Mr Archd Boyd at Maghera, Mr Robert Thompson of Belturbet, Ministers, and Mr Robert Stuart in Tyrone Presbytery, Mr Samuel Irwin in Monaghan Presbytery, Probationers, and Mr Thomas Strawbridge, upon his first trials in Derry Presbytery, can all speak Irish; and it is believed that most of them in less than twelve months, if diligent, may be qualified for preaching in Irish. Mr Archbald MacLaine at Market Hill, Mr James McGrigor at Aghadowey, Mr Patrick Simpson at Dundalk, Ministers, have oft preached in Irish.[12]

This list gives a total of fourteen individuals counted as Irish-speakers out of 129 ministers in the Synod, more than one in ten. But this must be looked on as an underestimate because, for whatever reason, other Irish-speakers are not included. None of the great number with a working knowledge of Irish was, of course, included, because the language skills required for preaching are of a high order. Those on the list who could not yet preach in Irish were invited to learn to do so and in order to help them two societies were formed. The first one was to meet in Dungiven and the six members of that group were Messrs McGregor, Higginbotham, Archibald Boyd, Dunlop, Lynd and Strawbridge. McGregor was to preach a sermon in Irish. The second group of nine members, to meet at Armagh, consisted of Messrs MacLaine, Simpson, Wilson, Humphrey Thompson, Robert Thompson, Moses Cherrie, Plunkett, Stuart and Irwin. MacLaine was to preach a sermon in Irish to the group. These societies were to meet every two months.

That was not the end of the plans about Irish, however, and a number of other decisions were taken. Mr Simpson of Dundalk was to preach in Dublin in the Irish language for a period of three months. A letter was to be written to the Synod of Argyll, asking them to send over a probationer qualified to preach in Irish and asking that a second probationer be sent later. Alexander Sinclair and Captain Malcolm McNeill, an Irish-speaker from Ballymascanlon, were to write the letter, presumably in Gaelic.

Messrs McGregor, Higginbotham and MacLaine were to preach in Irish, when and where as judged by the Presbytery. Furthermore, a school was to be set up in Dundalk, for teaching the reading of Irish. Each Presbytery was ordered to give twenty shillings for its support. Dundalk was Patrick Simpson's congregation and was enjoined to play a large part in these plans. He was asked to supervise the printing of a Catechism in Irish which would have, as an appendix, a grammar of Irish. Each minister in the Synod was commanded to take and pay for 30 copies and the print run was to be over 3000 copies.[13]

To find out the result of these ambitious plans, we turn to the reports of the following Synod, held at Belfast 18 June, 1717.[14] Although the two societies, at Dungiven and Armagh, had not met as frequently as every two months, it was reported that Samuel Dunlop had improved so much in his fluency with Irish that he could now preach in it. Messrs Lynd and Strawbridge could now read Irish. Higginbotham, since the last Synod, had preached in Irish very often. On the debit side, the Dundalk School for Irish had not got off the ground, because a good master had not yet been identified. Mr Simpson announced that there had been problems in getting a good translation of the catechism, but that these were now overcome and a translation was now available.

The Irish Committee of the Synod laid down directives for extensive tours of preaching in Irish.[15] Each of the Irish-speaking ministers appointed to preach was given a geographical area. Higginbotham was to preach in Athlone and Dublin; MacLaine was given parts of counties Armagh, Monaghan and Tyrone, to include Benburb, Dungannon, Stewartstown, Cookstown, Minterbirn, Kinaird, Vinecash, Loughgall, Keady and Monaghan town. Simpson was directed to preach to the Irish-speaking audiences and congregations in Co. Down and in the parts of counties Armagh and Monaghan not covered by MacLaine. Counties Derry, Antrim and part of Tyrone were the responsibility of McGregor and included Maghera, Dawson's Bridge, Coagh and Moneymore. Dunlop was to preach in Irish in Co. Donegal and particularly in the area of the Convoy Presbytery. The Presbyteries of Antrim and Belfast were jointly charged with the care of preaching in Irish in Killilagh and Kilmakevat. This resolution points to the areas with a high concentration of Irish-speakers and, interestingly, includes Antrim and Down, the two counties with the highest density of Presbyterians.

At the 1718 Synod there were more references to Irish. Archibald MacLaine, probationer from the Synod of Argyll, made a complaint that he had not been paid, as promised, for preaching in Irish.[16] We discover that the famed John Abernethy (see later) was an Irish-speaker and that there was some consternation among his Irish-speaking audience when the Synod directed that he be transferred to Dublin.[17]

The Synod of 1719 received a request from the Scottish Highlanders and Irish-speakers in the Dublin area for ministers to preach in Irish. The Synod responded with a number of measures.[18] It appointed Messrs Higginbotham, Dunlop and Simpson each to spend three month spells preaching in Irish to the Highlanders and native Irish in Dublin. An Irish Committee was set up to oversee the programme for preaching in Irish and to provide support. The two committees set up at the 1716 Synod were to be revived and were to make recommendations about how to prepare others to preach in Irish. Mr Simpson, who had seen the catechism in Irish through a second printing, was to have it distributed to all the presbyteries, for which he would have his expenses remunerated.[19]

In 1720 the Synod of Ulster reported that the three ministers who had been instructed to go to Dublin to preach in Irish to the Highlanders and Irish had indeed fulfilled their obligations.[20] It appears that Simpson of Dundalk was having difficulty in being recompensed for the Irish catechisms, at least by some of the congregations. However, the plan for preaching in Irish seemed to be, on the whole, successful. Not mentioned before, Belfast was included for this activity and the relevant minute reads: 'Mr Higinbottam if he be in town, is to preach an Irish sermon tomorrow. If he go out of town, Mr Simpson is to preach an Irish sermon in this town.'[21]

Another request for help was made by the Highlanders and Irish Roman Catholics who attended the preaching in Irish in and about the city of Dublin.[22] Once more the request was complied with and Simpson, Higginbotham and Dunlop were instructed to do three months preaching each. Their absences from their own congregations had to be filled by other ministers and judging by the complex arrangements made by the Synod for *locums*, this was quite a manpower strain on the church generally. Presumably, the Synod could not afford to have a panel of supernumerary ministers whose only purpose was to carry out peripatetic preaching.

Towards the end of the business of the Synod, there was a lengthy report on the progress of Irish-preaching. The Society formed to support preaching in Irish had provided a commodious place for these preachings. It was reported by Higginbotham, however, that the two societies formed in the north in 1716 had not been revived because Mr McGrigor, as his name was spelt, had gone to America in 1718 and others were taken up with preaching in Dublin. Once again, those ministers who had the Irish tongue, substantially more in number than those who could preach in the language, were petitioned to improve their command of the language to such an extent that they could preach with ease in Irish. The Committee for Irish-speakers in Dublin, which had been appointed at the previous Synod was reappointed.[23]

Stothers regards the year 1720 as a flowering of the Presbyterian involvement with the Irish language.

> Thus we have in 1720 a picture of the small Irish Presbyterian Church using its resources to the best of its ability in persuing a vigorous and organised programme of evangelism among their Irish-speaking countrymen, and of supplying the needs of Gaelic-speaking immigrants. Where appropriate they co-operated with their co-religionists in Dublin, and when necessary they requested help from the Mother-Kirk in Scotland.

Stothers furthermore pointed out that from early times until 1720 all the Presbyterian approaches to Catholics were in Irish.[24] Centuries later the Rev. J.E. Davey was to comment:

So did the Church seek to undo one of the great mistakes of the Reformation, that of refusing the scriptures in Irish to the Irish people at a time when Irish was still the main spoken language in the country.[25]

In addition the Presbyterian Church was involved in providing Irish-preaching to Presbyterians.

After 1720, the question of the Non-Subscription controversy was to distract the Synod from all other issues and the Irish language faded into the background.[26] It was to take more than a century before the Presbyterian Church, as a body, once more gave special attention to the Irish language.

As mentioned before, 17 Irish-speaking ministers have been identified in the period 1710–1720. Some details of these individuals which now follow will give a better understanding of this interesting period in Presbyterian Church history.

JOHN ABERNETHY (1680–1740)

This eminent Presbyterian divine was an Irish-speaker and used the language naturally and '... as a matter of course to speak to native Irish and Highlanders'.[27] He was born on 19 October 1680 at Brigh, Co. Tyrone,[28] where his father, John Abernethy Senior, was a Presbyterian minister.[29] His mother was a daughter of John Walkinshaw of Renfrewshire. When the young John was just over one year old his father, who had been minister in Moneymore, was installed in Coleraine (First).

At the age of 13 he became a student at Glasgow University, where he was awarded the degree of M.A. From there he went to Edinburgh University, where he made a great impression.[30] In 1703 he was appointed to the key congregation of Antrim. In 1705 he founded the Belfast Society,[31] an association of ministers which had the objective of improving the theological knowledge of its members.[32] The members came to the conclusion that the Church had no right to require candidates for the ministry to subscribe to a 'man-made' confession of faith. Yet, it took a number of years before these conclusions were publicised. In 1720 appeared the pamphlet written by Abernethy, which is said to have started the subscription controversy.[33] A tragic event, namely the death of his wife, occurred in 1712 leaving him desolate and sad for some time.[34] By 1716 many early problems encountered by the Presbyterians had been solved and circumstances were much more favourable. In this more relaxed climate, the Synod turned its attention to '... preaching to their countrymen in the Irish language'.[35]

It was at this time that Abernethy received two calls, one from Usher's Quay, Dublin, and the other from the Old Congregation in Belfast.[36] The congregation at Antrim, however, did not want to lose him and pointed out, in the discussion at the Synod, that Abernethy was most successful in his '... labours amongst the Irish Papists of Killilagh and

Killmakevat'.[37] Killmakevat was part of the congregation of Glenavy. The townland of Killilagh (Killealy) was the site of the original church in the parish of Killead. These two parishes touch the eastern shore of Lough Neagh. There were people from these areas at the Synod meeting and they were allowed to address the Synod and make a case for retaining Abernethy. Subsequently Archibald MacLaine and Patrick Simpson were instructed to go out and inform them that the Synod was very satisfied with their case and wished to reassure them of the Synod's high regard for them. As the two ministers were Irish-speakers, and this is mentioned in the minutes, it must be presumed that these people from the Glenavy area had little, if any, English. After much deliberation the final decision was that Abernethy was to go to Dublin. The Synod, however, ruled that, 'The Presbytries of Antrim and Belfast are appointed joyntly to take care of preaching to the Irish in Killilagh and Killmakevat.'[38]

It is a Presbyterian tradition that the number of people with native Irish surnames who are also Presbyterians still in the area touching the eastern shore of Lough Neagh is largely due to the work of John Abernethy. At that time there was a relative shortage of Catholic priests and the likes of Abernethy filled a great need.

There is no doubt whatever that Abernethy was a fluent Irish-speaker who could also preach in the language with great effect. Stothers points out the strange anomaly that little reference that is made to this in the minutes of the Synod.[39] Although Abernethy was appointed to the committee relating to preaching in Irish as far back as 1717,[40] that is the first reference to his preaching regularly in Irish. Stothers wonders how many other ministers could speak Irish but about whom we will never know.[41]

Abernethy was a very important figure in the history of Irish Presbyterianism. It was he who largely began the subscription debate which arose from what he saw as the dictatorial decision of the Synod of Ulster to send him to Dublin. After spending three months at Usher's Quay in Dublin, he simply returned to Antrim, in open revolt against the authoritative decision of the Synod. As expressed by the *D.N.B.*, 'Such a thing as disobedience to a decision of the supreme court of the church had never been heard or dreamed of as possible.' The outcome was that in 1726 the Antrim Presbytery were cut off from the main body of the 'Orthodox' Church, on the grounds that they refused to subscribe to the Westminster Confession of Faith. His grandson, John Abernethy (1764–1831), became a well-known surgeon.

ARCHIBALD BOYD

The Rev. Boyd is on Stothers' list of Irish-speaking ministers for the period 1710–1720.[42] He was born near Dervock, which lies between Coleraine and Ballycastle in the parish of Derrykeighan. He was educated at Glasgow, 1697 and was ordained to Maghera in 1703. An Irish-speaker, he was also able to preach in the language.[43] He was one of the seven ministers in the Synod of Ulster nominated to preach in Irish.[44] Unfortunately, he had an adulterous affair and, in August 1716, had to be deposed. Subsequently, he emigrated to Colonial North America and settled in Boston.

JOHN DUNLOP (OR DELAP)

Born in Co. Donegal, where the native name Ó Lapáin, is usually anglicised to either Delap, or Dunlop,[45] he could have been of native stock. He is listed as one of the Irish-speaking Presbyterian ministers in the period 1710–1720.[46, 47]

He started his third-level education in Glasgow in 1699 and was licensed by Convoy Presbytery in 1706.[48] At the General Synod in Antrim, 3 June 1707, it was announced that Convoy was to enter Mr John Dunlop on trials, with a view to ordination. Dunlop was ordained to Donegal on 15 September 1710.[49]

He died on 29 November 1713, having been only three years in his ministry.

SAMUEL DUNLOP (OR DELAP), M.A. (1680–1762)

The Rev. Samuel Dunlop is listed as one of the seventeen Presbyterian ministers known to be Irish-speakers in the period 1710–1720.[50] Nine of them, including Samuel Dunlop, were sent out to preach in Irish following the Synod of 1710.[51]

Although the surname Delap, from Ó Lapáin, is that of a Donegal sept,[52] Witherow traced Samuel's lineage back to a great grandfather, Hugh Delap, who came from Irvine in Ayreshire and settled in Sligo.[53] Born about 1680, his father was Robert Delap, a merchant in Ballyshannon, Co. Donegal and his mother was Anne Lindsay. In 1706 he was licensed by the Presbytery of Derry, and he was ordained in Letterkenny on 13 Aug. 1707.[54] He was the third minister in Letterkenny First, an old congregation going back to 1647.[55] Although he had been declared competent to preach the Gospel in Irish in 1710, it is not known to what extent he employed this talent.[56] He died on 30 August 1762 and his widow, Sarah Campbell, survived him by only two weeks.[57]

ROBERT HIGGINBOTHAM (C. 1682–1770)

This Presbyterian minister was a talented Irish-speaker and he translated several parts of the Scriptures into Irish. These were circulated both in Scotland and in Ireland.[58] He was born in Co. Antrim about 1682. In 1707 he graduated M.A. from Glasgow and he was ordained at Coleraine in 1710.[59] Mr Higginbotham, at this time a probationer, was a native Irish-speaker and so he was sent out with a senior minister to preach the Gospel to the Irish Papists. Irish-speaking missionaries were to be paid 20 shillings a week. They were to be provided with Bibles, Confessions of Faith and Catechisms printed in Dublin in Irish and had a '... little short Irish Grammar of a leaf or two subjoyned to it', and every minister in the Synod was expected to pay for 30 copies. As only some of the ministers could speak Irish every Presbytery was exhorted to endeavour '... to obtain Irish who may be educated in our way, thereby they may be usefull in obtaining this Desirable End'.[60]

In 1714 Higginbotham married Martha Woods of Fourloanends, Belfast,[61] and they had a daughter Anne Elizabeth. She married a person with the same surname, Rev. Thomas Higginbotham, Church of Ireland rector of Pettigo.[62] They left four children, Thomas, Robert, Martha and Sarah.[63] It was reported in 1717 that Mr Higginbotham had often preached in Irish. He had improved substantially since the Synod of the previous year[64] and at this time he was instructed to preach in Athlone and Dublin. Again, two years later he was appointed to preach to the Highlanders and Irish in Dublin. In the following year, 1720, he had a similar appointment for another three months. He was sympathetic to the Non-subscribers, but stayed in the Synod. In 1725 he wrote a pamphlet supporting non-subscription. He later took a prominent part in opposing the Seceders. Reid recounts that a Mr John Swanston, a licentiate of the secession, had attracted much attention in the Coleraine area by his attacks on the orthodox Presbyterians.[65] Robert Higginbotham, '... was a person of rather irritable temperament and though pretty far advanced in life ...' could not tolerate the insults of this Scottish probationer. He felt it his duty as moderator of the General Synod to meet Swanston face to face in a public debate. This took place at Ballyrashane in 1747, but it is not known definitely who was the victor. Mrs Higginbotham lived to be aged 80, and Robert, who was two years younger, died on 1770, 6 October, aged 88.[66]

Julia Mullin in her essay on Higginbotham wrote; 'Why this Co. Antrim man should have known Irish is a puzzle'.[67] This is an interesting comment because it displays surprise. Yet, if we remind ourselves about the language of the population in 1710, a mere 100 years after the Plantation of Ulster, it could not have been so unusual. Firstly, the native Irish population would still have been virtually 100 per cent Irish-speaking, and they would have been in daily contact with their Presbyterian neighbours, so for purely practical reasons Presbyterians would have had to have at least some Irish to been able to communicate. In addition, many of the Presbyterians came originally from Gaelic-speaking areas in Scotland and many would still have been native speakers of the language. Stother's analysis of Abernethy's ability to speak Irish shows that the number of Presbyterians who could speak Irish was most likely a significant underestimate. Furthermore it was never part of Presbyterian policy to eradicate the Irish language. On the contrary, many Presbyterians saw the language as an extra dimension in their understanding of a wider community. Bearing these factors in mind, could the question be re-phrased as, 'Why are there not many more Presbyterians, lay and clerical, recorded as being proficient in Irish?'

SAMUEL IRWIN (d. 1729)

Samuel Irwin was born in Killeshandra, Co. Cavan. He graduated from Glasgow University with a M.A. in 1708. Licensed by Monaghan Presbytery in 1716, he was ordained by the Augher Presbytery as minister to Lislooney in October 1718. He was the first minister to this congregation.[68] An Irish-speaker, he could also give sermons in the language.[69, 70] In the subscription controversy, he stayed with the Synod.[71] He died in Lislooney on 6 October 1729.

CHARLES LYND (1681–1751)

It is said that Charles Lynd, minister of Coleraine, was of Huguenot extraction. His father, Matthew Lynd, and family settled on the shores of Lough Swilly, in Rathmullan, where Charles was born in 1681.[72] He was educated in Edinburgh where he qualified M.A. in 1701. He was ordained at Clondevaddock on 25 February 1708 and became minister of Fannet. Twenty years later he became minister to the new congregation of Coleraine.

In 1716 he was listed by the General Synod of Ulster as a person who was fluent in speaking Irish and who, with less than a year's preparation, could be commissioned to preach in the language.[72] Subsequently, he became completely qualified to preach in Irish.[73, 74] He was born and reared in a totally Irish-speaking community and this would explain, despite his father being Huguenot, why he was an Irish-speaker.[75]

He was installed in Coleraine, New Row, on 27 February 1728.[76] His home was at Hatton Lodge in the town.[77] The General Assembly elected him as Moderator in 1733. In 1749 he published a pamphlet, *Short and Plain Vindication of Several Scriptural Principles*. He died on 21 December 1751.[78] His wife was Grace Bell and they had two sons and five daughters.[79]

It is interesting that one of his sons, Charles Lynd from Coleraine, donated a Bible in Irish to the Linen Hall Library in the period 1788/98.[80] His gift was mentioned in a minute of the Library dated 2 March 1793, as an important indication that the Library should be in the business of collecting not only books in Irish but also manuscripts in the Irish language. A Mr Calwell was delegated to undertake the task of gathering such publications on behalf of the Library and the budget was to be ten guineas.[81]

ARCHIBALD MacLAINE, (OR McCLEAN) (d. 1734)

It was said of him that he in '... his day was considered one of the best masters of the Irish language'.[82] MacLaine's father, the Rev. Alexander MacLaine, M.A., of Kilmaglass, had been a minister both in Argyll and Bute, both Gaelic-language areas of Scotland, so that it was hardly surprising that the son, Archibald, was fluent in Irish. He was ordained in Argyllshire in the year 1685, but came to Ireland in 1700 when he was installed in Markethill.[83] Later in that year he was included in the group of nine who were instructed by the General Synod to preach in the Irish language.[84] In 1711 he was elected Moderator of the General Assembly, a substantial honour to someone who had only recently arrived in the country.

Archibald MacLaine was the first Presbyterian minister in Ireland to be prosecuted by the Ecclesiastical courts of the Established Church for celebrating marriages according to the Presbyterian form.[85] He died on 20 July 1734 leaving three sons, all of whom became Presbyterian ministers.[86] One of them was Alexander MacLaine, minister at Ballynahinch and Antrim, who married a daughter of the celebrated John Abernethy, an Irish-speaker.[87] His son Thomas was ordained minister of Monaghan in 1718.[88] The other son, Archibald, was minister to Banbridge (Scarva Street) until his death on 23 February 1740.[89]

JAMES McGREGOR (1677–1729)

A tall man of commanding appearance, McGregor was one of several Irish-speaking Presbyterian ministers who lived in the early part of the eighteenth century. He was the son of a Captain McGregor and was born in Magilligan in 1677. As a youth he had been in Derry at the time of the Siege and is reputed to have discharged the gun which announced the arrival of the relief ships.[90, 91]

Educated at Glasgow, he was ordained in 1701 and became minister to Aghadowey. He was the first Aghadowey minister to have been born in Ireland. Mr McGregor often preached in Irish in Co. Derry,

Co. Antrim, and part of Co. Tyrone. Individual places included Maghera, Coagh, Dawson's Bridge and Moneymore.[92, 93]

He married Marion, a daughter of Captain David Cargill of Aghadowey, and they had ten children, including the Rev. David McGregor, minister of the West Parish, Londonderry.[94]

In 1718 McGregor, accompanied by a section of the Aghadowey congregation, emigrated to North America. Before leaving he preached to his people and in the course of the sermon described their reasons for departure: 'First, to avoid oppression and cruel bondage; second, to shun persecution and designed ruin; third, to withdraw from the communion of idolators; and lastly, to have freedom of worship.'[95]

No doubt, economic factors were also important. He and his people founded a city in New Hampshire and called it Londonderry, to commemorate the city which they had defended in 1689.[96] He died, aged 52, following an attack of fever, on 5 March 1729, and was buried at Londonderry. The Rev. Matthew Clarke married his widow, Marion.[97]

Of him it was said; 'His name and memory were most tenderly cherished by his beloved flock, and succeeding generations, and the effects of his labours among them were long and widely felt.'[98]

PATRICK PLUNKETT (d. 1759)

He was one of the nine ministers sent out by the Synod of Ulster in 1710 to preach the Gospel in Irish.[99] Hamilton gives the number as ten: seven ministers and three probationers.[100]

The son of a Catholic, Patrick Plunkett, of Drain's Bog, Cairncastle, he converted to Presbyterianism early in his youth.[101] After graduating M.A. from Edinburgh in 1704, he was licensed by the Antrim Presbytery and ordained at Scarnagiroch (Emyvale), Co. Monaghan, on 11 May 1714.[102] Until his retirement in 1757, he was minister of Glennan.[103] He regularly preached in Irish.[104, 105]

He married a Miss Baxter and their son Thomas was also a Presbyterian minister, who spent 21 years in Enniskillen, and then in 1769 moved to the Strand St. congregation in Dublin. This Thomas was father of Lord William Conyngham Plunkett, Lord Chancellor of Ireland.[106] While Lord Plunkett remained a Presbyterian, his son, the second baron, became the Anglican Lord Bishop of Tuam.[107, 108] The Rev. Patrick Plunkett died on 22 April 1759.[109]

PATRICK SIMPSON (1682–1781)

In 1713 the Dundalk congregation had been without a minister for some time when they extended a call to Mr Patrick Simpson, a native of Islay, Argyllshire, a Gaelic-speaking area.[110] He was educated at Glasgow where he graduated M.A. in 1707. On 30 December he was ordained to Dundalk.[111] He was an Irish-speaker and preached in Irish.[112, 113, 114] In 1716 he was ordered by the Synod of Ulster to preach in Irish in Dublin for three months.[115]

He married a woman from Ballymascanlon who was the sister of Malcolm and Archibald MacNeill, previously officers in the army of William III. These two brothers had come from Scotland in 1688 and had purchased the lordship of Ballymascanlon. They brought over ministers from the Gaelic-speaking island of Islay, including the Rev. Simpson.[116] He appears to have had an important position in the Church and the Synod in 1717 entrusted a major commitment to Dundalk when it agreed '… to erect a school for teaching to read Irish in the Town of Dundalk, to which each Presbytery was to contribute a certain sum.' They further resolved '… to print editions of the catechism and a short grammar in the Irish tongue'.[117]

He became unhappy about the meaness of his stipend and resigned because of this in 1721. He was persuaded to continue on but later left the General Synod and joined the Non-Subscribing Presbytery of Antrim in 1726. He retired in 1761. He died in Nov. 1781 and is buried at Ballymascanlon. Patteson says that he d. 1760 aged 99.[118]

His daughter married a MacNeill of Ballymascanlon. On 18 January 1737, Malcolm MacNeill gave the Rev. Mr Simpson a lease of 134 acres in Aghaboys forever, which Simpson devised by deed to his son-in-law Hamilton Gordon. He in turn was ordained in 1779 and demised the lands of Mount Pleasant to Captain Torquil Parks MacNeill.[119]

ROBERT STEWART (d. 1746)

Another Irish-speaking minister,[120] he was born near Carland, between Donaghmore and Coalisland, Co. Tyrone. He was the great-great-grandson of Andrew, second Lord Ochiltree.[121] He was ordained at Carland in August 1720. Not only could he speak Irish, he could preach in it as well. In 1726, he married the daughter of Captain Robert Edwards, of Castlederg, who had fought with King William III's army in the late wars. Stewart died on 11 April 1746 and was buried in Newmills.[122]

THOMAS STRAWBRIDGE (d. 1762)

Son of James Strawbridge, Thomas was born near Burt, Co. Donegal. He was educated at Glasgow University from which he graduated in 1708 with the degree of M.A.

In 1721 he was ordained to the congregation of Carndonagh, Co. Donegal.[123] He was the third minister to serve this congregation.[124] It is known that he was an Irish-speaker who could also preach in Irish.[125] Irish would have been necessary for normal communication in the area in which he was reared. In the controversy about subscription, he stayed in the Synod.[126] He died on 2 April 1762.

JAMES STUART (d. 1719)

This Rev. Stuart is listed by Stothers as one of the Irish-speaking ministers during this period.[127] He was apparently a native of Scotland.

He had his education at Glasgow University where he graduated M.A. in the year 1685. After a number of years, he was ordained at Mochrum, Wigtonshire in the year 1693. However, he resigned from that congregation in 1696 and after another delay, during which time he arrived in Ireland, he moved to Macosquin, where he was installed in 1701.[128] In 1705 the people of Macosquin were building a meeting house and in the same year Mr Stuart was suspended 'for indiscretions', but although the suspension was removed the congregation remained dissatisfied and in 1708 he resigned.[129]

Finally, he settled in Cushendall, where he was installed in 1708, but the people were not able to support a minister[130] and he had to survive with the help of a Special Synodical Fund, which was paid until his death. He regularly preached in Irish and Richardson held him up as an example of what the Church of Ireland should be doing.[131] He died in Cushendall on 22 March 1719.

HUMPHREY THOMPSON (d. 1744)

The earliest known minister to the First Ballybay Congregation was Humphrey Thompson.[132] He was educated at Glasgow and was ordained to Ballybay in 1699.[133] He preached in Irish every second Sunday to his own congregation in Ballybay.[134] He was also engaged in preaching in Irish in more remote areas.

Thompson must have been a very good preacher because in 1700 he was chosen as one of a group by the Synod to go on a tour preaching the Gospel to the '... upper County about Inniskillin'.[135] At that time this area would have been Irish-speaking. John McIvor said that an old record stated that Thompson '... had the Irish language ...' and pointed out that this was a direct translation from Irish, Bhí an Ghaeilge aige.[136] He married a daughter of William Elliott, a niece of David Cairns of Knockmany and Derry.[137] Among Shirley's transcriptions of gravestones in Aughnamullen is one to the Thompson family:

> John Thompson died in June 1771, aged 70. Thomas Humphrey Thompson died April 17th aged 73. Josiah Thompson died the 8th August 1771 aged 34 years Eunice Thompson, died March 28, 1777, aged 38 years.[138]

For some reason, the year of death for Thomas Humphrey Thompson, above, has been omitted; it was probably 1771. Therefore, this could be a son of the Irish-speaking minister.

He was a regular attender at the General Synod, until shortly before he died. His name was put forward, on one occasion, as a candidate for Moderator.[139] He died at Monantin, Ballybay, on 7 April 1744.[140, 141]

ROBERT THOMPSON (d. 1739)

He was another one of the group of Irish-speaking ministers who were able to preach, in the period 1710–1720.[142]

Educated at Glasgow 1705, he was licensed by the Monaghan Presbytery in 1709 and was ordained to the Belturbet congregation in Co. Cavan in 1713.[143] After eight years he found his stipend insufficient and, even worse, the stipend had fallen into three years' arrears. In June 1721, he handed in his resignation, but the Synod stepped in to make good the deficit, paying him £25 in that year and £20 in the following year, and so he stayed on. In

1725, he was once more in arrears and this time his resignation was accepted.[144] He answered a call from Minterburn, Co. Tyrone, where he was installed in May 1726. He remained there until 1736 and died on 5 June 1739.[145]

JOHN WILSON (1667–1733)

Born in Scotland in 1667, John Wilson was educated in Glasgow and in Edinburgh. He graduated M.A. from the latter university in 1690. In 1700 he was ordained to Dundalk and Carlingford, but he resigned from Dundalk in 1702. From then onwards he was responsible for Carlingford and Narrow-water.[146]

Wilson regularly preached in Irish and he was named as one of the eight ministers chosen by the Synod of Ulster to preach the Gospel in Irish.[147, 148] However, he emigrated to America in 1729. He was aged 66 when he died in Boston on 6 June 1733.

CALEB THRELKELD (d. 1728)

Dr Threlkeld was not associated with the previous Irish-preaching Ulstermen, but had an interest in Irish for purely cultural reasons.

He was a Protestant dissenting minister, also described as a '... nonconformist, with fundamentalist views about Christian faith and morality'.[149] However it is not because of these characteristics that he is best known. He was a most unusual individual, nearly impossible to categorise.

In 1726 he published a book, *Being A Short Treatise of Native Plants* including Latin, English and Irish Names.[150] Towards the end of the book there are extensive lists of names of plants in Irish, as well as in the other two languages. From the linguistic point of view these terms are most valuable.

In addition, the main text deals in detail with each plant and the Irish terms are discussed. For example, his account of clover goes:

TRIFOLIUM PRATENSE ALBUM, *White Flowered Meadow Trefoyl.* The *Meadow Trefoyls* are called in *Irish* Shamrocks ... The Word *Seamar Leaune* and *Seamar-oge*, being in signification the same, the first signifying the *Child's Trefoyl,* the other the *Young Trefoyl,* to distinguish them from the *Seamar Capuil,* or *Horse Trefoyl* as I suppose.

Nelson, in his monograph on the Shamrock, discovered that Threlkeld, in this account, was the first person to record in print the tradition that St Patrick used the shamrock to explain the Holy Trinity. By searching wide and far, Nelson also showed that Threlkeld was the first to record clearly the custom of drowning the shamrock. In tones of the preacher he put it as follows:

> However that be, when they wet their *Seamar-oge*, they often commit Excess in Liquor, which is not a right keeping of a Day to the Lord; Error generally leading to Debauchery.

It is interesting that these contributions to the understanding of the national culture and folklore came from a native of Cumberland. Threlkeld was not an Irishman: he came to Ireland in 1713 and, being also qualified in medicine, he practised both professions in the district of the Coombe in Dublin. It was said that he was sadly missed by the poor when he died in 1728.[151]

III B

Second Part of Eighteenth Century

CULTURAL FLOWERING

GENERAL

The latter part of the eighteenth century saw a great cultural awakening among northern Presbyterians. This related particularly to Irish music and language. Previous interest in Irish was usually either practical in approach or missionary in intent; this movement was quite independent of either element and was aimed at the '... revival and extension of Irish itself'.[1] It happened to correspond in time with a rise in republican sentiment in Belfast, a trend which included approval of the French Revolution of 1789. However the number of individuals who do not fit into both movements is great. Wolfe Tone, the Protestant republican separatist, showed no interest in the Irish language. With regard to Irish music, he was moved to write in his diary after dropping in on the Belfast Harp Festival of 13 July 1792: 'The Harpers again. Strum, strum and be hanged.'[2] A recent biographer of his said:

> Indeed the romantic Ossianic revival sweeping Europe in the latter decades of the century and spawning something of a Gaelic revival among the Irish intelligentsia seems entirely to have bypassed Tone.[3]

On the other hand, Dr James MacDonnell, an Irish-speaking Protestant, lover of Irish music and loyal to the British connection, is said to have timed the organisation of the Harp Festival in a way as to provide a counter attraction to the celebrations of the storming of the Bastille.[4, 5] The Rev. William Neilson, lover of the Irish language, was also loyal to the British connection and Dr Samuel Bryson, a talented scribe in Irish, was completely apolitical.

Indeed, it would be difficult to identify any individuals at that time who were both republicans and lovers of Irish language and culture. Thomas Russell, who was executed in Downpatrick for being a United

Irishman, had gone to Irish classes, but was never proficient in the language.[6] If one were to list the prominent United Irishmen – Wolfe Tone, Russell, Jemmy Hope, Henry Joy McCracken etc. – their lack of involvement with Irish would be immediately apparent. Nevertheless, the attitude of the *Northern Star* was an exception. It was the organ of the United Irishmen, and published 'Bolg an tSoláir', the first Irish language magazine. The newspaper was founded on 4 January 1792 with Samuel Neilson as editor. Eleven of the twelve proprietors were Presbyterians.[7]

The Belfast Harp Festival took place on 11, 12 and 13 July 1792, at the Exchange Rooms, Belfast. Its purpose was to attempt '... to revive and perpetuate the Ancient Music and Poetry of Ireland'.[8] Only for this harp gathering, and its being recorded, this ancient music would have disappeared for ever and the harp tradition which has come down to us today, would not exist. Edward Bunting, William Weare and John Sharpe were to record the musical notation.[9]

The songs sung by the harpers were actually poetry put to music and required a different kind of special expertise; so it was proposed that '... a person well versed in the Language and Antiquities of the Nation, should attend ...'.[10, 11] The person selected for this work was the Rev. Andrew Bryson, Presbyterian minister to Dundalk. It is noteworthy that this project was perhaps the first attempt in Ireland to actively rejuvenate the native Gaelic culture, and it occurred in Presbyterian Belfast with a Presbyterian Minister as the Gaelic authority asked to share his expertise.[12] All of the ten harpers present at the historic meeting were doubtlessly Irish-speakers, as were all their predecessors, and so a talented Irish scholar would be needed to record accurately the words of their songs, but it appears that the Rev. Andrew Bryson, unfortunately, did not attend the meeting, nor did anyone come in his place.[13]

Writing down the words of the songs was a major reason for holding the Festival in the first place, so Bunting and the McCrackens arranged for Patrick Lynch to do a tour of the countryside in order to collect the words of the old songs. Lynch was also able to record music and eventually he was able to put together a fine collection.[14]

The Presbyterian, Henry Joy (1754–1835), author of *Historical*

Collections relative to the Town of Belfast, who was an uncle of Henry Joy McCracken, was one of the organisers of the Harp Festival.[15] He was editor of the *Belfast News Letter* which gave an account of the festival. The *Northern Star* reported on the tunes played by the harpers.[16]

McNeill, in her biography of Mary Ann McCracken, said about these musical and language activities:

> Here in Rosemary lane, in the bosom of rationalist Presbyterian Belfast, the renaissance of Irish music took place, the precursor by a century of the Irish Gaelic Revival, which was to exert such a lasting influence on the course of the Irish nation.[17]

She pointed out that the Gaelic League was not formed until 1893. The house in Rosemary Lane was the home of Mary Ann McCracken and it was Bunting's headquarters. From there he organised his work and made trips through the country to collect the music. That is where he wrote his great books; Mary Ann corrected the proofs and her brother John wrote part of the preface for him and drew the pictures for the books. It was the McCrackens who organised the journeys of Bunting and Patrick Lynch to go to the people and record the Irish words of the songs and it was to Mary Ann that they wrote back the letters about their progress through the land.[18] At this period in Belfast history the town was referred to as the 'Athens of the North'.[19] It was fashionable to be involved in literary and cultural affairs. Lord Castlereagh, whose family name was Robert Stewart (1769–1822), was a Presbyterian.[20] He was Irish Chief Secretary in 1800 and eased the passage of the Act of Union through the House of Commons. He was very anxious to be associated with cultural activities and it was said of him:

> Lord Castlereagh was a munificient patron of literary talent, and particularly of that of his own country. The collection of Irish Melodies, made by the able Mr Bunting of Belfast, from the ancient bards of Ireland, was undertaken at his suggestion; and the translations from Carolan were moulded into their present shape by his masterly hand. Lord Castlereagh was the means of establishing in Dublin a 'Gaelic Society', the object of which was to encourage writers in the ancient Erse, and translations from scarce works in verse and prose. This society went on well for some time; and a volume of their proceedings was printed. Theophilis O'Hannegan was the Secretary, a man who was quite a genius, and a scholar of

unrivalled attainments, but who possessed not an atom of discretion. The removal of Lord Castlereagh to England withdrew his attention from this local institution, and it was, in consequence, discontinued. The last service he rendered it was releasing poor O' Hannigan from the Sheriff's, where he was confined for a considerable debt.'[21]

This posthumous tribute to Castlereagh, who had the reputation of being cold and uncaring, must be viewed with some scepticism. The suggestion that these activities relied so heavily on Castlereagh strains our credulity. Also, Theophilus O'Flanagan, who edited the *Transactions of the Gaelic Society of Dublin* (1808), had his surname recorded inaccurately above. Castlereagh's half-brother, Charles Vane, who wrote the above eulogy, seems to suggest that the Viscount translated O Carolan's songs from Irish. Whatever the truth in any of these assertions, the important conclusion is that, writing in 1848, Charles Vane, third Marquess of Londonderry, who idolised his half-brother, believed that one of the ways of reflecting his brother in a very good light was to depict him as a patron of Irish language and culture.

In the 1790s many in Belfast wanted to learn Irish and Patrick Lynch was much in demand as a teacher. A notice in the *Northern Star* of 16 April 1795 made detailed references to Lynch and what he was trying to do:

An attempt to revive the grammatical and critical knowledge of the Irish language in this town is generously made by Mr Lynch; he teaches publically in the Academy and privately in several families.

This language ... is particularly interesting to all who wish for the improvement and Union of this neglected and divided Kingdom. By our understanding and speaking it we could more easily and effectually communicate our sentiments and instructions to all our Countrymen; and thus mutually improve and conciliate each other's affections.

The merchant and artist would reap great benefit from the knowledge of it. They would then be qualified for carrying on Trade and Manufactures in every part of their native country.

Such knowledge we understand, could be easily acquired in three or four months by the assistance of Mr Lynch.[22]

Patrick Lynch, *hibernice* Pádraig Ó Loingsigh, ran an Irish School in Loughinisland, Co. Down. As a talented Irish scholar, he was an important language resource. He taught Irish in the Belfast Academy, which then had aspirations to become a College for training Presbyterian clerical students. He was responsible for the editorial aspects of Bolg an tSoláir published by the *Northern Star*. In addition he taught privately and in 1796 he made a phonetic script version of the New Testament for Whitley Stokes. In 1800 he was copying manuscripts written by Peadar Ó Doirnín, a well known South Armagh poet who wrote in Irish, and by Pádraig Ó Prontaigh. This he was doing for Samuel Coulter of Dundalk, at the price of thirteen pence a leaf. [23] The Rev. Moses Neilson who ran the Academy at Rademon, himself an Irish-speaker, was friendly with Lynch and his son William Neilson benefited greatly from Lynch's help in the production of 'Neilson's Grammar'. Lynch was at the centre of a wide circle of Presbyterians and others who were working for cultural rejuvenation.

Consideration of the extent of these activities taking place in mainly Presbyterian Belfast in the last decade of the eighteenth century, including the cultivation of the Irish language, the reclamation of Irish music and the spread of radical and liberal politics, makes it is easy to understand why a Belfast person wrote one hundred years afterwards: 'At that period our town numbered only some 18,000 inhabitants, but it was a focus of intellectual life and progress in Ireland.' [24]

A more detailed account follows of some of the personalities who were active in promoting Irish at their time. Some of them, of course, lived and carried on their activities well into the nineteenth century, and in turn these were continued by others.

The individuals concerned were:

ANDREW BRYSON (d. 1797)

Andrew Bryson was one of a succession of Irish-speaking Presbyterian clergymen serving the Dundalk congregation. [25] He was the second son of the Rev. James Bryson of Belfast and a brother of Dr Samuel Bryson. [26] He matriculated in the University of Glasgow in 1779 [27] and graduated M.A. in 1782. He was licensed by the Bangor Presbytery on 6 September

1785. On 15 August 1786 he was ordained to Dundalk. He frequently gave sermons in Irish and could write the language with ease. At a meeting of the committee called to organise the Harpers' Festival, held on 23 April 1792, it was agreed that '... the Reverend Mr Andrew Bryson, of Dundalk, be requested to assist, as a person versed in the language and antiquities of the Nation'.[28] The idea was that he would be able to understand the musical terms used by the harpers and be able to record them with appropriate orthography. It was also understood that he would be able to write down the words of any songs that might be sung. However, it appears that he was unable to be present.[29] The notes made by Bunting were very good considering his lack of proficiency in Irish, but since he used English phonetics they were most difficult to decipher.

His signature 'Andreas Brison in Dungannon 12 raos(sic) 1786', appears in an Irish manuscript numbered 37 in the Belfast Public Library.[30] A longer note in Irish appears in his own copy of an Irish Catechism, as follows: 'Is leabhar so le Aindrias Brison a mBaile-ath-cliath Dia-ceadaoin cead lá Feabhra 1786'.[31] A further signature is to be found in one of the Bryson manuscripts, a copy of Andrew's own sermons: 'Aindrias Brison a bhFachaird Dia Sathairn 9 adh ló don 7 adh mhí 1786'.[32] Each of these signatures gives the date and the place.

In 1786 he married a Miss McGlatley from near Dundalk and they had a number of children. One of their daughters married Charles Mellsop. It was said of his political leanings:

> He exercised an ardent and earnest ministry during a time of strenuous political struggle in Ireland. In the year 1782 he joined with his flock in boldly asserting the independence of the then Irish Legislature, and at the same time proclaimed their joy at the relaxation of the Penal Laws affecting their Roman Catholic fellow subjects.[33]

Andrew's family were closely associated with Holywood, Co. Down.[34] Statements that they came from Fourtowns,[35] Poyntzpass,[36] or Glenwherry[37] are all erroneous.

The Rev. Bryson retired on 22 June 1796 and died in March 1797. He was buried at Ballymascanlon, Co. Louth.

SAMUEL BRYSON (1776–1853)

Samuel Maziere Bryson, son of a Presbyterian minister, is remembered for his abilities as a notable collector of important manuscripts in Irish and for his skills as a talented scribe and Irish scholar. Many of his valuable manuscripts now form part of the Robert MacAdam Collection housed in the Belfast Public Library. The credit for first publicising the important work of Samuel Bryson in collecting and transcribing manuscripts in Irish goes to Henry Morris[38] and F.J. Bigger[39] who virtually simultaneously, in 1921, gave the first biographies of this Ulster medical Irish scholar. Since then, some further details have been added by another article by F.J. Bigger[40] and accounts from Ó Casaide,[41] Simms,[42] and more recently, from Arthurs,[43] Deirdre Mortún,[44] and Ó Buachalla,[45] who has also made a detailed study of the Bryson manuscripts, have appeared.[46]

His father, James, and his grandfather, John, were both Presbyterian ministers and his own brother, Andrew, was an Irish-speaking minister to the Dundalk congregation.[47]

Samuel was born, the twenty-first son of the Rev. James Bryson, on 9 March 1776.[48] It is not known if his mother was the first or the second wife of his father. His birthplace appears to have been Holywood, Co. Down, with which the family had been associated over preceding generations.[49] He went to Edinburgh to study medicine and when aged about 24 (c. 1800), qualified as a Licentiate of the Royal College of Surgeons (L.R.C.S.). On 16 May 1806, he also qualified as a Licentiate of Apothecaries (Lic. Ap.) of Ireland.[50] This permitted him to open a shop and practise as an apothecary.

In previous reports our subject has been confounded with his son, Samuel Bryson M.D. (1810–1858), who was also a physician, leading to the misconception that there was an anomaly in the father's medical qualifications. Bigger, writing in 1921, said that it '... was not known what medical degrees he had ...',[51] but this is incorrect and arose from the confusion of father with son. Samuel Bryson's qualifications are quite unambiguously recorded, as previously stated.

Samuel junior was qualified M.D. The disparate qualifications help to distinguish between father and son. It was probably the son who held the hospital appointment and not the father.[52, 53]

As early as 1803, when he was aged 27, Dr Samuel Bryson senior was engaged in collecting and transcribing Irish manuscripts. He supported himself at first by running what we would now call a chemist shop, but apothecaries in those days were most versatile and he sold not only drugs, many made up by himself, but also 'oils and colours'. However, he was married in October 1805 and this along with his full qualification as an apothecary in May 1806 would explain why he regularised his professional activities in August 1806, by dissolving his business and turning over to full time apothecary practice.[54] His surgery then was at 50 High Street, Belfast.

DISSOLUTION OF PARTNERSHIP.

THE PARTNERSHIP hitherto carried on in the DRUG, OIL, and COLOUR BUSINESS. under the Firm of SAMUEL BRYSON & CO. was dissolved by mutual consent on the First of May last. The Debts due to the above Firm. are requested to be discharged immediately ; and those to whom they are indebted, will please furnish their accounts to SAMUEL BRYSON, Apothecary, No. 50, High-street, who is duly authorised to receive and discharge the same.

Belfast, July 26.

SAMUEL BRYSON

TAKES the liberty of informing his Friends and the Public, that he has commenced the APOTHECARY BU-SINESS in that central situation, No. 50, High-street, and hopes by being constantly supplied with DRUGS of the best Quality, and from his designing to dedicate his time solely to the PREPARATION and COMPOSITION of MEDICINE, to merit a share of Public layout. Belfast, July 26.

Advertisement in *Belfast News Letter*, 1806

In the course of time he and his wife, Alice Standfield, had four known children. Robert, born in 1806, died young; Alice died unmarried in 1862. The other two sons, Joseph Wallace (1807–1855), and Samuel (1810–1858) grew up to eventually qualify in medicine; throughout the 1830s and 1840s the father and two sons practised medicine in partnership at 98 High Street, until Samuel Senior retired in 1848.

In later life his private residence was a house called 'Cluan' situated in Ballymacarrett and corresponding to modern Bryson Street, which is called after him. In the map of the first Ordnance Survey, dated 1834, this house is shown standing alone in the green fields of what is now Ballymacarrett. Samuel had no connection, however, with the family after which Bryson House in Bedford Street is named. A plaque inside the building indicates that the family concerned is entirely different. Yet, it is clear that Cluan Place is called after Dr Bryson's house. He was the owner of land on the east side of South Parade and of May's Dock, Belfast.[55]

On the occasion of his death a notice appeared in the *Belfast News Letter*.[56] 'Died February 28 at his late residence, Cluan, Ballymacarrett, Samuel Bryson, Esq., aged 77 years, late Apothecary, formerly Assistant-Surgeon in the 32nd Regiment.' This evidence further verifies his year of birth as being 1776, but despite a miscalculation by Francis Joseph Bigger, subsequent writers have uncritically reproduced Bryson's year of birth as 1778. Samuel Bryson was buried in Holywood[57] and, according to his great-grand-daughter, Miss Alice Bryson, the most likely spot for his burial is the grave marked by the memorial to her own father, Samuel Bryson (1847–1906), i.e. Plot No. 20, in the extension to the old Holywood graveyard.[58]

Our subject, Samuel Bryson Senior, had more than ordinary facility with Irish. He was an adviser on technical points in the language. For example, he advised William Hamilton Drummond, a Presbyterian minister, in his major work *The Giant's Causeway*. Drummond acknowledges this: 'From my esteemed friend, Mr S Bryson, I have received most of the derivations of the Irish names which occur in the notes.'[59] The notes section is voluminous, encompassing 95 pages, and discusses the meaning of placenames in great detail. For example, in these notes,[60] he says that the name of Co. Antrim is probably derived from Tír na nUaimh, the land of caves. The notes on placenames are extensive and it is clear that these have been contributed by Bryson.

In a later section, Bryson[61], after discussion, gives Carrick-a-rede as derived from *Carraig an Dhroichid*, The Bridge Rock. Having given a long list of original Irish versions of other locations on this Antrim coast, he comes to Port Moon, for which he has to say 'Perhaps

Mumhan, Munster-harbour. But why? better Mahone, a word of rather indelicate meaning'. By this Bryson meant Mo Thóin, my backside. He continues: 'Several waterfalls in the county of Antrim are known to the natives by a strange appelation, which may be rendered in Latin by *equa mingens.*' *Equa* means a mare and *mingens* means voiding urine. He then says: 'The names of the caves in the cliffs of Lirrybann will not bear even a translation.' Leaving such details aside, the amount of work and expertise on placename meanings in these notes is truly prodigious. Clearly Bryson was a major authority on place names in his time.

Another author who gave him credit was James Stuart (1764–1840), who wrote the famous *Historical Memoirs of the City of Armagh*,[62] and who was later editor of the *Belfast News Letter*.

Some of the material in Stuart's *Armagh* was submitted by Samuel Bryson. On page 629 information on the descendants of Aodh Buí Ó Néill is listed. The oration over the grave of the last descendant of the Clandeboy O'Neills was one of Dr Bryson's own manuscripts. There are references to other Irish language manuscripts and an account of the O'Neills of Clandeboy. Two verses in Irish, beginning 'Míle fáilte dhuitse a Chuinn', praising the generosity of Conn an Aithne Ó Néill, are reproduced. He says that one of the branches of these O'Neills gave Port a Ghiolla Ghruama, i.e. Groomsport, and adjacent lands to the Maol Craoives, or Rices; and Ard McCriosq, or Holywood, to the Gilmores.

It is interesting that Bryson, who again provided topographical information, this time to Stuart, returns to his theme of 'vulgarity' in placenames. In the footnote to p. 491, part of the section dealing with early Presbyterianism in Armagh he has written:

> Eanach Buidhe (pronounced anach bwyee) signifies 'the yellow marsh or moor'. English writers have corrupted the word into Annagh-boy, which they interpret "the yellow island"; but Annagh does not signify an island, and Annagh-boy seems devoid of meaning. In like manner, the words Baile na owen, i.e. the town of Owen, is corrupted into Ballynahone – a vulgar and somewhat obscene term.

However, the word tóin (thone), occurring in placenames usually refers to a type of hill or alternatively, low-lying or bottom lands.[63] After some delay succeeding the death of James Stuart on 28 September 1840, at the age of 76, a monument was erected to his memory in 1854. Samuel Bryson, shortly before his own death, was one of the contributors to the cost of a monument for him erected in the north-east aisle of Christ Church, Belfast.[64] James Stuart was buried in Clifton Street Graveyard in Belfast.[65]

Samuel Bryson from his commitment to Irish language and history was a member of many relevant societies and a financial contributor to various publications. He was a subscriber to William Neilson's *Introduction to the Irish Language*, 1808.[66] He subscribed to O' Reilly's *Irish Dictionary*[67], published in 1821. He was a member of the Irish Archaelogical Society, of which Prince Albert was a Life Member and Patron[68]. This was in 1841, the year of the first publication, and he was still a member in 1849. We find him among the list of subscribers to Owen Connellan's *Gospel of St John in Irish* (1830)[69].

He was responsible for laying down the nucleus of the valuable collection of Irish language manuscripts now held in the Belfast City Library. These were first reported on by P.J. O' Shea, 'Conductor of the Celtic Class in the Belfast Naturalists' Field Club', who had this to say in 1895:

> I have examined the above MSS, which were the property of the late Dr Bryson, and were by him presented to the Museum. They are well bound, the hand writing is excellent, and the contractions common in Irish manuscripts are so well imitated that one sees at a glance the copies are the work of practised scribes ... .[70]

The full collection is now known as the MacAdam Manuscripts and comes to 43 in number. Those numbered 35–40 were presented by Dr Bryson and at least four of these were written by himself. He showed very fine calligraphy. In 1803, he wrote a copy of *Oidhe Chlainne Lir* (*The Tragic Story of the Children of Lir*),and *Oidhe Chlainne Thuireann* (*The Tragic Story of the Children of Tuireann*). By 15 May of the following year he had completed transcribing O'Clery's *Irish Vocabulary* and on 16 April of the next year, 1805, he finished his transcription of the Funeral Oration in Irish made over Owen O'Neill of the House of Clandeboy, who died in 1744. Later this was edited and published by Douglas Hyde in *U.J.A.*[71] His transcription of *The Wars of the Romans* has been described as 'a beautiful specimen of clear, perfect and artistic calligraphy'.[72] His translation from Irish of the story of Deirdre was recently published.[73] He was also a friend of other scribes, for example, Simon Macken of Monaghan.[74] His energy and diligence in saving old Irish manuscripts pointed the way to Robert MacAdam, who later hired scribes to write manuscripts, some of which turned out to be exceptionally important.

A person of great drive, he was also very active in medical work in Belfast. He was admitted as a member of the Belfast Medical Society on 1 July 1822 and did much to help the rejuvenation of that organisation.[75] He was also a major subscriber to the Belfast Charitable Society.[76] On 1 November 1835 he was recorded as being a member of the Statistical Society of Ulster.[77]

Samuel Bryson was one of the original subscribers to the Irish Harp Society. The first meeting was in Linn's Hotel, the White Cross, No. 1 Castle Street on 17 Mar 1808. Drs Bryson, Tennant and MacDonnell drew up the rules. The society not only ran harp lessons but had classes for learning Irish.[78]

He has the unusual distinction of having had two laudatory poems in Irish composed in his honour. Both of these were composed by Aodh Mac Domhnaill. The first, 'In praise of Dr Bryson' (*Moladh an Dr Bríse*), thanks the doctor for having successfully treated his chest condition.[79] Aodh describes the hacking cough which kept him awake at night and contrasts that situation with his complete recovery after taking Dr Bryson's medicine. Aodh describes the doctor as *carthannach* (kind) and *caoimhiúl* (pleasant). Similar terms are used in the other poem, 'Two Belfastians' (*Beirt Bhéal-Feirsdeach*).[80] The same poem appears in *Duanaire na Midhe*[81] under the title of 'Comórtas na Toite' (The Smoking Competition). In this, Bryson is described as 'Flaithiúl' (generous). The other person praised in the same poem is Leary Duff, and many terms are used to describe both Samuel Bryson and Leary Duff. In translation they approximate to: noble; level-headed; cheerful; agreeable; kind; virtuous; pleasant and material of champions. Allowing for some sycophantic adulation, it seems clear that

John Abernethy
1680–1740

James Bryson
1730–1796

William Neilson
1774–1821

William H. Drummond
1778–1865

John Edgar D.D. L.L.D.
1798–1866

Norman McLeod D.D.
1783–1862

Dr Reuben J. Bryce
1797–1888

James MacAdam
1801–1861

Billy Parish Church.
Burial place of the Rev. Jeremiah O'Quinn

'Cleas an Chopáin' (Cup Tossing) based on the original painting by
N.J. Crowley, 1842. Mary Ann McCracken is said to have sat for the gypsy

Samuel Bryson was popular, kind, and generally well-liked. An indirect compliment was paid to him by the Central Library, Belfast, in their leaflet about the Irish language collection.[82]

> The jewel in the crown of the Irish language collection is a set of 43 manuscripts collected by Robert MacAdam and Samuel Bryson in the 19th century, containing songs, genealogies, prayers, sermons and poems. It can be viewed on microfilm.

Samuel Simms paid him the following tribute,

> It seems to me that he was the first Belfast citizen to actively encourage the study of the Irish Language and Irish Literature, and he shares with Dr James MacDonnell (1762–1845) and Robert MacAdam (1808–1895) the honour of preserving in this city the language and literature of his native land ... .[83]

THE BRYSON FAMILY

In the contemporary Ireland of Samuel Bryson (1776–1853), when monoglot Irish-speakers were measured in millions, it would not be very suprising for any citizen, including a Presbyterian, to be able to understand Irish or even to speak it fairly well. Since there was no education in Irish at the time it would, however, be surprising to meet a citizen who could read or write in Irish. Yet, both Samuel and his brother Andrew were exceptionally literate in the language. One possible reason for them, and also perhaps for their father James, being so proficient in Irish was that the family was an Irish-speaking one. While, of course Presbyterian families who were Irish-speaking were by no means the norm even in the early 1800s, we do know that some did exist. In some pockets, such as areas of North Antrim, the Dundalk district and in the Rademon and Castlewellan areas of Co. Down, there were Irish-speaking Presbyterian families. These are the ones who are documented, but there must have been a great many others. The *Dictionary of National Biography* (*D.N.B.*) says that Samuel's grandfather John (1685–1788) came from Donegal,[84] which at that time was uniformly Irish-speaking and this is a possible explanation for the extent of polished Irish in the Bryson family. The contributor to the *D.N.B.* was the Rev. Alexander Gordon , generally considered to be very reliable. Another factor to consider is that, according to McLysaght, the surname Bryson (Briceson), is used as an anglicisation for the Donegal surnames, Ó Breasláin (Breslin), and Ó Muirgheasáin (O' Morison).[85] Even today the surname Bryson is quite common in Co. Donegal.

John Bryson is so far the earliest member of the family to be identified.[86] Born around the year 1685, his place of birth could have been, as mentioned, in Donegal. He is said to have become a Presbyterian minister, but is not listed as a minister in the *Fasti*, or in the history of congregations. MacConnell, giving him as the father of James, does not refer to him as 'Rev'.[87] He lived in Holywood, Co Down, where he died on 23 Nov. 1788 at the age of 103 years.[88]

His son, James Bryson, was born about 1730, in Holywood, Co. Down. Cathal O'Byrne, without giving any evidence, said that he was educated by the Lynches of Loughinisland (who were noted Irish scholars) and that '... the knowledge thus gained was passed on by the reverend gentleman to his son, Samuel.[89] Ó Casaide said that the Rev. James Bryson '... may have been an Irish speaker himself as his family were intimate with the Rev. William Neilson, and one of his sons, Samuel, who transcribed several Irish MSS in his own handwriting.[90] These two facts seem hardly sufficient evidence for James Bryson being an Irish speaker. Yet, Ó Snodaigh goes further and states unequivocally that he was an Irish-speaker, quoting Ó Casaide,[91] above mentioned, and Bigger (1921),[92] who made no statements about James's language ability. For the other reasons, already given, it is a possibility that James and his father John were of native Irish stock and were an Irish-speaking family.

On 1 June 1762, James Bryson was licensed by the Armagh Presbytery at Clare, Co. Armagh. He was ordained into the First Lisburn Presbyterian Congregation on 6 June, 1764.[93] He removed to Second (Rosemary Street) Congregation of Belfast (1774–1792) and finally to the Fourth (Donegall Street) Congregation (1792–1796).

The Rev. James Bryson was a well known figure in the Belfast of his day. He was noted for his liberality,[94] and had an aphorism, 'All the children of God are our brethren'. On St. Patrick's Day 1778, the first Company of Belfast Volunteers was enrolled[95] and in November of the same year the Rev. Bryson preached them a sermon. He became chairman and chaplain to the Belfast First Volunteer Company.[96] In 1782 he became a Mason when he joined the Orange (Masonic) Lodge No 257, and on the 24 June of that year he preached them a sermon. Indeed, he was famous for his sermons, many of which appeared in print.[97]

He published a volume of sermons in 1778, dedicated to 'The Rev. William Brison of Antrim ... my friend and kinsman'. We do not know the exact relationship between them, but it seems that they were first cousins.[98] The *D.N.B.* entry for him states that he too is said '... to have come of a Donegal family'.[99]

William Bryson married a daughter of the Rev. Alexander MacLaine. It is of the greatest interest that both her grandfathers were Irish-speaking Presbyterian ministers who were also able to preach in that language with great facility. On her mother's side was the famous Rev. John Abernethy.[100] Her paternal grandfather was the Rev. Archibald MacLaine who was installed in 1700 in the Markethill congregation[101], and who was considered to be '... one of the best masters of the Irish language'.[102]

The association of this Bryson family with Holywood, Co. Down, has been consistent over many generations. The entry in the *D.N.B.* for James Bryson mentions a gravestone, in the Holywood Graveyard, which indicated that James's father John died in 1788, aged 103 years. This stone no longer exists. However, by chance, a letter was found in a newspaper[103] referring to the inscriptions on the stone. The details show that this family were in Holywood from about the middle of the eighteenth century. Another stone has been erected, probably on the same site, indicating that Brysons were still in Holywood in the early part of the twentieth century.

The last person to be buried in this grave was Samuel Bryson (1847–1906), the grandson of Dr Samuel Bryson (1776–1853), the scribe and Irish scholar. He was married to Mary Duncan, a native of Magherafelt and they lived with their three daughters in 'Woodbank', Ballymenoch, off the Croft Road in Holywood. It was this Samuel who possessed an oil painting of his great-grandfather, the Rev. James Bryson (1730–1796). He loaned it to S. Shannon Millin for use in his history of the Second Congregation (1900). The same picture was reproduced in Craig's *History of Presbyterianism in Lisburn* (1960).

One of the three daughters mentioned above, Alice, lived until 19 January 1987, when she died at the age of 96 years. In a letter to the author[104] she said that she had a silver snuff box which had belonged to her great-grandfather Dr Samuel Bryson. On it were inscribed his initials 'S.B'.

WILLIAM NEILSON (1774–1821) D.D. (1805), M.R.I.A. (1808)

William Neilson was a Presbyterian minister, who is best remembered for his remarkable *Introduction to the Irish Language*, also called *Neilson's Grammar*.[105] The author was born the fourth of seven sons,[106] on 12 September 1774,[107] at Rademon, Kilmore, Co Down, where his father, the celebrated Rev. Moses Neilson, D.D., ministered to a Presbyterian congregation, many of whom were Irish-speaking, and also ran a famous Classical Academy whose students were drawn from all the denominations.[108] William's mother, Catherine Welsh, was a direct descendant of the great John Knox.[109] His father, Moses, traced his descent from the O'Neills of Ulster and that is why he changed his surname to Neilson.

The young William, who resembled his father in many ways,[110] from an early age showed a taste for knowledge and the study of languages. He was the only one of the Neilsons to adopt his father's spelling of the surname.[111] He may have been reared with Irish because his father was a fluent Irish-speaker,[112] or he may have learned the language as a boy. O'Laverty seemed in no doubt that William was a pupil of Patrick Lynch (Ó Loinsigh) of Loughinisland who ran a school of Classics and Irish language.[113]

After attending the University of Glasgow (1789–1793), he helped his father with teaching in the Academy at Rademon, apparently for about three years.[114] During this time he continued to study and wrote a Grammar of the English language which was published some time later and was used throughout the province of Ulster.[115] He also at that time collected the material for his *Greek Exercises*.

Eventually, he was licensed by the Presbytery of Antrim and afterwards ordained a minister on his appointment to the Presbyterian congregation of Dundalk, Co. Louth. This was on 21 December 1796.[116] It is worth remembering that the Irish-speaking population of Ireland at that time numbered over three million. Large stretches of Co. Down were Irish-speaking. Therefore, it is not surprising to note that many of these were Presbyterians. Indeed, the Dundalk congregation was basically Irish-speaking and from 1700 to that time every minister appointed had been Gaelic speaking. Neilson was only twenty two on his appointment to Dundalk, but the fact that he was an Irish-speaker was in his favour, for 'It was considered essential that the minister of this congregation should be able to speak Irish ...'.[117]

In Dundalk, Neilson, with his kindly and charitable disposition, was very popular among all classes and creeds.[118] His fluency in Irish, both in writing and in conversation, made him particularly popular with the common people.[119] At the same time, through his scholarship and expert knowledge of languages, he was well known in academic circles, not only in the British Isles, but also in wider Europe.

He ran an inter-denominational academy, along the lines of that of his father's in Rademon. One of his many famous pupils was Nicholas Joseph Callan (1799–1864), a native of Darver, Drumiskin, Dundalk. He was a priest, scientist and inventor. Among his more notable inventions were the induction coil, which led to the modern transformer, and types of galvanic batteries. He independently discovered Ohm's Law.[120] Another of his famous pupils was the Irish-speaking Lord O'Hagan, the first Roman Catholic Lord Chancellor of Ireland in modern times.

In 1804 Neilson published at Dundalk his *Greek Exercises*, a very popular text which saw eight editions, the last one at London in 1846.[121] Neilson was very fond of preaching in Irish and indeed was not put off by actually being arrested on one occasion in 1798, when he was delivering a sermon to his father's congregation in Rademon. This was an embarrassing blunder on the part of the authorities, for it was subsequently proved that, not only was he simply preaching the Gospel, but that William was also verified as being a loyal subject of the King![122, 123]

The Rev. Neilson continued to preach in Irish. In July 1805 he went on an Irish-preaching tour of the North. For example it is recorded that on Thursday 11 July 1805, 'Dr Neilson preached a sermon in Irish in the Donegall Street Meeting House in Belfast, to a numerous and respectable audience.'[124] He appeared to give sermons regularly in that Meeting House.[125] Ó Snodaigh[126] has shown that he was still preaching in Irish in 1813.[127]

A person of true scholarly attributes, William penned an extensive manuscript, while in Dundalk, consisting of an edited version of Begley and MacCurtin's *English-Irish Dictionary*, which had been printed in Paris in 1732.[128] This document is in the National Library of Ireland, and is dated 1798.[129]

It was while he was in Dundalk, in 1808, that he published his famous *Introduction to the Irish Language*, a work which is said to have been begun by his father in 1769.[130] It was dedicated to Philip, Earl of Hardewicke who was Lord Lieutenant of Ireland from 1801 to 1805.[131] Neilson described him as patron of the work.

The book is a unique repository of the Irish language of Co. Down. According to O'Rahilly,[132] Neilson, like many grammarians, tried very hard to avoid dialect, but he did not always succeed and this is one of the reasons that the book is still valuable today. O'Rahilly went on to say: 'He devotes a page to provincial varieties in pronunciation, and is the first to remark on the difference of accentuation between North and South.' O'Rahilly was able to infer, by studying Neilson's book, that the people of south-east Ulster normally used the Scottish Gaelic form of 'not', i.e. 'cha', instead of the usual Irish form 'ní'. O'Rahilly relied very substantially on Neilson's work to describe and contrast the Irish of south-east Ulster with other dialects.

Neilson's work also included the earliest printed folk-tale in Irish, recounting the abduction of a Co. Galway woman by the fairies and her liberation by Thady Hughes of Knock-na-Feadalea, Co. Down. Furthermore, this is the only folk-tale in Irish we have from Co. Down.[133] Apparently, Neilson gathered the stories from Patrick Lynch, the Irish-teacher of Loughinisland.[134] This book was pioneering in its use of everyday familiar dialogue as a method of teaching. Hyde said that Neilson was the only person ever, up to that time, who had done anything for the spoken Irish of the people.[135] Furthermore, Neilson's *Grammar* has left us today with a detailed and fascinating picture of social life in pre-famine Co. Down.

A review of Neilson's Grammar appeared in the *Belfast Monthly Magazine*, March 1809.[136] The author ('H') said that he approved of the study of Irish. 'A language which is spoken by at least one third of the inhabitants of the British Isles and by more than three fourths of the natives of Ireland, has some claim to attention'.

The critic pointed out that the language had been the subject of a propaganda war, by enemies who used every imaginable distortion to attack it. When Queen Anne had proposed to establish professorships in Irish in her universities, the Duke of Ormond devised a plan to thwart her and put together an absurd concoction to dissuade her, 'D'ith damh dubh ubh amh ar neamh', which he tried to parade as a typical piece of the Irish language. This meaningless gibberish is equally absurd in any language, 'A black ox ate a raw egg in Heaven'.

This person, 'H', reminded his readers that among the *cognoscenti*, the Irish language rivalled ancient Greek in its harmony, copiousness and strength. He furthermore quoted the rather extravagant claim that '... it is the root of the Latin of the Twelve Tables; that it was spoken by Hamilcar and by Hannibal; and that it is not only the primitive language of Europe and of a great part of Asia and of Africa, but of Paradise itself.'

The author did not agree that the language was '... quite so old ...' but continued on to quote General Vallencey who did thorough studies into the antiquity of Irish. He welcomed publications in the language, including Dr Neilson's *Grammar*.

> That he has rendered a service to the cause of Irish letters the work before us clearly evinces. It is a work of time, labour and an accurate knowledge of the language. It is also the most copious we have seen. Indeed we think it faulty in this respect ... and are rather surprised that he has extended the declension of the verb 'Bí', through no less than five octavo pages, and 'Buail' through eight and a half.

The writer continued with detailed grammatical criticism.

'H' also criticised the *Grammar* for the loose translations accompanying some of the texts, on the grounds that these would confuse a beginner. He accused Neilson of over-fastidiousness when he omitted to translate a passage where Deirdre was described as praising the delight she had in feasting on a brock (badger). He furthermore chided Neilson for having, in the title page, described the first part of the work as an original grammar. He felt that this did not do credit to previous grammars.

Dr Neilson replied to these points in a letter from Dundalk dated 5 May.[137] About originality he said:

> I rest my pretensions to originality upon the conviction that at least nine tenths of my work consists of material that was never before published. A coincidence with other writers, in some things, must appear, even where there was nothing borrowed.

He answered the grammatical criticisms very effectively and in detail. 'H' had alleged he was too copious, to which he replied 'Indeed copiousness has been my object throughout; as I conceived it more useful to publish a book which a man might consult, than one that a child might get by rote'.

To the objection about looseness in translation, he pointed out that only three songs fell into this category and that these had been selected to show a free approach, '... which is observed in the most elegant translations'.

Finally 'H' had upbraided him for having different orthography (spelling standards) from other authors, to which he replied:

> The standard ... I have always followed, is the Irish Bible published nearly 130 years ago, by Bishop Bedell. When a better shall be invented, I shall readily adopt it; in the mean time, it is sufficient to observe that the ancient manuscripts afford no one such standard.

In 1828 Scurry wrote a treatise on Irish grammars and dictionaries, in which he commented in detail on Neilson's *Grammar*, going through every section in turn.[138] He had a number of criticisms to make, but gave praise as well. In general he felt that the work assumed too much prior knowledge in the reader and he would like to have seen definitions of the grammatical terms. However, in general, he commended this work, of which he said: 'His labours for the preservation and improvement of our language deserve considerable praise.'

Writing in 1845, John O'Donovan, nearly 40 years later, said that Patrick Lynch, a native of the parish of Inch, near Castlewellan, had helped Neilson with this grammar, but that Lynch, although having a good knowledge of the Irish of east Ulster, was a 'rude scholar'.[139] Continuing in this vein, while praising the layout of the book, he criticised the examples given as 'provincial and barbaric'. O'Donovan was an eminent scholar of Irish but devoted himself generally to a frozen, 'classical' Irish which even in his day was completely out of touch with the everyday spoken Irish of the people. In his own *Grammar* (1845), the examples of Irish literature which he gave began in the seventh century and, incredibly for a grammar of modern Irish, stopped short at 1567.

It is notable that the great O' Donovan has not left us any significant writings of his own creation in the Irish language. It is also a matter of record that O'Donovan's children knew no Irish. Therefore, it is hard to escape the conclusion that his interest in Irish was mainly antiquarian. Robert MacAdam could not understand why O'Donovan would not co-operate in establishing a monthly journal in Irish, but an insight into his attitude is shown in a letter published by Ó Buachalla, where he argued against teaching modern Irish in the Queen's College, Belfast, where he had been appointed Professor of Celtic. He felt that teaching historical and antiquarian topics would be more suitable. Indeed, he predicted that Irish would have disappeared by the beginning of the the twentieth century![140] His criticisms of Neilson's *Grammar* must be seen in this light.

There is substantial evidence to show that Patrick Lynch certainly contributed to Neilson's *Grammar*, but that he could not be considered a co-author. Clearly Neilson conceived and devised the shape and form of the *Grammar* himself. In 1810 he published a second Irish book.[141] This was at the request of the London Hibernian Society. A translation of the title would be, 'A First Irish Book. Printed for the Public good of Ireland. At the request and expense of the Hibernian Society 1810'.

Both these books, but particularly the first, earned the author a substantial reputation as an Irish scholar.[142]

Dr Neilson's status in classical literature ranked so high that in 1805 the University of Glasgow conferred on him the degree of Doctor of Divinity. It is believed that this was in recognition of his significant contribution to the study of Irish that he was awarded the membership of the Royal Academy of Ireland (M.R.I.A.), to which he was elected on 30 November 1808.[143] His devotion to Irish never faltered during his lifetime. He was a keen collector of manuscripts in Irish and is recorded as having offered 40 guineas '... for a perfect copy of the ballad *The Independent Man* by Peadar Ó Doirnín'.[144] He was a founder member of the Gaelic Society of Dublin formed in December 1806, as was reported by the Society's secretary, Edward O'Reilly.[145]

So highly thought of was Neilson by his colleagues that at the General Synod at Cookstown on 24 June 1806 he was elected to the highest honour, that of Moderator.[146] In this capacity he signed, on behalf of the Presbyterian Church, an address to the Lord Lieutenant of Ireland, congratulating him on his recent appointment to that office. The address committed the Presbyterians to '... an inviolable attachment to his Majesty's person, family and government ...'. His term of office was completed at the next General Synod on 30 June 1807, which he opened with a sermon based on Psalm CXXX.

He resigned his post in Dundalk on 23 July 1818, when at the age of 44 he was appointed Headmaster of the Classical School and Professor of the Classical, Hebrew and Irish Languages in the Belfast Academical Institution.[147] The College had been founded only four years previously. Although his responsibilities were onerous, Neilson made special attempts with the teaching of Irish. His class was held three times a week and the account which he gave of the objectives included the following explanatory note:

> As the Irish language is considered the best preserved dialect of the ancient Celtic, a knowledge of it is highly important to the philological scholar and the antiquarian. It enables the latter to explain ancient names of almost all the places in the West of Europe and the former to ascertain the meaning of many words particularly in the Latin language that are derived from Celtic. A knowledge of

modern Irish is also indispensible in travelling through many parts
of Ireland where this language is still spoken. The Irish class was
established with a view to both these objects ... .[148]

It is noteworthy that, although he was a minister of religion, Neilson
had no evangelistic motives in his use of Irish.[149] Rather, he loved the
language for its inherent merits and because of the concern he felt for
the well-being of his countrymen and fellow Irish-speakers.[150, 151] In
addition, Stothers makes the point that the General Synod as a whole
was not, at this time, interested in evangelism through Irish, a
movement which did not come until the 1830s.[152]

With regard to wider interests, he was a member of the Belfast
Literary Society and was elected president for the period 1819–1820.
On 1 May 1820 he read to the Society a paper entitled, 'Remarks on
Gaelic Authors and Antiquities, particularly upon Ossian'.[153]
Theologically, William Neilson held 'New Light' views. The term is
more or less synonymous with 'Non-subscription', and 'Unitarianism'.
Such elements in the Presbyterian Church tended to be more liberal
and tolerant and less likely to be aligned politically with the established
Church. They tended to believe in the 'Unity' of God rather than the
Trinity. However, the anonymous writer of his obituary in the Dublin
Christian Instructor believed that before his death the Rev. Neilson's
beliefs had undergone a change and that '... he publicly declared ... he
felt himself overcome by the force of evidence, and was obliged to rest
on the atonement of Jesus Christ'.[154]

His tenure of the post in the Academical Institution was to be all too
short, for after only three years he died, '... due to a violent rheumatic
fever ...'[155] at the early age of 47. His eulogist, McEwan, said: 'The
period was short, from his appointment to his dissolution; yet long
enough to enable him to rise the classical literature of Ulster to a high
rank in public estimation.' On his death bed the news was brought to
him that he had been offered the Chair of Greek in Glasgow. The great
size of his funeral, reputedly numbering 15,000 mourners,[156] reflected
the esteem in which he was held. He was buried in the family tomb at
Kilmore, near Downpatrick.

THE NEILSON-NELSON FAMILY

The Rev. Moses Neilson, Presbyterian minister and headmaster of a famous Academy, along with his son William, the Irish grammarian, seem to be the only two members of this family who regularly spelled their surname as Neilson. According to a descendant, the Rev. Moses traced his ancestry to Niall of the Nine Hostages, the first of the O'Neills, and therefore concluded that the spelling should be Neilson. This descendant, Dr Joseph Nelson, his great-grandson, referred to a relevant letter written by the Rev. Moses to the Secretary of the Belfast Academical Institution, dated 7 October 1821. By comparing two different inscriptions in the Meeting-house at Rademon, Joseph concluded that his great-grandfather had changed his surname some time between 1787 and 1789.[157, 158]

The two Neilsons were associated with Rademon, a townland in the Parish of Kilmore, Co. Down. Moses, the father, was born in March 1739, in Craigmonaghan, Castlederg[159] and in 1767 he graduated M.A. from the University of Glasgow. In the same year, on 21 May, he married Catherine Welsh, said to be a direct descendent of the Rev. Josias Welsh, the grandson of the Great Reformer, John Knox.

Moses Neilson instituted a Classical Academy in Rademon, which quickly grew in reputation. Its characteristics were quality of tuition and liberality.[160] Young men were prepared for the ministry and many for the Catholic priesthood. A warm tribute was paid to the school and its principal by Luke Walsh, parish priest of Culfeightrim, Co. Antrim, writing in a letter dated 1 January 1844.

I was educated myself by a Presbyterian clergyman, a man of as great moral worth and sterling integrity as Ireland could boast of, the late Dr Moses Nelson of Redemon, in the county Down, well known as one of the first classical scholars of his day. I was for seven years under his parental care and tuition; and, even yet, I cling to his memory with filial love and affection.[161]

Most of the Rademon congregation were Irish-speaking. It is recorded that Moses' son, William, gave sermons in Irish to this congregation.[162] Recent research by Seery[163] has verified this and in addition shows quite clearly that Moses himself was a fluent Irish-speaker. The evidence comes from an article written by Colin Johnston Robb in which he quoted from a document written by the local landlord, Arthur Johnston, in 1784.

> The Dissenting minister of this place, Moses Neilson ... a man of much culture and learning ... is perfection in Latin, Greek and Hebrew, and in the native Irish tongue. The Dissenters and Papists of this place mostly speak in that language ... He has collected much of the ancient fables and ballads, and is labouring on a grammatical account of Irish.[164]

There is no possibility of confusion here with the son William, because he was only ten years old at the time. However, the young William grew up to be very like his father in many ways and it would seem likely that Irish would have been spoken between them in the home.

At age 71 the Rev. Moses Neilson retired because of failing sight. When his son William died in 1821, he was aged 82, but despite his age and being nearly blind, out of loyalty to his son, he took on himself the burden of continuing his son's work at Inst until a replacement could be found. The following advertisememt appeared in the *Belfast News Letter*:

BELFAST INSTITUTION

CLASSICAL SCHOOL

> During the vacancy occasioned by the death of Dr Neilson, the CLASSICAL SCHOOL will be conducted under the superintendence of Dr Neilson, sen., and Professors Young and Cairns. The Ushers previously selected by the late Dr Neilson himself will continue to assist. And every attention will be given to secure to the Pupils the advantages of substantial and accurate instructions.[165]

Moses died on 23 April 1823 and his wife Catherine in June 1827. Altogether they had seven sons and only one daughter. The daughter was called Jane (1777–1834), and married John Getty, surgeon and apothecary of Dundalk. Her eldest brother, James (1768–1838), was minister to the Stream Street congregation in Downpatrick and he also ran a classical school, sometimes called the Down Academy, in Downpatrick. It was situated at the junction of Scotch Street and Saul street.[166]

The second son of Moses and Catherine, Joseph Andrew (1770–1835), was a doctor of Physic in Dundalk so, for a number of years there were three Nelson siblings living in that town. The next son John, born 1772, emigrated to Canada and the fourth son was William, the Irish grammarian. The next two sons were Andrew (1779–1860) and Robert (1781–1837). The youngest child was Arthur, born 1785, who succeeded his father as minister of Rademon in 1810 and continued with the Rademon Classical Academy after the death of his father in 1823. He, along with his congregation, left the Synod in 1829 to take part in the new Remonstrant (Non-Subscribing) Synod of Ulster.[167] He died of fever on 20 June 1831.[168]

His elder brother, James (1768–1838), already mentioned, had 'New Light' ideas, like most of the Nelsons, but was not on the list of seventeen ministers who withdrew from the General Synod to form the Remonstrant Synod,[169] because he was already in the Non-Subscribing Synod of Antrim. In emulation of his father's Classical School in Rademon, James ran an Academy in Downpatrick, described as being '... one of the best classical schools in the North of Ireland'.[170] Like his distinguished brother, William in Dundalk, James was a talented linguist and master of the classics. Apparently his Academy in Downpatrick was the main training school for local Roman Catholic youths going on for the priesthood. One of his most distinguished pupils was William Crolly from Ballykilbeg, who subsequently became Bishop of Down and Connor (1825–1835) and afterwards Primate of Armagh (1835–1849).[171]

James Nelson had married Alicia Craig of Carricknab in 1794[172] and they had five sons and six daughters. A number died young. On 11 April 1821, their son Collingwood died at the age of only twelve years, to be followed in the next month (4 May) by Horatio who was aged only twenty.[173]

One of the best-known of the children of James and Alicia was their eldest son, Samuel Craig Nelson, who was born on 24 February 1800. On 17 March 1825 he was ordained at Dromore. While there, in conjunction with Bishop Saurin (C. of I.) and the parish priest Dr McConvill, he organised the first national school established in Dromore which, like all early national schools, was run on a strictly non-sectarian basis.[174] While Mr. Nelson was minister of the Dromore congregation, the Subscription controversy in the Presbyterian church was at its height, and on 25 May 1830 was entered on the roll of the Remonstrant Synod the name of the Dromore congregation and the names of Rev. Samuel Craig Nelson as minister and Robert Dickson as elder. He removed to Downpatrick in 1835 and he lived at The Hill, Saul Street, Downpatrick.

Samuel Craig Nelson, one of the most prominent ministers identified with the Unitarian Church in the North of Ireland[175] was a fluent Irish speaker, but he does not seem to have learned it directly from his Irish-speaking elders, uncle William or grandfather Moses. No doubt they would have been an influence on him, but it is recorded quite unambiguously that at the age of 21 Samuel Craig, with only one intention in mind, spent a long holiday in Co. Mayo, where he learned to speak Irish fluently.[176] As recounted by his eulogist, it was clearly important for the Rev. S.C. Nelson that he should be proficient in Irish. Indeed, before he went on that extended holiday in Co. Mayo, he had already spent some time in what was the then Gaeltacht of West Meath as a tutor with the family of Featherstonehaugh.[177]

This Rev. Nelson was a pupil at his father's school and later an assistant. At an early age he graduated at the University of Glasgow. His biographer described the difficulties in travelling;

> but those were not the days of railways or steam-boats and in order to reach Glasgow a very serious journey had to be undertaken. Mr Nelson walked on foot from Downpatrick to Donaghadee, carrying with him his slender wardrobe and store of books. At Donaghadee he awaited the sailing of the packet, which often was days behind time. Scotland thus reached, another long journey on foot awaited him before he reached his university, where he was amongst the brightest of its sons.[178]

In time he ran his father's school, the Down Academy, and it carried on the established standards of excellence and liberality. Two of his young pupils later became Catholic bishops, Cornelius Denvir of Ballee, Bishop of Down and Connor from 1835 to 1865, and Patrick Dorrian, who succeeded Denvir.[179] Another pupil was Dr J.F. Hodges (1815–1899), the first Professor of Agriculture at Queen's College, Belfast.[180]

In 1833 he married Mary Cleland McCaw, a relation of the Clelands of Tobar Mhuire, Crossgar and they had nine children. The famous Dr Henry Cooke was a close personal friend of the Rev. Samuel Craig Nelson, despite the strong theological differences between them. The friendship dated back to the time when they were students together in Glasgow. They were in the same class as medical students. Neither qualified M.D., but the Rev. Nelson in later life frequently advised on medical matters and dispensed medicines. As far as his political beliefs were concerned he was a Liberal, yet also a strong opponent of Home Rule. He approved of Catholic Emancipation, but was a Unionist. He believed that his country's safety and welfare depended on its union with Great Britain, 'under the flag that had braved a thousand years the battle and the breeze'.[181]

This remarkable reverend lived to the age of 91, having contributed substantially, both in a spiritual sense and in a material manner, to the well-being of his flock and of others in the greater community. His funeral on 29 January 1891 was attended by a wide cross-section of the same community. Among the mourners was the young Robert Lyttle, of Moneyrea, a fellow Irish-speaking Unitarian.[182]

He and his wife had nine children. One of the most colourful was Dr Joseph Nelson, M.D. (1840–1910), who wrote a biography of his grand-uncle, William Neilson, the Irish grammarian. At the age of twenty,

> ... inspired by the heroic ideals of the Italian revolution, he and another student, Robert Blakeley Patterson, put aside their books and set out for Italy to join the forces of Red Shirts rallying to the banner of Giuseppe Garibaldi at Genoa. Commissioned Lieutenant in the famous *Regimento Inglese*, he campaigned through Sicily and Italy and took part in the battle of Volturno, received the Sword of Honour from the great patriot himself and medals commemorating the victorious campaign from the new King of Italy, Victor Emmanuele.[183]

Back in Belfast he became known by his colleagues and students as 'Garibaldi Nelson'. He qualified M.D. in 1866 and then spent fourteen years in India. He returned home at the age of 37 and then studied ophthalmology in Dublin and did a course of German. Armed with these skills he went to Vienna and studied under two world authorities in ophthalmology, Carl von Arlt and Ernst Fuchs. On returning home to Belfast, he founded the Eye, Ear and Throat department in the Children's Hospital. His home was at 29 Wellington Place, where he died on 31 August 1910.[184]

There are still many Nelson descendants in the Ulster area and the characteristics of independence, liberality and idealism live on in the family.

WHITLEY STOKES, M.D. (1763–1845)

Dr Stokes was born in Waterford in 1763, son of Gabriel Stokes and Susan Boswell. His father was a Fellow of Trinity College, Dublin, prebendary of Elphin, chancellor of Waterford and he was rector of Desertmartin in the diocese of Derry.[185] However, his son Whitley left the Church of Ireland and became a non-conformist. He was a member of the Strand Street Non-Subscribing Presbyterian congregation in Dublin.[186, 187]

Educated at the Endowed School in Waterford[188] he qualified B.A from Trinity College, Dublin in 1783 and M.A. in 1789. He finally graduated M.B. and M.D. in 1793. Subsequently, in 1800, he became Professor of Practice of Medicine in the Royal College of Surgeons of Ireland. It was while he was here that he published the first ever description of *ecthyma terebrans*, a febrile skin disease in children.[189]

Then, in 1830, he was made Regius Professor of Physic, in Trinity College,[190] a position which he held until 1843. While pursuing an active medical career, he still had time for other activities, one of the most impressive of which was his publications in and on the Irish language. The first was in 1799, when he edited the Gospel of Luke and the Acts of the Apostles in Irish.[191] The most remarkable aspect of this publication was that it was the first issue of any part of the Bible in Irish since the year 1690, when the last edition of the Bible had been published. Also in 1799 he published a pamphlet,[192] in which he attempted to estimate the prevalence of Irish-speaking and came to the conclusion that there were 2.4 million out of a total population of 4.8 million.

In 1806 he published the four Gospels along with the Acts of the Apostles in two volumes.[193] In 1814 he caused to be printed, at his own personal expense, an English-Irish Dictionary. It happens that such a dictionary was published by Connellan in the same year, so perhaps that is the dictionary in question.[194] In 1810, he was the author of a pamphlet, *Observations on the Necessity of publishing the Scriptures in the Irish Language*.[195] In this essay he reported on estimates of the numbers of Irish-speakers, by county, for Ulster and Leinster.[196] Some time after this, he helped to form the Irish Society, the organisation established to help Irish-speakers read the Bible in their own language. Finally, in 1815, he published the Proverbs of Solomon in Irish and in English.[197]

The Stokes family produced many other notable individuals. Perhaps the best known is Whitley's son, William (1804–1878), who has his name attached to two medical syndromes, Stokes-Adams disease and Cheyne-Stokes breathing. However, his achievements beyond this, were many, including his three classic books on the stethoscope (1825), on chest disease (1837), and on the heart (1854).[198] William had a son, also called Whitley Stokes (1830–1909), who was a renowned Celtic scholar. Whitley's sister, Margaret, was also a Celtic scholar of international repute.

The first Whitley Stokes was in close contact with Irish-language circles in the Belfast area. A series of letters, dated March–May 1796, deposited in Trinity College Library,[199] showed him to be on friendly terms with Dr James MacDonnell, an Irish-speaker from the Glens, and with Patrick Lynch, the Irish scholar from Loughinisland. The main purpose of the correspondence[200] was to enlist the help of Lynch in producing a phonetic Irish edition of St Luke's Gospel and the Acts of the Apostles. The basis for this new version was a copy of either the first edition (1602) or the second edition (1681) of the first translation of the New Testament into Irish; both the work of William Daniel (Ó Domhnaill). Stokes had sent his own copy to Lynch, and because of the great rarity of copies, even at that time, was most concerned that it should not be mislaid or lost. The letters show much disquiet about the health of James MacDonnell's wife, who was evidently very ill at that time.

When the work finally appeared some three years later, it was printed in parallel columns, one of them in English and the other in Irish, but with Roman script and semi-phonetic orthography. Two thousand copies were published, and the Dublin Association for Discountenancing Vice, of which Stokes was a member, supported the cost of publication by contributing ten guineas. This work gives clues to the pronunciation of Co. Down Irish in the late eighteenth century.[201] His other Irish publications have already been mentioned. Ó Casaide was of the opinion that Lynch was associated only with the first publication in Irish and that the others were his own work.[202]

Whitley Stokes was married to Mary Anne Picknell of Loughgall, Co. Armagh and they had nine children. Their home was at Harcourt Street, Dublin and that is where Whitley died on 13 April 1845.

If interest in Irish can be crudely divided into the two oversimplified categories, missionary efforts on the one hand and cultural on the other, then we should remember that running parallel with all the cultural activities, Irish still continued to be used for preaching and for conducting services in the Presbyterian Church. William Laing exemplified this model.

WILLIAM LAING (d. 1806)

Ó Snodaigh mentioned that the Rev. William Laing, a native of Perth, preached in Irish in the Newry district from 1780 to 1816 (*recte* 1806) and was also called on to preach in Irish to the Presbyterian Ayrshire settlers about Ballymascanlon in Co. Louth.[203] His source for this information was Mac Con Midhe, who wrote an article in 1968, but who gave no references for this information. Mac Con Midhe said that Laing came as a minister to the old church in Well Lane in 1780.[204]

The history of congregations recounts that 'Mr William Laing of Newry Second, (Lic. Associate Presbytery 1772) was ordained on the 25 October 1780'. This source tells us that he was a Scot who could preach in Gaelic and did so at Ballymascanlon. Furthermore it is stated that in '... 1782 he got a site in Newry and moved there with his congregation as soon as the church was built'. The statement goes on to say: 'He was a zealous, devout and strictly orthodox man.'[205] He died on 22 July 1806.

JAMES STEELE (1792–1859)

James Steele was born near Raphoe, Co. Donegal,[206] and was ordained on 8 Nov. 1821 as assistant and successor to the Rev. James Neilson, minister to the Stranorlar congregation, who had become infirm. On the death of Neilson in September 1826, Steele became the fifth minister of Stranorlar.[207] He was Clerk of the Donegal Presbytery for 16 years.

The Rev. Dr Steele (he received a D.D. from the U.S.A.), is recorded as being accustomed to preach in Irish to his own congregation on alternate Sundays[208] which says much about his proficiency with the language and even more about the extent to which Irish-speaking was willingly prevalent among ordinary Presbyterians.

IV
NINETEENTH CENTURY
A
MISSIONARY ACTIVITY

GENERAL

For the first third of the nineteenth century a number of features relating to the Irish language are apparent. First, there was a continuation of the wave of enthusiasm for Irish language and culture which had arisen principally in Belfast at the end of the previous century. A small coterie carried on the tradition which had been started – Bryson, McDonnell etc. For example, an Irish Language School was founded in 1809, in Pottinger's Entry, Belfast, under the aegis of the Irish Harp Society. They used Neilson's *Grammar* as a text.[1] Another theme was the Presbyterian ministers who were still preaching in Irish to their own or to other congregations, on a regular or intermittent basis. Examples were James Steele of Stranorlar, Andrew Bryson of Dundalk, and his successor, William Neilson. And then in the 1830s two new movements began. One had its earlier impetus from Christopher Anderson, through his publications which stressed the need for Irish-speakers to have the Bible in their own language. The other was the formation of the Ulster Gaelic Society, which was first called the Belfast Gaelic Society, and is considered to be an important forerunner of the Gaelic League. This in turn was a stimulant to the work of William Hamilton Drummond and Sir Samuel Ferguson. James MacKnight, journalist and editor of the *Belfast News Letter*, also did much to promote Irish. The remaining strand was missionary in nature but nevertheless incorporated an important educational element. For this period, just before the Great Famine, it is important to recall that at that time Ireland was inhabited by the greatest number of monoglot Irish-speakers ever in her history, over three and a half million.

After 1720 there was no mention, at meetings of the Synod of Ulster, of preaching in Irish, or of any missionary activity until almost a century later when in 1818 (30 June) a letter was received from the Presbyterian Synod of Munster congratulating the Synod of Ulster for its missionary activity in the south of Ireland and offering cooperation.[2] As a result of this letter the Synod decided to strengthen the congregation at Carlow. Thanks were extended to Messrs Henry Cooke of Donegore, Robert Stewart of Broughshane and James Horner of Capel Street, Dublin.[3] This marked a revival of missionary spirit within the Synod of Ulster.[4]

It was resolved in 1820 that a committee of eight ministers would be appointed annually for promoting the cause of Presbyterianism in the south and west of Ireland. The missionary objective at the beginning was directed mainly towards wayward Presbyterians and in that sense was a true home mission. These aims were thus explained in the minutes in the General Synod for 1826:

> ... to supply with religious instruction and the ordinance of the Gospel such Presbyterians as are scattered through various districts in the South and West of Ireland, and who, from their isolated situation, are destitute of the pastoral attention of stated ministers of their own communion ... they have not sent forth their missionaries, with the view of interfering with Christians of any other denomination.[5]

Bowen, in his analysis of religious conflict, tended to agree that the Presbyterians were not keen on making converts from Catholicism:

> The truth was that, although the Presbyterians of Ulster were willing to help Roman Catholics during the famine years, they were not urgently concerned about converting their traditional foes.[6]

Stothers found it hard to believe that evangelism was not taking place. He pointed out that the places to which the ministers were being sent in the south and west were for the most part Irish-speaking. One of these was Fethard in Co. Tipperary, to which a Mr Ferris was sent. The Synod minute read:

> Mr Ferris, one of the probationers of the Synod of Ulster, was ordained there by the Synod of Munster ... under his ministry, the congregation of Fethard, Co. Tipperary is in a thriving state. We understand that he devoted himself assiduously to the study of the Irish language, which is universally spoken in that district, with the

view of qualifying himself as a candidate to fill the situation of Irish Preacher, on the foundation appointed by the Rev. Dr Williams.[7]

The above Mr Robert Ferris was ordained to Fethard in 1825 and was incumbent there until his death in 1850.[8]

Perhaps the missionary objectives of the Presbyterian church at that time were ambivalent. On the whole, however, strife and conflict were consciously avoided and there was a genuine concern to communicate with the people and to teach them to read the Bible in their own language. This attitude can be contrasted with that of the Anglican Rev. Alexander Dallas who, in 1845, came from England to wage an anti-Catholic Crusade. He formed the Society for Irish Church Missions to the Roman Catholics. He and his organisation lacked understanding of the Irish people and true compassion for their needs. 'Dallas never lost the mind of a soldier and, in his reckoning, he was enlisted in the army of righteousness opposing the powers of darkness.'[9]

His campaign was counter-productive because it had the effect of provoking a reaction in the Catholic Church which led to its being restructured, with a strengthening of its organisation and authority and of bringing the Irish Church more under the control of the Vatican.[10] All of this was epitomised by Cardinal Paul Cullen, who was appointed by the Pope to carry out these changes. From the Protestant point of view Dallas had strengthened, not weakened, Irish Catholicism; he was also one of the forces which helped to align Irish nationalism with Catholicism, a process already begun by Daniel O'Connell.

On the whole the Presbyterian approach was much more understanding of the issues involved. After all they themselves had also been persecuted by the Established Church. The outreach, however, to the Catholic native Irish was very tentative in the beginning, because the work of the Synod became disrupted by the controversy about Subscription and at one stage there were two missionary groups within the Synod, each having the same functions. The fact that the Home Mission had members who were Arian (Non-Subscribing) had irked the Subscribers, who formed a new group called The Presbyterian Society for Ireland.[11] When finally, in 1829, the New Light or Arian Party led by Henry Montgomery left the Synod to form the Remonstrance Synod, a period of stability ensued. At the subsequent Synod of the Orthodox Presbyterians in 1830, it was agreed to unite the two missionary agencies under the name of the Presbyterian Missionary Society. This was still mainly a home mission to Presbyterians and there was no mention of evangelising Roman Catholics.[12] Within a few years the interest in preaching in Irish grew substantially. The first signs had been in 1828 when, at the meeting in Cookstown, Co Tyrone, the Synod very strongly recommended that candidates for the ministry should apply themselves to the study of the Irish language.[13]

When the Presbyterian Missionary Society reported to the Meeting of the Synod held at Cookstown in June 1833, one of the recommendations was that the missionary work, up to then dealing mainly with fellow Presbyterians, should be extended to include preaching in Irish. It was also recommended that steps be taken to have a proportion of the Presbyterian Licentiates and Students instructed in the Irish language.[14] When the subject was discussed at the full meeting of the Synod it was clearly considered not to have gone far enough, because the final decision of Synod was more radical, namely: '... that all Students under the care of this Synod, shall be required to study the Irish language, during a period equal at least to one session of College.'[15] It would appear that most of the Synod still felt that much more could be done, for a special Synod was then held the following September in Dublin, lasting three days.

Two eminent Gaelic-speakers from Scotland had been invited to be present as advisers. These were Rev. Dr Norman McLeod, minister of Campsie and Rev. Duncan Macfarlane, minister of Renfrew. A resolution was passed.

> That, as it was once the laudable custom of this Church to encourage qualified ministers to preach the Gospel in the Irish language; and, as we acknowledge, with sorrow, that this duty has long been culpably neglected, yet, while we rejoice in the success of those Societies which are engaged in disseminating religious instruction throughout the kingdom, in the Irish tongue, this Synod resolve to resume the former practice of our Church, by assisting in the circulation of the Irish Scriptures – sending out Ministers qualified to preach in Irish – and encouraging our Students to acquire a knowledge of that language.[16]

The most important of the Societies referred to above was the Irish Society for Promoting the Education of the Native Irish Through the Medium of Their Own Language, which had been founded in 1816, largely as the result of the publications of Christopher Anderson. Dr McLeod was asked to go to the Galway mission station for a period of three weeks and to use that as a base for peripatetic preaching in Irish. He was to report back to the Directors of the Missionary Society who would confer with him '... on the best means of providing for the extension of religious knowledge through the medium of the Irish language.'[17] There is no doubt that the Synod was taking the use of Irish seriously. In October of the same year Tomás Ó Fiannachtaigh (Thomas O'Feenachty) was appointed to teach Irish in the Belfast Academical Institution which was the main training college for student ministers. He was already involved with the work of The Ulster Gaelic Society. The third report of the Missionary Society, in 1834, referred to the resolution on the use of Irish, passed at the previous Synod as,'one of the most important ever recorded by it.'[18] Yet much preparatory work was still required before the scheme could get going. Getting enough qualified preachers was a problem. Dr McLeod had suggested employing Gaelic-speaking ministers from Scotland to preach, provided they were understood by the native Irish. He had gone to the west to find out if his Gaelic would be understood. He reported that he could converse well on ordinary affairs of life, but although the Gaelic and Irish languages were essentially the same, he could not go further than fairly basic communication. Nevertheless, he was certain that a Gaelic-speaker would require only a few months tuition to master Irish and speak it clearly and acceptably. In a very short time he could preach in Irish as fluently as a native Irishman.[19] So until young men, natives of Ireland, could be found to preach the Gospel to their countrymen in their own language, the experiment of sending out some Gaelic preachers, was to be tried. At the Synod held at Londonderry in June 1834, both Norman McLeod and Robert Winning of Ervey addressed the assembly on the importance of making greater efforts to spread '... the Gospel throughout Ireland, through the medium of the Irish language'. They furthermore recommended that the Synod should undertake the publication of the metrical version of the Psalms in

Irish. This the Synod readily agreed to do and, before the close of business, James Shields had collected over £80 from the members towards the cost of publication.

The Synod reaffirmed their command of the previous year that students must study the Irish language, with the following addition:

> That all Students who, at present are about to enter the Moral Philosophy Class, together with all future students entering college under care of this Church, shall be required to possess a competent knowledge of the Irish language before commencing their theological course; and that with regard to all other students at present attending college, it be earnestly recommended to them to become acquainted with the Irish language before the termination of their college course.[20]

Appended to the report of the Synod was a copy of a letter, dated 20 June 1834, from Joseph Stevenson, secretary to The Royal Belfast Academical Institution. Included in this letter was a recommendation about the teaching of Irish:

> The desire repeatedly expressed by the Synod, that their Students should acquire a knowledge of the Irish language, induced the Joint Boards to appoint a teacher of that ancient language; and on the 22nd of October last they appointed Mr Thomas Feenachty to that situation, a gentleman well qualified to fill that office ... Few of the Students in the last Session availed themselves of his appointment; but if the Synod makes a knowledge of the Irish language a necessary acquirement by their Students, Mr Feenachty may reckon confidently on a numerous class in the insuing Session.[21]

In 1835 the name of the organisation was now the Home Mission of the Synod of Ulster and Irish-speaking George Field of Belfast was appointed as its general agent. The target groups were identified as

1)   Presbyterians scattered throughout the South and West of Ireland,
2)   Presbyterians in the north who were inadequately supplied with religious instruction and
3)   ... the ignorant of our countrymen of all sects, especially the Irish-speaking population.[22]

The methods of reaching these groups were 1) Itinerant ministers, 2) Catechists or Readers and 3) Irish Schools.

The latter schools were directed towards Irish-speakers. At this time they operated only in the north and had been initiated by the Presbytery of Tyrone. They had taken the idea from the Irish schools run by the Irish Society, previously mentioned. Permission had been sought from the Directors of the Home Mission in November 1834, in order that Irish schools be established in the Irish-speaking areas of Tyrone and Derry. Approval was readily given and a study was undertaken to find out the feelings and desires of the Irish-speaking people. In February visits were made to the small number of schools of the Irish Society, which formed the Tyrone and Derry branch of the Kingscourt district of Co. Cavan, but under the superintendence of some Presbyterian ministers.

After these preliminary investigations, a programme for establishing Irish schools was begun and by July 1835 thirty schools were in place, twenty-two of which had been in operation for nearly four months, having on their rolls 1,010 pupils. The remaining eight had just been started, but it was estimated that they catered for another 390 pupils. Arrangements were made to provide books for teachers and pupils. From the Irish Society 500 Irish primers were purchased at cost price. The primer concerned was almost certainly that produced by Thaddaeus Connellan for the Irish Society.[23] The Hibernian Bible Society generously donated 200 New Testaments in Irish and promised a further grant when required. Robert Allen, as superintendent, wrote to the British and Foreign Bible Society asking for ... 'a free grant of 500 portions or parts of the Irish New Testament, in the Irish character; and as many whole New Testaments as [the Society] may be disposed to add to them.' As a result they provided many hundreds of copies free of charge.[24]

It was being reported that some of the Roman Catholic clergy were hostile to the Irish schools. Teachers and scholars were being refused the sacraments and an aged lady with no English was refused confession in Irish.[25] It was found that, among the people, the opportunity to read the Bible in Irish was everywhere being welcomed. The Mission warmly welcomed the publication in 1836 of the Psalms of David in Irish. This was to be used in the Irish Schools. By this time there were 50 schools in Tyrone and 13 in the neighbourhood of Cushendall. This corresponded to 2,598 scholars on the rolls. In the space of eighteen months a total of 1,412 persons, from fifteen to fifty years of age, had been successful in learning how to read Irish.[26] By now the schools had a reasonable range of textbooks in Irish to fall back on: Connellan's *Primer*, Miss Alexander's *Sinner's Friend* in Irish, also her Irish Hymnbook, and of course Bedell's *Old Testament* and Daniel's *New Testament*. Before long these were joined by George Field's Catechism in Irish and then his grammar, called *Casán na Gaeilge*. Other Presbyterian publications in Irish are discussed in a section especially devoted to that subject.

The saintly William Bedell (1571–1642) had always been held in high esteem by Irish-speaking Catholics. An Englishman by birth and breeding, he was well in his fifties when he came to Ireland. He became Bishop of Kilmore in 1629. He deplored the oppression of the Catholics.[27] At Trinity College, Dublin he brought in a rule that Irish-born divinity students should be able to preach in Irish, that they might serve their flock better. He learned Irish himself and had the Old Testament translated into Irish. Published in 1685, it remained the only full Irish translation until the Maynooth Bible was published in 1981. When Bedell was being buried, a Catholic priest stood at his graveside and cried out, *O sit anima mea cum Bedello*! (Oh, that my soul could be with Bedell.)[28]

Presbtyerians also felt an affinity for Bedell. Stothers has drawn attention to Reid's analysis of Bedell's Presbyterian leanings.[29] Boylan points out that he rejected bishops having plural dioceses.[30] He maintained the identity of both bishop and presbyter and he disliked episcopal vestments and instrumental music in worship.[31]

It comes as no surprise to learn that the Bedell Bible was popular with the Irish schools. Page after page of the Mission reports annotate the joyful reception of this book by the native Irish, many of whom had never seen a printed book in Irish before and most of whom were eager to be able to read their native language, especially in the form of the Bible. In 1837 there were 74 schools in Tyrone and 18 at Cushendall. The numbers continued to grow until in the period 1844–1846, there were around 300 Irish schools in operation. This was the peak activity period and the advent of the Great Famine substantially reduced their numbers, until they reached zero in 1855.[32] Perhaps the most contentious episode in the history of the Irish schools was the problem which arose in the Glens of Antrim, when the Catholic priests began to intervene. This is dealt with later as a separate section. Stothers points out that the main organisational weakness in the Irish school system was the principle of paying Roman Catholics to teach Irish because, quite simply, it was open to abuse. The Irish teachers were under impossible pressures. On the one hand, some of them were very poor indeed and needed the money badly.[33] On the other hand, if word got out about what they were doing they were in dire trouble with the Catholic clergy and in danger of excommunication.

On the Presbyterian side, the schools were under-financed, because many ordinary members of the congregation were suspicious of this fraternisation. Nor were they wealthy enough to support the extra preachers required to carry out this work. Stothers concluded, however, that the Presbyterian worthies, Robert Allen, John Edgar and the Directors of the Home Mission, were simply trying to live up to the spirit of Matthew 28.19: 'Go ye therefore and teach all nations ...'. Stothers also reminds us that in using the Bible in Irish schools, Presbyterians were being true to their colours. They held that the Bible was an essential ingredient in education. Indeed, it would have been remarkable for them not to use it, especially as there was so little choice of printed literature in Irish at the time.[34]

CHRISTOPHER ANDERSON (1782–1852)

Anderson was not a Presbyterian, but his ideas were influential on Presbyterian policy in the early eighteenth century. He was born in Edinburgh of Baptist stock. From his visit to the Highlands of Scotland in 1810 he discovered that the vast majority of Gaelic-speakers could not read their own language and that '... there are no Gaelic schools in existence, nor a spelling-book for teaching them to read their mother tongue.'[35]

He became Secretary to the Society for the Support of Gaelic

Schools in Scotland. Later he turned his attention to Ireland and, arising out of an extensive tour which he made throughout the country in 1814, he published in the following year a small pamphlet appealing for the education of the native Irish through their own language.[36] This was the forerunner of increasingly more detailed publications on the same subject. His nephew, Hugh Anderson, referred to this pamphlet as a seminal publication in the following terms:

> The facts disclosed were startling, and the reasoning on them so conclusive, that few who were interested in the subject at all, but were astonished and convinced. It was addressed to no sect or party, nor could anyone learn from the pamphlet itself to what section of Protestantism its author belonged ... More than one of those benevolent societies which have laboured for nearly forty years to impart instruction to the Irish in their own language, derive their origin from that publication, or from the correspondence to which it led ...[37]

Christopher Anderson continued to publish on the subject, and followed with a further pamphlet in 1819.[38] Then in 1828 came his major work, *Historical sketches of the ancient native Irish*.[39] This, and its subsequent editions, had a significant impact on Protestant thought in Ireland. These publications are still an indispensible source in understanding the position of Irish in pre-famine Ireland. There was an excellent account of printing in the Irish language and statistical information on the number of Irish-speakers and where they are distributed. He gave a detailed account of the previous printings of the Bible and made recommendations for the kind of Irish books that were urgently needed in great numbers, the Bible, Bunyan's *Pilgrim's Progress*, Newton's *Life*, Scott's *Essays*, etc. As a person who believed in what he taught, it is interesting that he himself undertook the translation of *The Pilgrim's Progress*.[40]

Perhaps the most important result of his publications was the formation of the Irish Society, a group formed chiefly by members of the Anglican Church in Ireland for '... promoting the education of the native Irish through the medium of their own language.' This was instituted in the year 1818, lasting until nearly 1860. It set about the production and distribution of works in Irish: bibles, catechisms, prayer-books, readers, grammars, dictionaries and even books on rural economy (e.g. beekeeping). Many of these were produced by Thaddeus Connellan, an Irish scholar who was a convert. The Society provided teachers and readers to instruct the many persons who were illiterate in Irish. Local schools were formed on the plan of the Gaelic School Society in Scotland.

There was a genuine educational feeling among the organisers and a reluctance to be overtly evangelical, in case they would provoke the Catholic clergy. In contrast, the Roman Catholic Church did very little to encourage the use of Irish, because Daniel O'Connell and other leaders and clergy believed that the use of English would help the people to better themselves socially and economically.[41] The Presbyterian Synod was encouraged, both directly by Anderson's works and also by the example of the Irish Society, to start Presbyterian Irish schools for Bible reading and education in Irish, under the Home Mission.

THE IRISH SOCIETY

The year of foundation of this society was stated in early annual reports as 1816[42] but the year is usually taken as 1818. The full title of the organisation was The Irish Society for Promoting the Education of the Native Irish through the Medium of Their Own Language.

The London Hibernian Society, which was mainly an English language Bible society, gave a useful and mutually agreed description of the aims and methods of their sister organisation:

> The Irish Society teaches all its Scholars primarily to read the Irish Language. It seeks out the Irish speaking-people as the sole objects of its care; and teaches English only in the way of translation from the Irish. Its Scholars are principally Adults, though it instructs some Children. Its Schools are rarely stated Schools, but the pupils are taught either in their own houses, or in the Masters' houses, on Sundays, holidays or in the evenings; and thus prepared for the periodical examination of the Inspector, on whose report of progress they are paid for. It employs the unoccupied time of the Inspectors, in visiting the houses of the Irish peasantry, reading to them the Scriptures and exciting a thirst for instruction in the Irish Language exclusively; and distributes the Holy Scriptures in Irish, together with Irish Prayer Books, where acceptable.[43]

It seems clear that the formation of the Society was, at least in part, a response to the pamphlet written in 1815 by Christopher Anderson, the Baptist minister from Scotland, who had made a prolonged tour of observation in Ireland during 1814. He noted how few Irish speakers could read and write in that language and how little printed reading material was available, especially in the form of the Bible. He had already, in 1810, been instrumental in setting up the Gaelic School Society, to remedy a similar problem in Gaelic-speaking Scotland.[44]

The headquarters of the Irish Society was at 16 Upper Sackville Street, Dublin. The first Secretary was Henry Joseph Monck Mason (1778–1858), LL.D., M.R.I.A., a prolific writer, particularly on the Irish language and the author of an Irish *Grammar*. He encouraged the cultivation and study of Irish and was instrumental in founding a chair of Irish in Trinity College, Dublin.[45] The organisation was an arm of the Established Church, but avoided direct proselytism. In 1823 there were just under 3,000 scholars on the rolls of the Irish schools; by the late 1840s this had risen to nearly 18,000. In 1849 the number of books, mostly in Irish, distributed to the teachers and scholars was more than 30,000. More than two-thirds of these were primers (21,155), grammars (28) or dictionaries (219), underlining the essentially educational character of the Society.[46]

When the Presbyterian Home Mission started in earnest after 1830, the Irish Society had already been in the field for many years, and so the Home Mission turned to the Society as a model and for cooperation. The Presbyterian Irish schools followed closely the example of the Irish Society. Both bodies agreed that they would not operate in the same areas and so the Glens of Antrim, and most of Co. Tyrone and Co. Derry came under the aegis of the Home Mission.

NORMAN McLEOD (1783–1862)

The Rev. Dr Norman McLeod had a major impact on the Irish Presbyterian Church in the period just before the Great Famine. It was widely appreciated that millions of inhabitants of Ireland were Irish-speakers, yet the approaches made by religious groups tended to be in the English language. Both he and the Rev. Duncan Macfarlane (1793–1853) of Renfrew, ministers of the Church of Scotland, came expressly to attend the Special Synod held in Mary's Abbey, Dublin, September 1833, which had been called to consider the best means of developing the missionary activities of the Presbyterian Church in Ireland. In an earnest and animated address to the Synod, Dr McLeod, himself a distinguished Gaelic scholar, urged the more systematic use of the Irish language. He undertook to visit the West of Ireland, to discover personally the problems involved and to see how Gaelic preachers would be received and understood by the Irish-speaking population. He also offered to ensure that an Irish translation of the metrical Psalms would be made and put into print.[47] As seen elsewhwere Dr McLeod carried through these proposals successfully and his energy, expertise and moral weight induced a great feeling of optimism in the Synod of Ulster.

He was born of a Gaelic family in a Gaelic-speaking area, Morven in Argyleshire, on 2 December 1783. He was the eldest son of Norman McLeod, the minister of that congregation. On completion of his education in the University of Glasgow, he was licensed by the Presbytery of Mull on 23 June 1806.[48] Eventually he was ordained to Campbeltown on 12 June 1808. It was in 1825 that he removed to the congregation with which he has always been closely associated, Campsie in Glasgow. This parish had been founded because the Synod of Argyll had caused money to be collected to build a place of worship for the Gaelic-speaking people of Glasgow. Among Gaelic-speakers he was called *Caraid nan Gaidheal* (Friend of the Gaels), because of his much-appreciated work in the Highlands on education and for organising relief during the distress of the 1830s and 1840s.[49]

He was a productive writer both in English and in Gaelic. His most important works included, *A Gaelic Collection for the Use of Schools* (1828–34), and two magazines, *An Teachdaire Gaelach* (1829–31), and *Cuairtear nan Gleann* (1840–43). Along with Daniel Dewar he wrote a *Dictionary of the Gaelic Language* (1831 and other editions). His *Leabhar nan Cnoc* was published in 1834. A posthumous selection of his Gaelic writings was published by the Rev. A. Clerk in 1867, under the title of *Caraid nan Gaidheal*. It went into many editions.[50] Máirtín Ó Cadhain, the Irish writer, said of this last publication that it was, '... ar cheann de na trí shaothar próis is toirtiúla i nGaeilge na hAlban'. i.e. that it was one of the three bulkiest works of prose in Scottish Gaelic.[51]

In his assessment of McLeod, John MacInnes placed him as one of the leading figures in the history of Gaelic prose and said '... he created a genuinely popular readership and the standards that he set influenced Gaelic writers for over a century.'[52]

GEORGE BELLIS (1800–1885)

When the Presbyterian Missionary Society of the Synod of Ulster was formed in 1830, George Bellis, of Belfast, became its first secretary.[53] He was secretary of the Home Mission from 1841 to 1885 and was editor of the *Missionary Herald* from 1843 to 1855. Stothers notes that his influence was always used to promote the use of Irish in the evangelical approaches to Roman Catholics.[54]

Born in 1800, he was the fourth son of James Bellis, farmer, Ballyarton, Coleraine. He was educated at the the Old College Belfast, where he was awarded the General Certificate in 1820. He was licensed to the Route Presbytery in 1823 and ordained to the Donegall Street congregation (Cliftonville), Belfast on 24 May 1825. After his appointment as Secretary to the Home Mission in 1841, he resigned his pastorate so that he could pay full attention to the missionary work.[55] In 1835 he married the daughter of a surgeon, Samuel Arnott of Belfast.

At the time of the Presbyterian Union in 1840, with Dr Edgar, he helped to turn the Synod in the direction of Irish Mission Work. He became the Missionary Secretary of the Synod of Ulster and, afterwards of the General Assembly. As editor of the *Missionary Herald* he did his utmost to encourage the use of Irish to reach out to his fellow Irish-speaking countrymen.[56] When aged 80 he was awarded the degree of Doctor of Divinity by the University of Kingston, U.S.A.[57] He died on 18 August 1885.

ROBERT ALLEN (1789–1865)

He was an Irish-speaking minister, born 1 October 1789, in Cookstown, Co. Tyrone, the youngest son of Robert Allen, a merchant.[58] He had his early education in Cookstown Academy.[59] Educated at Glasgow University, he graduated M.A. from there in 1809. He was licensed to Tyrone in 1811. Allen was ordained in Stewartstown on the 7 June 1814, and ministered to that congregation until 1848.

While minister of Stewartstown, because of his interest in the Irish language, he applied in November 1834 to the Mission Directors for permission to start Irish schools in the Irish-speaking areas of Cos Tyrone and Derry.[60] The Church of Ireland had been running its own Irish Schools since 1818 when the Irish Society was formed and Robert Allen had been present at a recent meeting in Dublin where stirring statements had been made about the success of these Irish Schools.[61] He received permission and before long the schools were progressing very successfully.

He made visits to Irish-speaking areas and has described his experiences in his journal. For the whole month of October in 1838 he visited the Irish teachers, reading in their houses and conversing with them, their neighbours and their pupils. On one of these visits he was stressing the importance of reading the scriptures and went on to say:

> But I will read a little of his word in the 119th Psalm, where he speaks in praise of his own word, and I will read it in the sweet voice of our country. The people in the house seemed very much delighted when I read in that language, and afterwards paid double the attention.[62]

Within one year of their foundation the schools numbered 30, with a total of 1,400 pupils. By 1843, the movement was so successful that there were now 120 Irish schools in existence run by the Presbyterian Church. In 1842 the number of teachers had gone up to 200, with an attendance of 10,000 pupils.[63]

It was around this time that some Catholic priests led by Luke Walsh began to complain about the Home Mission in the Glens of Antrim. His main thrust was that the Irish teachers, who were being paid by the Home Mission, were pocketing the money and doing nothing. They were sending in falsified returns about the numbers of schools and pupils, according to Luke Walsh.

The whole debate was carried out publicly in the press and Walsh published all the letters in the form of a book.[64] As Superintendent of the Home Mission, Robert Allen wrote the letters supporting the Home Mission and its work. As is always the case in such contests, the outcome was confused but it is fair to state that Allen conducted the debate in a most restrained and gentlemanly fashion. Ó Buachalla, who has analysed this contest in detail, made the point that, although the main protagonists were Irish-speaking and the debate was about Irish, the whole affair was carried out in English.[65] Although it is clear that Mr Allen had a heavy workload with his responsibility to the Home Mission, his congregation in Stewartstown were entirely behind him.

For many years he had given little consideration to the west of Ireland, until he received an unexpected letter from a person unknown, drawing his attention to Mayo. He then paid a visit to Killala and it was as a result of this experience that the Irish Schools in Connaught were established in 1845.[66] In his Connaught ventures, Allen was fortunate in having the help of Michael Brannigan, a fellow Irish-speaking minister and himself a native of the Stewartstown area.[67] It is told that, at some time in the late 1830s, Brannigan, as a Roman Catholic youth, got into discussions with the Irish teachers in his area. In order to get support for his arguments, he began to study the Irish Bible. It is said that the more he studied the more he doubted his own faith. He went through agonies of self-examination. At last he resolved to go to Stewartstown to hear the Rev. Robert Allen preach. Apparently this had a dramatic effect on him, so that he turned Presbyterian. Later he was ordained.[68]

Robert Allen made continuous reports available about his activities in the *Missionary Herald*. From 1845 Mr Allen directed the Connaught Mission from his home in the Square in Stewartstown, but in 1848 he resigned his position at Stewartstown and became Superintendent of the Connaught Mission. At the age of 59 he set off for Killalla, Co. Mayo to join with Michael Brannigan. He was considered to be the person best suited for the work in Connaught. Among his qualifications were:

> His experience in Irish Mission work was ... altogether unique. He was full of the kindliest sympathy with the Irish people, whose grievances he thoroughly understood and whose many good qualities he heartily appreciated.[69]

In the period 1855–1856 he was Moderator of the General Assembly.[70] His wife was Sarah Jane Little and she bore him six children,[71] one of whom was Surgeon-Major Robert Austen Allen (1829–76) M.D.(Glasg. 1853).[72]

It was in Ballina that he finally died, on April 1865, aged 75, and his body was brought from Ballina to be buried in the Donaghendry graveyard, Stewartstown, Co. Tyrone.

He was described after his death as '... truly a Christian gentleman; he did so much, unostentatiously, for the benefit of his generation; and by sound judgment and untiring vigilance, contributed greatly to the prosperity of the Connaught Mission.'[73]

JOHN KNOX LESLIE (1810–1902)

This Presbyterian minister had the distinction of becoming the first missionary to be sent out under the care of the Home Mission.[74] He was born near Ballymoney in 1810. In August 1834 he was ordained to the Home Mission.[75] Subsequently he, in the company of Dr Henry Cooke, visited many places in the south and west of Ireland, where they preached at various mission stations. All of these seem to have been already long established. There is no record of Irish being used, or of Irish-speakers being preached to. Yet this was the beginning of what developed with time into extensive preaching in Irish.

Leslie resigned from the mission in 1835 and was installed in Cookstown (Third Congregation) on 11 November 1835.[76] His successful ministry there lasted 67 years. He retired in January 1893 and died on 13 May 1902. At the time of his death he was 'father' of the General Assembly, at the age of 92 years.[77]

HENRY COOKE (1788–1868)

The Rev. Henry Cooke, third son of John Cooke, farmer, and Jane Howie, was born (as Henry McCook), in Grillagh, near Maghera, Co. Londonderry, on 11 May 1788.[78] His first school was the hedge school of Joe Poak at Ballymacillcur. Later, he attended the school of Frank Glass, a spoiled priest, at Tobermore.[79, 80]

He was on very friendly terms with the officers of the Ulster Gaelic

Society, particularly the President, Lord Downshire and the Rev. R. J. Bryce its co-secretary. In October 1832, Dr Henry Cooke moved a motion at the General Synod favouring '... the cultivation of the native language'. This was adopted. The *Belfast News Letter*, however, in an editorial comment felt that the '... Northern Presbyterians could have done more.'[81]

In 1836 the Church of Scotland received the Synod of Ulster into its communion and Dr Cooke made the celebratory speech before the Assembly.[82] His speech was sprinkled with Irish words and phrases and listing the Synod's aims he said: 'Our last object is in our country generally; and especially those Roman Catholics who speak exclusively or generally in the native Irish tongue. For this end we have joined ... At our last report our Irish schools amounted to forty: they are since increased.'

He then told a story of an Irish-speaker who came to him to borrow a shilling to buy Dr Chalmers' *Scripture References*. Cooke took down from his shelf a copy of the Testament in Irish to see if he could read it. The man was able to read it, translate it and comment on it intelligently, so Cooke gave him five different books. He went on to say:

> For advancing and perpetuating this part of our work, the Synod has lately enacted, '... that all her students must study the Irish language' (Hear, hear) ... And trust you may yet be spared to see the day, when on visiting the Synod of Ulster, you may adopt the tongue of your native hills in addressing us, and not be necessitated to enquire at any of us, *An labhrann tú Gaeilge?*

It must be significant that Cooke did not need to translate this (Do you speak Irish?). It was on the same occasion that Cooke made an appeal for Gaelic-speaking ministers to come to preach to the Irish-speakers.

> The Earse of your Highlands is so nearly akin to the Gaeilge of Ireland, that a few months would enable many of you preachers to proclaim the gospel to our countrymen ... We will receive you into the heart of our humble hospitality, brotherly kindness and gratitude, and the *céad míle fáilte romhat* with which Ireland will meet you, will flow as warm from her heart as from the spirits of your Highland clansmen.

Some of this speech was published by Porter in the standard biography,[83] but the above sections were not included.

The meeting of the General Synod of Ulster which was held on the last Tuesday in August 1838, took place in the Rev. Dr Cooke's own meeting-house in May Street, Belfast.[84] A motion was passed thanking God for the success of the Home Mission. Then the Rev. Robert Allen of Stewartstown introduced three of the Irish Scripture Readers. Between them they read out in Irish the thirteenth Chapter of St Matthew's Gospel. Then they read it out again in Irish, but this time translating it into English as they went along. They then answered questions, and members of the Synod were duly impressed by their knowledge of the Scriptures. There were further readings following the same pattern and it is remarkable how much time and how much interest was devoted to the readings in Irish. Dr Cooke announced that:

> the attendance of the Synod's students at the Irish class was not so large as they had a right to expect, and that every student might expect that a part of a chapter of the Irish New Testament would form a portion of the examination before the Theological Committee.

After a long and eventful life Dr Cooke, one of Belfast's most famous figures, died at his home on Ormeau Road, Belfast on 13 December 1868. He is buried under a high granite sarcophagus in the Balmoral Cemetery[85] not far from his Irish-speaking kinsman, Sir William Porter MacArthur.

GEORGE FIELD

Field called himself Seoirse Ó Mhachaire in Irish. He was appointed as General Agent by the Home Mission of the General Synod of Ulster in August 1835, to organise the work of the auxiliary ministers and to coordinate scripture readers and Irish teachers.[86] He was a fluent Irish-speaker and undertook the translation of the Shorter Catechism into Irish.[87] As an Appendix to the 5th Report of the Home Mission, he published his first report, dated June 1836. One of his specific duties was to supervise the Irish Schools at Cushendall.[88]

In 1837 the sixth report of the Home Mission welcomed the

publication of the Westminster Shorter Catechism which had been translated into Irish by George Field, with the statement, 'It is well and faithfully executed.'[89]

Perhaps his most remarkable achievement was his *Irish Grammar*, where as author he modestly describes himself as 'S.Ó.Mh.' (i.e. Seoirse Ó Mhachaire). This lively publication, entitled in Irish 'Casán na Gaoidhilge' (The Irish Language way), has a very long title in English, *An Introduction to the Irish Language; compiled at the request of the Irish Teachers; under the Patronage of the General Assembly in Ireland, and dedicated to them, as a tribute of esteem for their zeal in preserving and extending the knowledge of our beloved mother-tongue, by their friend and countryman, S.Ó.Mh.* In the preface, dated Belfast, March 1841, Field explained that '... this work has been compiled for the use of the native Irish and for those who wish to acquire a knowledge of *our sweet and venerable mother-tongue.*' He ended the preface by inviting '... those who feel themselves competent to expose error ..., to undertake the definitive work and so to present the nation ... that long expected gift – a perfect Grammar of the Teanga Bhinn mhilis na hÉirionn.' (i.e. the sweet melodic language of Ireland).[90] According to Beckett, Field was assisted in the compilation of 'Casán na Gaeilge' by Aodh MacDomhnaill (Hugh MacDonnell).[91] It is not clear, however, if he was of more assistance than the other persons acknowledged in the Preface to the *Grammar*.

Field used to send songs in Irish to Robert MacAdam and some of these are in the Irish MSS collection of University College Galway.[92] His writings were not confined to Irish; he is known to have written on placenames in the Bible.[93] This was reviewed in the *Orthodox Presbyterian* shortly after he was appointed general agent.[94] His address was at Castle Street, Belfast and he appears to have later moved to Scotland, from where he continued to have correspondence with MacAdam.[95]

Although he was an undoubtedly important contributor to the story of Presbyterians and the Irish language, through his publications and his work with the Home Mission, very little is known about his personal life, unlike the ministers, whose lives are usually recorded.

HUGH GORDON

He was a Presbyterian master of a Co. Down school in the period 1824–1827. This school was connected with the Kildare Place Society and was situated at Clara in the parish of Loughinisland. Later Gordon is found as a Scripture reader in Irish in Killorglin, Kerry, in 1843. In 1852 he was still acting as an Irish Scripture reader, this time in Bunlahinch, Co. Mayo.[96] Gordon was mentioned in George Field's *Casán na Gaoidhilge*. In the Preface he was thanked with others for his part in assisting and instructing the author.[97]

MARY JANE ALEXANDER (1799–1874)

The publications of Miss Alexander, who translated hymns and religious material into Irish, were welcomed by Presbyterian clergy and laity alike. Her two publications in Irish were used extensively by the Presbyterian Irish Schools run by the Home Mission. There was a great dearth of printed material in Irish in the early nineteenth century and her works fulfilled an important need. She was born about 1799, the daughter of the Rev. Nathaniel Alexander, who became Bishop of Down and Connor in 1804, and of Anne Jackson, the first cousin of Lord O'Neill. Some of her youth was spent at Portglenone House, the residence of the bishop, her father, and later at the Bishop's Palace at Holywood, Co. Down. She was a shy and retiring person to the extent that her contemporaries knew very little about her. Mary Jane Alexander was a second cousin to the third Earl of Caledon. By coincidence she was also first cousin once removed to the husband of the famous English language hymnist, Mrs Cecil Frances (née Humphreys) Alexander, who wrote *There is a green hill far away*, etc.

When Miss Alexander published *Cláirseach Naomhtha na hÉireann* (*Sacred Harp of Ireland*)[98] in 1835, she was living with her father in Ardbreccan, Co. Meath, since he had settled there as Bishop of Meath in 1823. She was still only 36 years old at this time. This book of 53 hymns in Irish was praised by the *Orthodox Presbyterian*, and was reviewed favourably by the editor of the *Belfast News Letter*, James MacKnight, in August 1835. The introduction, written by herself, includes thanks to 'Eoghan Ó Connalláin, Scríbhneoir Gaoidhilge an

Righ', i.e. Owen Connellan, Irish Historiographer to His Majesty, as he used to call himself in English; and also she thanked Peadar Ó Dálaigh, i.e. Peter O'Daly, from the parish of Ardbreccan. Five other unnamed persons helped with the translations from English to Irish. We do not know where she herself learned Irish, but when we remember that Irish was spoken by about three million of the population at the time, it would not have been difficult to have access to a good tutor.

The Report of the Home Mission[99] had the following to say of her:

> As many of the Teachers and scholars are deriving much pleasure and, it is hoped, profit also, from singing the Irish hymns, which have been provided by Miss Alexander, we feel constrained to express our grateful acknowledgment of her liberal and zealous services in this good cause. *The Sinner's Friend*, a small book which has proved so extensively profitable to English readers, may shortly, through her labours, become a useful companion to the Bible, for the reader of the Irish tongue ... .

As had been predicted, the latter book[100] was published in the following year. The translation appears to have been the unaided work of Miss Alexander, except for a four-line verse on page 19, titled, 'Tá Súil Dé Ort. Glac Rabhadh' i.e. 'The Eye of God is on You. Be Warned'. It is signed by Peter O'Daly. She was noted for her generosity and on one occasion she presented the Home Mission with 100 Irish Testaments.

PATRICK MacMENAMY (d. 1860)

Patrick MacMenamy was born in Magherafelt and grew up as a native Irish-speaker. Educated at the Old College, Belfast he received the General Certificate in 1844. He became a convert from Roman Catholicism and was licensed at Belfast, 6 December 1844. He was ordained by the Presbytery of the Route and Ballymena, acting jointly, on 15 April 1845 to act as a missionary to the Glens of Antrim, under the Home Mission. Based in Ballycastle, he was on the roll of the Route Presbytery. There is little information on his work.[101] He resigned because of ill-health in 1846. In 1845 he married a daughter of John Elder, Portknock, Skye. He died in New York in July 1860.[102]

WILLIAM CHESTNUTT (1818–1888)

William Wallace Chestnutt was born in Dervock, parish of Derrykeighan, Co. Antrim, 1818, and educated at the Old College, Belfast, where he graduated with the General Certificate in 1843. In 1844 he was ordained as a missionary for the south and west and ran a missionary station in Tralee until the formation of an official congregation there in 1846. He was installed in his new role on 23 March of that year.[103]

He apparently was himself an Irish-speaker and when he needed help he asked for another Irish-speaker to service the area of Scartyglin.[104] The Kerry Mission extended over an area of some 180 square miles, and by 1847 he had mission stations in Ardfert, Laherin, Scartyglin as well as in Tralee.[105] A church and a manse were built in Tralee and he developed all the permanent aspects of a lasting congregation. He himself was highly respected in the area and remained a regarded minister for 45 years.

He married a Miss Stewart.[106] Due to poor health he had to retire in 1888. Shortly afterwards, on 29 July 1888, Chestnutt died.[107]

WILLIAM CROTTY (d. 1856)

William Crotty, an Irish-speaker, was originally a Catholic priest and began as a curate in the parish of Killaloe, but was transferred to Birr, Co. Offaly, in 1829,[108] at the request of his cousin, Michael Crotty, who had been in Birr since 1821 and who had just been appointed by his parishioners as parish priest of Birr, in opposition to the Catholic bishop. Michael and William Crotty refused to recognise the authority of Father T. Kennedy who had been appointed by the bishop, as administrator of the parish of Birr. There was considerable tension between the parties concerned, often ending in violence. For example, it was reported in the *Belfast News Letter* of 6 June 1834: 'The Rev. Mr Crotty, of Birr, King's Co. was arrested on Sunday last by Captain Vignolles, on depositions made by the Rev. Mr Kennedy. There was a general fight on this occasion in the chapel between the parties of both priests, who each contended for exclusive possession of the edifice and Capt. Vignolles put out by force all the rioters.'[109]

Michael Crotty was no stranger to controversy. He had been imprisoned and fined as a result of a number of contentious activities, mostly aimed at improving public morality by direct action.[110] In 1821 he was fined for assault and contempt of court. His loyal parishioners collected the money to pay the fine. In 1826, he and his parishioners were forcibly removed from the church at bayonet point. They built another church and set up in opposition to the orthodox Catholic Church. The Crottys began a Reformation in Birr and piece by piece altered the liturgy until, in May 1838, a Presbyterian order of service was introduced. Finally on 30 May 1839, through the mediation of the Rev. Joseph Fisher of Galway[111] (another Irish-speaker), William Crotty and his congregation of 130 persons transferred from the Catholic Church to become a congregation of the Irish Presbyterian Church in communion with the Synod of Ulster under the care of the Presbytery of Dublin. These events are described as unique.[112, 113]

On becoming a Presbyterian minister, Crotty did not have to be re-ordained, but was directly installed after answering a few simple questions, showing that the validity of Roman Orders was recognised by the Synod.[114, 115] Bowen has suggested that the motivation of the Crotty cousins had less to do with theology and much to do with their aversion to the Catholic Church being closely attached to O'Connell.[116] The dislike of O'Connell is very clear in Michael Crotty's 'Narrative'[117] and one of his first stands against the Bishop of Killaloe was to refuse to collect the 'O'Connell rent'.

William Crotty would have been very aware that O'Connell was an Irish-speaker, but that he nevertheless wanted the Irish people to speak English which, he hinted, would bring about for them a Utopia. The attitude of O'Connell is summed up in one of his statements, which went as follows; '... although the Irish language is connected with many recollections that twine around the hearts of Irishmen (sic), yet the superior utility of the English tongue, as the medium of all modern communication, is so great that I can witness without a sigh the gradual disuse of the Irish'.[118] Rodgers, in his analysis,[119] suggests that the events above recorded, itemising the revolt of the Crottys against the Catholic Church and the translation of a whole congregation to

Presbyterianism, was simply a matter of pique to annoy the Catholic bishop. Certainly, William Crotty's own account of the events would suggest that the beginnings of the disputes centred around the attempts of Dr McMahon, the coadjutor Bishop, to prevent Michael and, in turn, William from being ordained. This was a petty-minded tactic to get at William's uncle, the Rev. Michael Crotty senior, parish priest of Castle Connell, who had refused to collect the O'Connell rent.

In 1840 William Crotty went to Roundstone, Co. Galway, an entirely Irish-speaking community, where his facility for preaching in Irish could be used to the full. The next year he married the daughter of Richard Dempsey of Mountmellick. In 1845 he was playing a large part in the Connaught Mission, always preaching in Irish. The Rev. Jonathan Simpson visited him in November 1848. He recounted how they were nearly mobbed by a crowd of roughs but that Crotty spoke to them in soothing tones in Irish, thus averting any danger.[120] The year 1852 saw him still conducting services in Irish. Towards the end of his life he was writing a diary, at the request of the *Missionary Herald*, in which extracts were published.

William Crotty spoke to the Assembly in 1853 and recounted how 64 Irish teachers with large families had been ... brought out of the Church of Rome ... and joined the Presbyterian Church.[121] The following is the entry from his diary for 21 March 1856:

> Met Mr P-, and had a long conversation with him on religious subjects, especially on the national observance of the Sabbath. Passed by the Fish Market (presumably in Galway City), and had an opportunity of speaking to the fish-women in Irish. The subject was fasting, this being Good Friday. One of the women asked me would I eat meat today. Explained the nature of fasting, spoke freely and was listened to with much attention. Distributed some tracts.[122]

His use of Irish is also described in other entries. Much lamented by the Church, he died on 25 July 1856 in Galway, leaving a widow and ten children, the eldest one only thirteen years of age. The *Missionary Herald* published a glowing obituary.[123] He was described as '... a man of unswerving integrity ... and of sincere and devoted attachment to the principles of the Protestant Reformation.'

JOHN EDGAR, D.D., LL.D. (1798–1866)

In 1842 John Edgar wrote,

> My highest and holiest ambition, my fervent wish and prayer for
> my two sons, is that they may faithfully and successfully preach in
> the Irish language to the Irish people.[124]

He was born near Ballynahinch in 1798, son of the Rev. Samuel Edgar
(1766–1826) and his wife Elizabeth McKee (1771–1839).[125] He shone
as a student at the Belfast Academical Institution where he carried off
four silver medals.[126] Edgar was noted for his humanity and his high
ideals and renowned as the originator of the Temperance Movement,
preceding by some years the work of the Rev. Fr Mathew (1838). His
letter to the *Belfast News Letter* on 14 August 1829 was the first appeal
on behalf of Temperance Societies that appeared in Europe.[127]

A person of strong social conscience, he was involved in the early
development of several of the public institutions in Belfast. Dr Orpen
of Dublin, a fluent Irish-speaker, had founded the first establishment
for deaf mutes in Ireland.[128] Dr Edgar was instrumental in getting the
Deaf, Dumb and Blind Institute in Belfast started. This was only one
of his many charitable ventures. He was sensitive to his cultural
environment and described in detail the custom of 'keening' (from the
Irish *caoin*, to cry or moan) for the deceased. He first heard it in Co.
Down, but felt that the Connemara keen was much superior.[129] His
well-known tract *A Cry from Connaught* was a best seller with 26,000
copies being printed. It first appeared in the *Missionary Herald* of
November 1846. He commented on the failure of the potato crop and
how it was spreading panic. However, there was as yet no inkling of
the devastating disaster still to strike. The work of the Irish schools was
progressing very well and he described the successes in much detail:

> In the district I visited there were 107 Irish Schools, which
> furnished for examination, last inspection, 2,053 pupils, but not
> less than 5,000 are under instruction.[130]

He criticised the attitude of the Anglican Church and in a paper read
at the 6th annual conference of the British organisation of the
Evangelical Alliance in August 1852, he said:

Is it at all surprising that the Reformation made small progress in Ireland when those in authority persisted in attempting to spread it by means of a language (English) which the people did not understand.[131]

In 1840 he was a member of the Secession Synod and Minister of Alfred Street congregation. In 1842 he was elected Moderator of the General Assembly.[132]

John Edgar resented the allegation that he was a proselytiser and that his objective was to turn Roman Catholics into Presbyterians. He pointed out that his sole aim was to give them living, saving, faith in the Son of God. Furthermore, the Home Mission, of which John Edgar was the Honorary secretary in 1847, could not be accused of using the Famine, which broke out in that year, as a means of getting a foothold in Connaught: they were already there.[133] He died in 1866 aged 68.

HENRY MacMANUS (C. 1817–1864)

The Rev. Henry MacManus was the first of the Irish-speaking missionaries to be active following the formation of the Presbyterian Missionary Society in 1830 and the Synod resolution in 1833 that all Divinity Students be required to learn Irish. Interest in preaching in Irish was very great at this time and the Synod had been deeply affected by the enthusiasm of Norman McLeod in his address to them. In many ways, therefore, MacManus was a man for his time. He pays tribute to Norman McLeod, Joseph Fisher, Robert Allen and Miss Charlotte Pringle of Edinburgh all of whom in their own way prepared the path towards the Connaught Mission.

Henry MacManus was born in Virginia, Co. Cavan and may have grown up as a native Irish-speaker. He was educated at the Old College, Belfast and received the General Certificate in 1837.[134] He was on first trials with the Presbytery of Cavan in 1839 when he first came to the attention of the General Synod. He was licensed from Dublin in 1840 and ordained to the Home Mission on 10 February 1841. He had already visited Connemara in the midsummer of 1840, so that he could get his Ulster Irish more attuned to the Irish of Connaught. His mentor in Galway at this time was Joseph Fisher.[135] He spent six months there perfecting his Irish. Apparently, his diligence was very worthwhile, because when he finally started his preaching tour of the West, he was everywhere received with great enthusiasm.

He was able to report to the General Assembly, later in 1841, the cordial reception given to him by the Irish-speaking people, who showed a great willingness to hear him preach in their language. Over the next few years he covered great areas of the West in his preaching tours and then he continued on into Kerry. However he began to suffer poor health and had to withdraw from Kerry in 1846. In the next year he was acting as a missionary in Athlone.[136] On September 1853 the congregation of Mountmellick came under his care.[137] He retired because of ill health on 7 Sept 1858 and went to live in Clontarf, Dublin, where he died on 14 October 1864.

The book he wrote of his experiences, *Sketches of the Irish Highlands*,[138] provides a vivid insight into the life and social background of the times and shows what it meant to be an itinerant preacher in pre-famine Ireland. About this book, Magee made the comment:

> In reading [it], we seem to be inhaling the invigorating breath of the Connemara mountains, and listening to the sweet music of the Gospel message tenderly spoken by a loving Celtic tongue.[139]

On the title page is found the motto *Erin my Country*. In the Preface MacManus acknowledged the special help he received from Robert Kane Esq., author of the translation of the New Testament into Munster Irish. This was published in 1858. It is not known if Kane, called Riobeárd Ó Catháin Ó Chontae Chláir, was a Presbyterian. In any case McManus described him as a '... worthy brother and true Christian patriot.'

In the first chapter he described his first visit, in 1840, to Connemara, scenes at a holy well and his first view of the mountains called the *Twelve Pins*. He saw red deer, wild badgers, barnacle geese, seals and got to know something of the local customs of the people. The last chapter recounted how welcome he was made feel, but referred to some of the opposition that he faced, particularly from the clergy. It is quite clear that MacManus identified closely with the Irish-speaking people of the West and saw himself as taking their part against the

Roman Catholic clergy, who, he believed, were trying to keep the people in subjection and had no sympathy with their true culture and language.

His first Irish sermon was on John 1.29: 'Féach Uan Dé a thógfas peacaidh an domhain'. (Behold the Lamb of God who takes away the sins of the world). He always spoke in terms that his fellow Irishmen would understand and he consistently respected their culture and intelligence. For example, he avoids using terms of abuse, so common at the time, such as 'superstition', when describing local customs and beliefs. In the first chapter he recounts in detail the belief held by the fishermen that it is wrong to kill a seal, because these creatures were actually people who had died, often one's own relatives, albeit now in a metamorphosed form. His concluding comments are:

> According to tradition, this is the pedigree of the tribe of the Coneelys, of whom there are still some in that country; and till a late period, it was often cast in their teeth by their enemies that they were, 'de chineál na róintigh', 'of the race of the seals'. Such is the story, a very wild one, no doubt – the creature of an oriental imagination; and yet it contains some touches of nature, which to the simple fisherman, give it the semblance of truth.

About the Irish language, he says that it is anything but barbarous;

> ... and in collaboration of my view, I might cite some of the greatest continental philologists, especially the German; but it will suffice to quote the well known testimony of our own great Ussher, who pronounces the Irish as 'Both elegant and copious;' and of the Rev. Mr Shaw author of the Gaelic Dictionary, who considers it, 'the greatest monument of antiquity which the world ever saw'; adding, that, the perfection to which the Gaelic attained in Ireland, in remote ages, is astonishing.

He spent much time explaining why the Irish Bible is so much more attractive to the native Irish than the English version. He discusses the reasons for this, including the inate imagery of the Irish language. It is of great interest that, when he discussed Irish orthography, the one example he gave of inflated spelling was the word 'tighearna' (lord), which he felt should be 'tiarna'. This is exactly the same one example that George Field gave in *Casán na Gaoidhilge*, indicating the interrelationship of these works. MacManus had an interest in manuscripts in Irish, and it is reported that he had in his possession an MS pedigree of the Maguire family largely written in Louvain in the year 1732.[140]

He spent much time explaining why he was preaching in Irish to spread the Gospel. His argument can be paraphrased as follows: it is important to bring the message to the Irish-speaking population, and, because of their lack of English, or on account of their regard for their own Irish language, it has to be done in Irish. The argument that Irish is due to die out and that it is therefore a waste of time to preach in Irish, does not make sense in the short term because it will be a long time before Irish expires. This would suggest that MacManus did not care about the language as such and that he treats it as just a medium to win souls. We must be very careful not to take his argument at face value. The prevailing Protestant attitude at the time was that there was hardly such a thing as the Irish language. This is reflected in social surveys of the time which usually stated something such as 'English is spoken by everybody in this parish' or 'Most of the natives understand the English language'. Such statements, illustrate conclusively that Irish was hugely prevalent at the time. The official attitude of the Established Church was that Irish did not exist. Incredibly, for a reformation Church, an edict had been issued to say that where English was not understood, the Anglican services should be conducted in Latin. The Latin Mass was one of the great reasons for the Reformation!

It is against a background such as this that we must gauge the argument of MacManus. He had to justify his preaching in Irish to officials whose prime aim was not so much the saving of souls as the subjection of the Irish people. It is clear that MacManus had a great love for the language and a respect for the traditions and culture of Irish speakers. Stothers aptly summarised his personality as follows:

> In his dealings with the people we see him as a man of kindness and compassion and full of Christ-like pity for their poverty, ignorance and sin.[141]

JOHN BARNETT (1826–1901)

He was born on 26 January 1826, son of Thomas Barnett of Ballough near Clogher, Co Tyrone.[142] John Barnett was taught Irish by Tomás

Ó Fiannachtaigh (Thomas Feenaghty) in the period 1846–1847, while he was attending the Old College, Belfast.[143] As a student he was a member of the Students' Missionary Society. In 1851 he became the second Irish-speaking missionary to be sent to Connaught under the scheme promoted by the Students' Missionary Society at the Presbyterian College, Belfast.[144]

He was licensed by Clogher, Co. Mayo and ordained there on 3 October 1852. The Rev. Henry MacManus had preached here as early as 1841.[145] Using the Irish Bible, he was active in a scheme for Colportage in Connaught. However, it was not long before he resigned from Clogher and in 1856 he was called to Carlow. In 1866 he went from there to Katesbridge, near Banbridge, where he became the first minister to that congregation.

His first wife was a daughter of Colonel Storey. After she died he married a Miss Mulligan of Katesbridge. His daughter married the Rev. S. Fullarton of Ahoghill.[146] Barnett died on 18 November 1901, in Katesbridge. He was considered to be an excellent preacher with the heart of an evangelist.[147]

MICHAEL BRANNIGAN (1816–1874)

He was born in 1816, near Stewartstown, Co. Tyrone. Originally, he was a Catholic studying for the priesthood.[148] His conversion to Presbyterianism was the result of cooperation between the Home Mission and the Irish Scriptural Schools Society. The latter, founded in 1818, aimed at teaching Irish-speakers to read and write in their own language through the use of the Irish Bible. The person most instrumental in his conversion was the Rev. Robert Allen.[149]

Brannigan, whose father had been a teacher in one of the Irish-speaking schools in Tyrone, became a Presbyterian and in 1845 was ordained a minister. His education in the Belfast Academical Institution and later in the Free Church College, Edinburgh was supported by The Scottish Ladies Society of Edinburgh, which had been founded by a Miss Pringle.[150] Eventually, Brannigan was licensed by Tyrone on 20 February 1845[151] and was ordained to Connaught on the following 24 June, one of a number of Irish-speaking Presbyterian ministers who directed their attentions to their fellow Irish-speaking compatriots. He was not re-baptised.[152]

He preached in Irish to many groups throughout the country, starting with Connaught. At the time of the famine Brannigan was in Sligo and Mayo, but his indomitable spirit, in the face of famine and adversity, resulted in his setting up some 140 Irish language Schools. He was specially assigned to the Irish School and Roman Catholic Mission Department in the year 1845 by the students of the General Assembly's Collegiate classes in Belfast, who had formed the Students' Missionary Association in February 1845 aimed at their fellow Roman Catholic countrymen. He was to oversee the Irish Schools and to act as an itinerant missionary over a large tract of country.[153]

In January 1846 he went on the Connaught Mission and altogether established 144 Irish Schools. The first congregation he founded was in 1846 at Dromore West. He is said to have introduced turnips into Ballinglen in 1847.[154] In the same year he addressed the General Assembly. When, in 1848, the Rev. Robert Allen moved from Stewartstown on his appointment as Superintendent of the Connaught Schools, Mr Brannigan was directed to confine his labours to the Ballinglen district.[155] It was Mr Brannigan who built the church in Ballinglen, which was opened by Dr Henry Cooke.

The Rev. Jonathan Simpson gave a poignant description of Brannigan's home in Ballinglen, Co. Mayo, when he visited Connaught in the late autumn of 1848.[156] Leaving Dromore West, Co. Sligo, the road was miserably kept, unfenced, and without any hedges. There was no bridge over the river and the open car was nearly swept away in the swollen river at the crossing point. When they, wet and cold, finally got into Mr Brannigan's house, it was only the owner's '... hearty Irish kindness and hospitality ...' which compensated for the inconveniences of that dismal abode. The rear of the house was built against the face of a hill, and water ran in streams down the wall inside. Yet Simpson described it as the best house in the neighbourhood. However the situation was very beautiful, with Nephin Mountain in the background and '... the murmur of the stream as it bubbled by in the valley below, and emptied into the North Atlantic Ocean ...'.

The Rev. Michael Brannigan resigned from the Connaught Mission in 1849. In 1860 he married Miss Dobbin, sister of two Presbyterian ministers, Alexander (Boardmills) and William Dobbin (Annaghlone). Two of his daughters married ministers, the Rev. Philip Flaherty of the Free Church Mission to Turkey, and the Rev. Robert Hall of Pittsburgh. He died on 15 November 1874, aged 58 and had been 29 years a minister.

JOSEPH FISHER

Joseph Fisher was the son of Walter Fisher of Kilgormley, Stonebridge near Clones, Co Monaghan. His two brothers also became ministers, John Fisher, who served from 1841 to 1843 in Moyvore, and Ringland Fisher, Raffrey (1843–1888). Educated at Old College, Belfast, he was awarded the General Certificate in 1832. He was ordained as minister of Galway on 3 June 1835.[157] No Presbyterian minister had settled there for over 110 years.[158] There were only 81 Presbyterians in the congregation, but Fisher was concerned not only with evangelism to his co-religionists but also to the Roman Catholics, most of whom were not English-speakers.[159] He reported to the Home Mission:

> On my coming to Galway, I found that the vast majority of the people, both in town and country, used the Irish language; and immediately I commenced to learn it. I found the difficulties to be very great, yet I persevered and have almost succeeded. I can now read it pretty correctly and translate it with the greatest ease; and I have so far advanced in the colloquial style, as occasionally to pass for one of their own Priests. I fear, however, that, if even spared to preach in Irish, the influence of the Priests will hinder me from being heard. The trial I am resolved to make, as I consider it my duty. The success and the blessing must all come from God.[160]

Fisher found that the Irish-speaking population were somewhat reluctant '... to come out to hear the Word, even when preached in their beloved tongue ...'. However, readers of the Scriptures usually found a welcome at the doorstep and were invited inside to read the Irish Scriptures. He established many Irish Schools in the West and in Connemara. Henry MacManus, the Irish-speaking preacher, was a friend and colleague. In 1842, Fisher married the daughter of James

Risk of Crommon Lodge, Co. Donegal. It is recorded that he was preaching in Irish in the year 1843. He resigned from Galway on 5 February 1845 and went from there to London, where he was installed in St George's, Southwark.

THOMAS ARMSTRONG (1822–1897)

Thomas Armstrong, son of John Armstrong, was born in the town of Monaghan on 6 March 1822. He received his education at the Old College, Belfast[161] and apparently was studying Irish in Belfast during the period 1837–1838.[162] He learned to read it with ease. Subsequently, he received the Edinburgh General Certificate in 1842. Licensed from Monaghan on 10 November 1844, he was ordained at Ballina, Co. Mayo, on 6 May 1846, the first permanent minister of Ballina. The little congregation had begun some ten years earlier as a mission station with Killala, Co. Mayo.

He succeeded the Rev. Archibald Lowry in the congregation of Ballina, Co. Mayo. Shortly after he arrived the Great Famine began and he was deeply disturbed by its effects on the helpless people of Connaught. He played a major part in alleviating their suffering and distress.[163] His account of his experiences, *My Life in Connaught*, is an excellent first-hand account of the Famine and one of the best accounts of the Connaught Mission.[164, 165]

He was a member of the local relief committee which included gentry and clergy of all the different denominations.[166] A policy of forced emigration had been introduced and Armstrong was horrified at the ruthlessness with which it was implemented. Of this he said:

> There would have been wisdom in this course if carried out with kindness and care. Provision should have been made for these humble people to enable them to emigrate with comfort to another land where their toil would be repaid by prosperity and comfort. But as a rule this is not done. Entire families were turned out on the roadside without a shelter, sometimes even in the cold and rain of the winter time. 'The Crowbar Brigade' unroofed the houses and broke down the walls, so that the poor creatures had nothing to protect them from the weather, even in the ruins of their own homes.[167]

All these unfortunate people were Irish-speakers, who were by far the hardest hit by the Famine and for many of them it must have seemed that Daniel O'Connell was right about the need to discard the language. Armstrong's knowledge of Irish made him identify with the people and sharpened his awareness of their plight.

He had to struggle to get his small congregation properly established. With diligence he finally managed to build a meeting house for his flock. This was formally declared open by the Rev. Henry Cooke in July 1851.[168] Greatly involved in the Irish Mission, Armstrong was able to read Irish, but not skilled enough to preach in the language.[169] While in Ballina, he was also Clerk to the Connaught Presbytery.

He resigned from Ballina in 1868 and became Superintendent of the Connaught Schools, succeeding the Rev. Robert Allen who had died in 1865. He was Superintendent for 27 years. For a short time (1873–1875) during this period he was also minister to Dromore West, which had been first organised by Michael Brannigan. His first wife was Theresa C. Smith, a daughter of Dr H. Smyth of Ballina. After she died he married in 1868, Jane F. Reid, a daughter of William Reid of Skibbereen, whose wife was a daughter of Dr Charles Neilson.[170] His second wife was also a great-grand-daughter of the Rev. Moses Neilson of Rademon, parish of Kilmore, Co Down.

In 1893 Armstrong's health began to deteriorate, but he persisted with his work. It was 1895 before he resigned from the Connaught Mission and he died at Bloomfield on 23 December 1897. His wife finished his biography. About his politics, she said that he was fair and unprejudiced, but that he was a strong Unionist.

MATTHEW KERR (1828–1900)

The son of Robert Kerr of Articlave, Co. Londonderry, Matthew Kerr was born on 1 January 1828. He was educated at the Old College, Belfast, where he qualified in 1846,[171] and he was ordained as a missionary to the Presbytery of Connaught on 8 August 1849.

He settled in Dromore West, Co. Sligo. This congregation was first organised by the Rev. Michael Brannigan in 1846,[172] who conducted regular services in Irish there, as well as at Ballinglen.[173] Up to 1847 the services were in a private house, but after this in a barn. Kerr himself carried out his work from a humble cottage in the bog which served him as a manse.[174] He served as a Connaught missionary until the congregation was formally organised in July 1848. He worked there until 11 July 1862 when he went to Tipperary to be an itinerant missionary. Later he was minister of Queen Street, Cork[175] where he was installed on 16 June 1874.[176]

It is not entirely clear if he preached in Irish.[177] But he did have Irish-speaking teachers and readers under his control. Kerr died on 5 February 1900.

GEORGE SHIRRA KEEGAN, (1823–1890)

George S. Keegan, was a native of Scotch Corner, Clontibret, Co. Monaghan where he was born in 1823.[178] His parents were respected farmers. An Irish-speaker from birth, in his early youth he was converted from Roman Catholicism largely through reading the Scriptures in Irish, at one of the Irish schools run by the Irish Society.[179]

After his education in Glasgow and Edinburgh, he spent a short period, 1852–1854, as an agent for the Anti-Popish Mission of the Free Church of Scotland. He was ordained as a missionary to the district around Newport, Co. Mayo, by the Presbytery of Connaught on 16 March 1854.[180] He regularly preached in Irish.[181] A proper church was opened for worship in Newport on 3 June 1857, with Rev. John MacNaughten of Belfast as special preacher. Mr Keegan's ministry lasted for 36 years.[182] He died on 10 May 1890 and it was said of him, 'He was much beloved, and his knowledge of the Irish language gave him ready access to many who were not connected with his own church'.[183]

HAMILTON MAGEE (1824–1902)

Born in 1824 the son of Henry Magee of Belfast, Hamilton Magee was destined to become a leading light in the Irish Mission.[184] He was educated at the Old College, Belfast, from which he obtained the General Certificate in 1845.

In July 1848 he was licensed at Belfast and on 8 August 1849 he was ordained to Killala, at the same time that Matthew Kerr, his close friend, was ordained to Dromore West. The two congregations were not far apart and the ministers used to see each other frequently. His other colleagues on the Connaught Mission were the Reverends John Hall and T.Y. Killen.

Magee favoured preaching in Irish, though he seems not to have been proficient enough to preach in it himself.[185] In 1853 the General Assembly decided to establish a mission in Dublin as part of its Irish Mission and Magee was asked to run it. So on 18 January 1854 he resigned from Killala and moved to Dublin to become Superintendent of the Dublin City Mission.[186]

In 1860 he married the daughter of the Rev. W.B. Kirkpatrick of Mary's Abbey, Dublin.[187] He had a talent with words and was editor of four different journals, all relating to the Irish Missions. They were *Plain Words*, which he edited for sixteen years, *Key of Truth* (1862–1876), *Presbyterian Churchman* (1877–1878), and *The Christian Irishman* (1883–1894).

In 1894 he retired from the Dublin City Mission and wrote his account of the Irish Home Missions, a most valuable description of the period. In this book he dealt extensively with preaching in Irish and included many biographical details of Irish-speaking ministers.[188]

He coined the motto of the Irish Mission, *Speaking the Truth in Love*. Stothers says about him: 'His book shows that he, like all the Irish Missioners, had a strong desire to see his fellow Irishmen come to Christ and that he had a strong love for his native land. His concern for the Connaught Mission never waned.'[189] He died on 11 October 1902.

IV B

In 1844 Fr Luke Walsh published a booklet under the title of *The Home Mission Unmasked*.[190] This publication and the alleged events reported in it did little credit to those concerned and it might be argued that, for this reason, they should be passed over. Yet, no account of the Home Mission would be complete without reference to the debate. In the booklet Fr Walsh published letters which he selected from two contemporary Belfast journals, one *The Vindicator* representing the Catholic interest and the other, *The Banner of Ulster*, being Presbyterian. His assertion was that when the Home Mission began to send teachers of Irish to the Glens of Antrim, he had understood that the sole purpose was to teach people to read in the language but, when he discovered that the true aim was proselytism, he and other priests set out to put an end to it. However, the main thrust of Fr Walsh's onslaught on the Home Mission was that, despite official Presbyterian statistics saying there were 20 Irish schools and 600 students in the Glens, there had not been, according to him, any schools or pupils for the previous four years. He alleged that the Irish teachers had continued to take money from the Assembly for doing nothing.

On 20 June 1842, four persons from the Glens of Antrim declared that they had dishonestly been getting money from the Synod of Ulster for teaching Irish, something they had not done for four years previously, i.e. since 1838.[191] The signatories of the letter were Patrick Macauley, Patrick Loughran, Patrick Quin and John McKeesick. They furthermore alleged that, contrary to the statistics of the Home Mission, there had been no Irish Schools in the same area, nor had any inspectors come with the purpose of inspecting such schools.

There followed a letter from Francis Brennan, who said he was an inspector under the General Assembly and that he did inspect an Irish School for Patrick Macauley, of Gruige, in his own barn on 28 January last, where 21 scholars were assembled and who read the gospels in

Irish and underwent other tests, satisfactorily. He said that he had
made similar inspections of the Irish Schools run by the other three
signatories.[192]

This was followed quickly by a letter of 18 July 1842, signed by the
same four Irish teachers.[193] This time they stated categorically that
they did teach and that the schools were inspected. This letter had
been forwarded to *The Vindicator* by Robert Allen, of Stewartstown,
Superintendent of the Home Mission. He believed that the four
teachers had not signed the first letter or, if they had, then they must
not have known of its contents. Allen enclosed a signed and witnessed
statement from the four teachers, saying:

> We ... do hereby certify ... that we have been, and are at present,
> employed, when opportunity serves, in teaching our neighbours
> and their children to read the Scriptures in our native language;
> and we also do declare, that our schools have been regularly visited
> by the local inspector each quarter, who has inspected and
> examined a great number of scholars in our schools under our
> instruction, for which we receive a gratuity from the Assembly's
> Home Mission ... .

The strange spectacle thus presented itself of the four Irish teachers
firstly asserting in a public letter that they had not been teaching, followed
a little later by another letter to the press saying precisely the opposite.

Subsequently a letter from the Rev. John Fitzsimons, parish priest of
Cushendall, dated 25 July 1842, was sent to Robert Allen.[194] He
quoted a witnessed statement from two residents of Gruige who
maintained that there was no Irish school in their district for the last
four years and therefore no inspection. He also quotes a statement
from Patrick Loughran who says:

> Having seen a document signed 'Francis Brennan', in which the
> writer states that he inspected an Irish School under me on the 2nd
> Feb. last and that I brought in five scholars to read for him in
> John's Gospel, I hereby declare, in the presence of witness, such a
> statement to be altogether false.

This letter of Fitzsimons also quoted similar statements from the
other Irish teachers, who collectively denied that they had taught at

any time during the previous four years. Fitzsimons ended by appealing to the Home Mission to give up its attempts '... of converting the Irish Catholics, through the medium of the Irish language, to the religion of Calvin and Knox.'

Robert Allen replied to this on 30 July 1842.[195] He said that he felt it very strange that Fitzsimons should feel so uneasy just because, as he believed, the Presbyterians were being deceived and that they were paying out money despite the work not being done. Allen said that he was not worried about the accusation that he was partner to a monstrous fabrication, because in the last analysis he was responsble to his own Master. He saw his duty as one of '... still continuing to seek the instruction to our Roman Catholic countrymen, through the teaching of the Irish Scriptures.'

He pointed out that the evidence of locals that they had seen no Irish schools was no proof that they did not exist. He also said that the Irish teachers went about their work in a quiet unobtrusive manner and therefore might not be noticed. In any case, he said, the Glens were a more extensive area than so far discussed, stretching from Ballycastle to Glenarm. He suggested that the four teachers had come under great clerical pressure to change their testimony. The latter part of Allen's letter was most conciliatory and appealed to Fitzsimons:

> If he would only give a little encouragement; if he would merely say from the altar, to his people, that all who were desirous of learning to read the Irish Scriptures might do so, and all who could teach his neighbours to read might teach him, I would undertake to furnish him, in a very short time, with the gratifying spectacle of some hundreds of them, old and young, heartily engaged in the work, and I would invite him to all our examinations, that he may witness, with delight, the aptness to learn, the readiness and shrewdness in answering, and the good sense and intelligence that characterise the Irish mind, when left at liberty to think, and judge and reason, without constraint and fear ... We could thus afford him pleasing proof that we are sincere and honest in our endeavours to do the work which we profess to do ...

Luke Walsh replied to Allen on 29 July.[196] He reserved his worst abuse for the Irish teachers for their dishonesty and for the agents of the Home

Mission. He did not directly attack the principle of teaching Irish-speakers to read, even if it was through the Bible. About falsification he said:

> I called no later than yesterday on some of these teachers, who told me they had not themselves, nor did they know of, a single Irish school in the parish. Some of them, indeed, told me that they had occasionally been giving lessons in Irish to their own children, to enable them to draw the salary; but, in this way, any man who can read Irish, and has a family, can be said to be a teacher.

Without waiting for a reply, Walsh wrote another letter to Robert Allen on 7 August.[197] He began by attacking Allen and the Home Mission and then quoted another letter from Irish teachers hired by the Home Mission. This was a different group, which included Patrick Sheals, Glenshesk, Hugh Sheals, Ballyucan, Francis McKendry, Ballypatrick, Robert McMichael, Ballyveradagh, Rose Duncan, Escart and Mary McDonnell, Ballyucan. They said they were heartily sorry because,

> We have received money from the agents of the Synod of Ulster for teaching the Irish tongue, although for the last twelve months we had no schools in existence, nor do we know of any in the parish; and we further declare, that it is our poverty and the manner in which it was pressed upon us caused us to receive it, as we were told that all the agents wanted was our names.

They promised to make restitution to the poor when in a position to do so. Fr Walsh reported that some of them had already paid him small sums of money. Walsh describes them as '... the very dregs and lees of the Catholic people.' His point was that for the Home Mission to use such people showed a lack of confidence in the scheme. He also attacked the inspectors appointed by the Assembly. According to him Mr Moloney was '... an unfortunate renegade Catholic.' He thought very little of Hugh McDonnell, another inspector, or of Francis Brennan. He said that they connived at deceiving the Assembly about the existence of Irish Schools and that they falsified returns about the numbers of students. He accused Robert Allen himself of either allowing himself to be deceived, or of actually being a party to the deception. He went further and said that either some part of the £3,519 raised for the Home Mission had gone into Allen's own pocket or he had acted gratuitously out of zeal for the propagation of the faith, but either way he had been guilty of a shameful neglect of duty. His final point was that even if the definition of the 'Glens' included Ballycastle, Ardmoy, Glenarm and Glenravel, there were still no Irish schools in that area. He quoted the parish priests of Armoy and Ballycastle to prove this.

On 6 August, one of the teachers, Patrick Loughran, published a letter to Robert Allen, who was now being subjected to a concerted attack from all sides.[198] He accused Allen of bribing him to sign the second letter sent by Francis Brennan, which stated that he ran an Irish school and taught a number of students. But he also gives the reason for signing as '... the whining solicitation of Brennan. He implored us to to do so merely to get him his salary.' Then in a letter of 10 August another parish priest, John McCourt of Glenarm, joined in the offensive against Robert Allen.[199] Like many of these letters it generated more heat than light, being a mixture of abuse and heavy sarcasm, for example:

> Neither I, nor the faithful people confided to my pastoral care, ever entertained the thought, until Mr Allen was obliging enough to enlighten us on that subject, that the Catholics of my united parishes enjoyed the opportunity of deriving religious instruction, through the agency of Irish schools, from that most learned and veracious company lately incorporated at Belfast, and known by the name of the General Assembly.

At last, on 15 August, Robert Allen gave a lengthy reply.[200] His letter was relatively free from personal attack and its tone conciliatory. He suggested that two documents dated 9 August 1842 were actually two years old. 'They have been nursed there, with paternal affection, for two whole years, while the Presbyterian public were cooly allowed to be fleeced during all this time ...'.

This is the first time that Allen conceded that Presbyterian funds might have been misused. He pointed out that the teachers were paid for teaching Irish when the scheme started some time ago. He admitted that the schools were not functioning for some time, but denied that the teachers continued to be paid after the work had stopped. Allen said he did not understand how the promise to make retribution would work. Did it mean that the teachers would not return the money until they themselves became rich?

He denied the suggestion that the Irish-teachers were not good readers, or that 'they do not know a letter of the Irish alphabet'. He knew this to be false because 'every person appointed a teacher and receiving gratuities has been examined by myself in reading and translating the Irish'.

This is convincing evidence that the teaching standard was satisfactory and also verifies that Allen himself was proficient in Irish. He quoted a letter to Fr Walsh from Hugh McDonnell, the Irish-teacher and scribe, denying the statements attributed to him by Fr Walsh and disavowing that he had sent him any letters on this subject. Allen also rejected the idea that he received any remuneration for this work.

The correspondence – 24 letters in all – continued on until December 1842. But most of these letters contained the text of other letters, some alleged by opponents to be forged. There is much repetition, which makes the thread difficult to follow at times. The Home Mission spokesmen repeatedly stressed the laudable objectives of the scheme. For example, on 27 August Robert Allen restated the aims of the Irish schools as seeking: '... to teach the Irish-speaking population to read the Irish Scriptures and thus promote among them a knowledge of the Word of God.'[201] Paradoxically, his opponents appeared to be concerned only with the prospect of the Presbyterians being cheated! As Allen said in the same letter, in which he caricatured the opponents' argument as follows:

> It is that the above official persons (Agents, local ministers etc.), with all the Directors of the Mission, annually chosen by the several Presbyteries do conspire to take the money of their own people to give it away to Roman Catholics, knowingly, for doing nothing and that the priests, having found out the cheat, have come forward as the honest disinterested conservatives of Presbyterian property; and not at all angry with us, or opposed to us because the Irish Scriptures are being read, but because the well-meaning Presbyterian people are cheated out of their money by their own ministers, who collect it from them, and give a little of their own, to throw it intentionally away on a few useless members of the Roman Catholic community?

Allen had put his finger on an irrational element in the arguments of his opponents. They were constantly on the attack, yet their concern about Presbyterians being cheated did not ring true. So what was really disturbing the Catholic priests? He felt that, contrary to assertions, the Irish teachers were still very active, but that the priests were not willing to admit it. The fact that on 18 August 1844, two years later, Fr Walsh solemnly excommunicated three of the Irish teachers for their activities proves beyond any doubt that Allen's suspicions were correct.

Arising out of a visit by Fr Walsh to Scotland in 1844, about the very same time that he excommunicated three of the teachers of Irish, the Rev. Jonathan Simpson, in his memoirs, summarised the controversy:

> Priest Luke Walsh had gone over to Scotland to prove to the Scottish people our Irish Home Mission was all a humbug and a cheat; but the shrewd people concluded if the lion hadn't been disturbed in his den he wouldn't have roared, and his mission was of essential service to our mission, and led the people to see we must be doing a good work among the Roman Catholic Irish.[202]

In addition, looking back at these events with a historical perspective, it seems clear that the Catholic priests were suffering from feelings of guilt and that it was important for them to create an effective diversionary smokescreen. The apparent characteristics of Walsh's attack were:

1   Walsh and his colleagues took the initiative in launching these verbal attacks on the Home Mission while the latter, in contrast, played a simply reactive role.

2   The main emphasis was placed on the current, complete absence of Irish Schools and pupils in the Glens and, arising from this, the dishonest fabrication of numbers and the claiming of money by the Irish teachers for work which they never carried out.

3   His tone was much more vindictive and personal than that from the Presbyterian side.

4   Despite his quarrel about the statistics, he did not make any reference to the number of Irish teachers in the Glens, whether these had decreased, or disappeared or what they were before. Yet, his main contention relates to the teachers and their fraudulent behaviour.

Postcard from Aden written in Irish by William MacArthur to his son

Sir William P. MacArthur (1884–1964) as a young officer
in the British Expeditionary Force, 1915. In the following year
he was wounded in the stomach at the Somme

The health caravan organised by Lady Aberdeen was inscribed with English on one side and Irish on the other. *c.* 1907

The prize-winning *seanchaí*, Bridget Costello,
at the 1910 Oireachtas captured by Robert Lynd

5   Although nodding in the direction of the desirability of teaching reading to Irish speakers, he does not seem to put a premium on this venture.

6   He used no Irish whatever in his discourses.

7   Walsh's poor opinion of Hugh McDonnell suggests that the parish priest was out of touch with the Irish language world. He apparently had no appreciation of McDonnell's work as a scribe, as a poet and as a naturalist in the Irish language. McDonnell worked for Robert MacAdam in the collection and saving of Irish literature.

Most of the Roman Catholic clergy were strong supporters of O'Connell's policy. He was promising Irish-speakers progress and a better standard of living, or even a form of Utopia, if they would give up the language. There was no suggestion that bi-lingualism was an option. There is in print a contemporary account of the Catholic Church's attitude. In a publication called *Songs of the Irish*, the author, in the September 1843 issue, says:

> I have seen an Irish bishop, with mitre on head, and crozier in hand, delivering an elaborate English discourse to an Irish congregation, while a priest stood in the pulpit interpreting it sentence by sentence. This prelate was the son of an Irish peasant, born and reared in one of the most Irish districts in Ireland. Many of his audience might have been, and very probably were, his playmates in childhood and boyhood, and must have heard him speak the language of the vulgar herd he had left below.[203]

With this and other evidence, it is possible to suggest conclusions which are compatible with the facts of the dispute. It would appear that Fr Walsh was affected by guilt for not doing anything about teaching his Irish-speaking parishioners to read but, on the contrary, for promoting English, a language entirely strange to them. His resentment, from seeing the Home Mission doing what was his own responsibility, would explain why he would want to attack the Home Mission on a less relevant issue, i.e.the Home Mission paying people who did not do the work they were paid for and the implied connivance of the inspectors and organisers of the Home Mission. At the moment, this conjecture is in keeping with the whole tone of the bitter debate and is almost proved by one major incident.

Despite writing polemic letters maintaining that the Home Mission was dead in his parish and that there were no Irish schools or pupils, Luke Walsh, on 18 August 1844, at a ceremony in the Catholic Church, solemnly pronounced excommunication on three Irish teachers in the following words: 'My curse, and God's curse on Charles McLoughlin, Hugh Shields, and John McCay, and on all who work with, and hold any communications with, the accursed teachers of the Irish Bible.'[204]

This statement and this act would appear to demonstrate beyond doubt that Walsh's arguments had been hollow, that the teachers were still operating in the Glens and that his accusations against the Home Mission were diversionary tactics to hide his own misguided policies. The pro-Catholic gloss on these events blamed the Home Mission for the demise of the Irish language in the Glens of Antrim. Yet, the language survived longer there than in South Armagh, where there was no Home Mission.

O'Laverty summarised the disputes[205] but, while publishing 25 letters, not even one of these is from the Home Mission, although Luke Walsh himself included at least five of Robert Allen's replies in his own pamphlet. Therefore 16 pages of O'Laverty's chapter on the subject are devoted to only one side of the discussion. O'Laverty referred to the court case taken by Charles McLoughlin against Fr Walsh in March 1846, but he did not draw the conclusion that Fr Walsh admitted effectively, by his excommunication of a number of Irish teachers, that the work of the Home Mission was still very active in the Glens.

A modern commentator, Breandán Ó Buachalla, took perhaps a more careful line, more in the spirit of a plague on both your houses, and made no judgements on one side or the other except to regret that neither side thought of conducting the debate in Irish.[206] Stothers appreciated Ó Buachalla's fairness, but felt that it was difficult to judge what was the truth of the matter.[207] However, Fitzsimons[208] put the blame totally on the Home Mission, but published only material favourable to Luke Walsh's case. It could be said that there was more honour on the side of the Home Mission, who acknowledged the reality of an Irish-speaking community in the Glens of Antrim and who tried their best to teach them to read in their own language.

In the late 1820s a movement started in Belfast to encourage the use of Irish, to save its ancient literature and to spread education in the language. It was this that led to the formation of the Ulster Gaelic Society in 1828.

THE ULSTER GAELIC SOCIETY (CUIDEACHTA GHAEILGE ULADH)

Although this was an interdenominational society, the two co-secretaries were Presbyterian. Ó Buachalla said that it was connected almost totally with the Presbyterian middle class, who were always among the most energetic and progressive groups in the town.[1] In many ways the society accorded with the Presbyterian philosophy of the time.

The most extensive account to date of the aims and objectives of the Ulster Gaelic Society was published in the *Newry Examiner* of 7 April 1830. The editor introduced the report as follows:

> It is with great pleasure that we direct public attention to the following detailed account of the object and purposes of the Society, which has been lately established in Belfast, for the cultivation of the Irish language.

It seems clear that the account had been submitted by the Society itself. It began by pointing out how many Irish-speakers there were in Ireland, 500,000 who spoke Irish only and another 1.5 million who spoke English but imperfectly. Because of the great scarcity of books in Irish and because of the lack of schools these people '... have no means of attaining intellectual cultivation.' The account continued:

> At different times, the idea of supplying these wants has been started by patriotic men but, from various causes, has never been fully carried into execution. Influenced by the wish of affording to two millions of their countrymen the blessings of education and encouraged by the success of similar undertakings in Scotland and Wales, a few persons in Belfast have formed themselves into a Society, for the purpose of promoting

the diffusion of elementary education and useful knowledge, through the medium of the Irish language. Their intentions are –

I   To establish Schools, where reading, writing and arithmetic may be taught by means of the Irish language.

II   To publish useful books in that tongue for the benefit of the lower classes.

III   To collect books and manuscripts, for an Irish library, with a view of promoting the last mentioned object.

IV   To maintain a teacher of the Irish language in Belfast, that the educated classes in this town may be enabled to take an interest in the operations of the Society and to judge of its performances. Several objections have been made to this plan, which it will be well to obviate.

The next section is a paraphrasing of a piece written by Thaddaeus Connellan as part of the *Preface* which he reproduced in a number of his publications, for example, *The King's Letter*,[2] and the *Irish-English Spelling Book*,[3] both published in 1825. The gist of the argument was that the promotion of Irish was not injurious to the spread of English. Indeed, the process of education involved in reading and writing Irish will help people to be language-conscious and so enable them to learn English more easily. Anyway, Irish was not all that rapidly in retreat. On the contrary:

> There is nothing to which a people clings so long, or with so much enthusiasm, as their language. Many centuries have not been able to establish the language of the sister island amongst our mountains and glens; and generations must pass away before the original one is entirely obliterated. And should we on this account defer the diffusion of knowledge and deny to the present and rising generations the means of education, merely because they cannot speak English?

These points were made in great detail reflecting ideas of education prevalent at the time. The argument appears to be very close to our modern concept of bi-lingualism. The last part of the account deals with the Society itself.

> Several meetings of the Ulster Gaelic Society have taken place and part of their plan has already been put in execution. They have opened an Irish class in Belfast, under the superintendence of a well qualified teacher. They have in progress a translation of two of

Miss Edgeworth's Tales; and they are making arrangements for establishing schools in the remote districts of Tyrone, Derry and Donegal where Irish is the only language spoken. The Society take this public opportunity of declaring, that they are determined not to interfere in the least degree with religion: they aim solely at affording the elementary parts of education. The works which they intend to publish, will be altogether of a neutral character. Some of the tales of Miss Edgeworth, Mrs E. Hamilton etc.: some approved books on rural economy, with elementary treatises on arithmetic and geography, are all that they have at present in contemplation ... .

It is clear from this account that the Society, although to some extent influenced by the educational theories of the day, was non-denominational and non-sectarian in its approach. The fact that the only two authors mentioned were women is of great interest. Mrs Elizabeth Hamilton (1758–1816), novelist, was a native of Belfast.[4] No doubt the novel intended for translation was the very popular *The Cottagers of Glenburnie* (1808) which went into many editions.[5]

Although the society appears from the above account to have been 'recently' instituted in 1830, Dr Bryce reported in a pamphlet dated 1828 that a society had been formed for the cultivation of the Irish language.[6] In addition, he quoted sections of a paper which the society had circulated in the previous few days, setting out its aims. This is the same document which was published in the press two years later and described above. Some of the ideas, as mentioned, were taken from publications of Thaddeus Connellan, who worked with the Irish Society.

Further evidence that the society was formed in 1828 comes from a letter dated 15 September 1828, from Thomas Feenachty to Robert MacAdam which referred to the Society as already being in existence.[7] The officers of this unique venture were of very different backgrounds: President: The third Marquis of Downshire; Chairman: Dr James MacDonnell; Secretaries: Dr Reuben John Bryce and Robert Shipboy MacAdam.[8]

It appears that they were much impressed by the works of Christopher Anderson, who had begun writing about the dearth of reading material in Irish, especially of the Bible, as far back as 1815.[9] This pamphlet led to much discussion at the time and resulted in the formation of the Irish

Society in 1816.[10] He published a book on the subject in 1828,[11] an enlarged second edition in 1830 and a third edition in 1846.[12]

Pádraig Ó Snodaigh (1973) has suggested that the Ulster Gaelic Society '... seems to have ceased effective functioning about 1843 ...', but he quotes no evidence for this.[13] Certainly the chairman, James MacDonnell, died in 1845 and this must have had some effect on the survival of the society. But if we remember that Reuben Bryce survived to late in the century and that Robert MacAdam continued with the aims of the *Cuideachta*, almost to the time of his death, it could be argued that the aims of the Ulster Gaelic Society were being pursued to near the end of the nineteenth century. An account of the life and efforts of Robert MacAdam will support this view.

In 1833 the society published Irish translations of two stories by Maria Edgeworth, *Rosanna*, and *Forgive and Forget*.[14] It has two title pages, one in English and the other in Irish. The Irish versions of the stories were printed by M. Goodwin of Dublin and the English versions by Mairs of Belfast. The dedication, signed by R.J. Bryce and R.S. MacAdam, is to the third Marquis of Downshire and offers the book to him '... as a sincere ... token of their respect for the patriotic interest you have taken in the resuscitation of our long lost national literature.'

The translator was Thomas Feenachty, who is acknowledged on the title page, where he is described as a teacher of Irish in Belfast. He was the teacher of the students for the ministry at the Belfast Academical Institution and he ran less-frequent classes at the Belfast Academy. We find him in 1828 trying to implement the first aim of the *Cuideachta Ghaeilge Uladh*, i.e. founding Irish schools; this one in Ballinascreen.[15]

Rosanna was the only official publication of the Society, but the officers, MacAdam and Feenachty and other Belfast people in the Irish language circle, had a substantial output over the space of a few years. Ó Buachalla remarked that, in the period 1830–1841, five Irish books were published from Belfast.[16] He further commented that there was no other town in Ireland at that time doing so much work concerned with Irish. It was said that the Ulster Gaelic Society inspired a little group of Belfastmen to take an interest in the native literature of Ireland.[17] This included Samuel Ferguson, Thomas O'Hagan, George

Fox and others. Certainly, it is noteworthy that Ferguson reported that his interest in Irish began in 1833,[18] the year that Rosanna was published.

The great number of poetry anthologies, translated from Irish, which appeared after this time, was attributed by Ó Buachalla to the inspiration of the *Cuideachta Ghaeilge Uladh*.[19] The list is long and includes Ferguson's own works, Matthew Graham's *The Giantess from the Irish of Oisín* (1833), *Early Native Irish Poetry* by Henry Riddell Montgomery in 1846, and William Hamilton Drummond's collection called *Ancient Irish Minstrelsy*. MacAdam lived until 1895 and he in many ways continued, while he lived, to carry out the aims of the Ulster Gaelic Society, particularly the collection of manuscripts. The aim to publish in Irish was not so successfully implemented. However, as founder and editor of the *Ulster Journal of Archaeology*, MacAdam was read by a wide audience for his articles in and about Irish.

ROBERT SHIPBOY MacADAM (1808–1895)

Robert MacAdam has left a significant and lasting imprint on the story of Irish in East Ulster. He was born in 1808 in the house of his father, James MacAdam (1775–1821) hardware merchant, in High Street, Belfast, two doors from Bridge Street, on the Castle Place side,[20] where he lived until 1833. His mother, Jane Shipboy (1774–1827), was the daughter of Robert Shipboy of Coleraine.[21]

Educated at the Royal Belfast Academical Institution it seems, however, that he was largely self-taught. Later he was for many years Hon. Secretary to that College.[22] In Inst William Neilson was teaching Irish, *inter alia*, in the period 1818–1821. Robert entered Inst at the age of 10 in 1818,[23] the same year that Neilson was appointed, so that it is not only possible but likely that he had formal lessons in the language from William Neilson. The sons of Samuel Bryson attended the school with him in this period. Another influence on him would have been his uncle Robert MacAdam, who appears to have known Irish and put together a compilation of songs in Irish.[24] Both Robert and his brother James were active and life-long members of the Non-Subscribing Presbyterian Congregation in Rosemary Street, Belfast.

Having left college, Robert was then apprenticed to his father's hardware business. His father died when he was only 13 years old, so that he had from then to make his own way in life. It was while making his frequent journeys throughout the country for the firm that he acquired fluency in the Irish language.[25] Many of the areas he visited, such as Tyrone, North Antrim, South Armagh, Donegal and the West of Ireland were monoglot Irish-speaking. According to Christopher Anderson's calculations,[26] based on material provided by Dr Graves of Trinity College Dublin, there were in 1820 some 141,004 Irish speakers in Co. Tyrone, amounting to 53.8% of the population; in Co. Down, 92,974 speakers (28.6%); in Co. Antrim, 56,327 (21.4%); in Co. Armagh, 56,406 (27.5%); in Co. Londonderry 27,696 (14.3%), and in Co. Fermanagh 18,714 Irish speakers (14.3%). It was in these places that Robert MacAdam began to collect manuscripts in Irish and, while still very young, saw the importance of recording stories and folklore. Few others at that time understood the significance of this kind of work and this made him very jealous of his own MSS – hardly surprising, as there was no other person in Ireland at the time who understood their value so well, or who had spent so much personal effort and expense in preserving these literary treasures.[27] It should also be mentioned that there would have been plenty of Irish-speakers in Belfast itself, as people had begun to come from rural areas to seek work in the city. Before long he had put together the first collection of Gaeltacht folktales. In the series of MacAdam MSS indexed by Ó Buachalla,[28] that numbered XXXI is the personal work of MacAdam and includes a collection in Irish of songs, proverbs, folktales, and folklore which he himself transcribed from Irish-speakers over the period 1828–1847. As the Ulster Gaelic Society was founded in 1828,[29] this period covers the peak of the active work of this society. The manuscript also includes a number of mottoes in Irish written for the visit of Queen Victoria to Belfast in 1849. Being a very thorough person, it was his frequent habit to record the name of the subject from whom the text was obtained, along with the date of the interview. For example, one of the recitations is titled, 'Oisín, arsa Pádraig, is binn do bhéal' (Ossian, said Patrick, your voice is melodious), to which he appended, 'Taken down from Tom Stokes, 1829'.

In 1830 Edward O'Reilly, the Gaelic scholar, died in Dublin and his magnificent collection of manuscripts in Irish was put up for sale. Robert MacAdam went to Dublin and came back with the best part of the assortment.[30] This was to be the major foundation of his own great collection. It included the fifteenth century medical treatise written by Dónal Óg Ó hIceadha (O'Hickey) which cost him £2.11s. Also he had bought, for eleven shillings, a manuscript written by Corc Óg Ó Cadhla in the sixteenth century. The scoop further included *Agallamh na Seanórach*, an ancient Irish text. Acting on behalf of the Ulster Gaelic Society, he frequently borrowed Irish manuscripts and had them copied. There is on record one of his many letters of thanks, written in his excellent Irish. Published by Ó Buachalla,[31] it mentions that his brother James was likewise active in collecting Irish language manuscripts.

A letter by MacAdam to a friend in Inishowen, Co. Donegal, dated 6 September 1833 indicates the nature of his mission at the time.[32] He said:

> ... in the meantime you will be good enough to accept from me the accompanying little publication in Irish, being the first book printed by the Ulster Gaelic Society to which I belong. If you would not think it too much trouble I would feel greatly obliged by your writing to me some time during the next month or two and letting me know whether you think Irish schools would be encouraged in Innishowen, or whether anything of the kind is already established. You were good enough in a former letter to mention ... the old poems and Fenian tales. I am particularly desirous to see these preserved and published and shall willingly take an opportunity of going down to Innishowen for the purpose of writing them down with you and your brother's assistance. During last week I was several days engaged in that manner in the Glens of the County Antrim and succeeded in writing a good number from the old people there.

The third Viscount O'Neill (John Bruce Richard O'Neill, 1780–1855), of Shane's Castle, had a valuable manuscript in Irish written by Friar Terence O'Mellan of Brantry, Co. Tyrone, Chaplain to Sir Felim O'Neill.[33] Robert MacAdam translated this into English and R.M. Young published the translation.[34] It is a first-hand account of the wars of 1641 and includes a detailed report of the Battle of Benburb.

The fact that he was able to copy, interpret and translate this seventeenth-century text in Irish, and that this should be passed as 'tolerably correct' by O'Donovan, shows how proficient in Irish he was.[35] It was not only with ancient antiquarian Irish that he had facility, but perhaps more importantly, with the contemporary Irish of his time. He understood, spoke and wrote modern Irish with the greatest ease. It must be remembered that, despite the great number of Irish-speakers, only a very few at that time could read and write Irish. He was anxious to promote the use of the language in the commercial world and implored of Philip Barron that he would '... not lose sight of an improved current handwriting fit for business and the like'.[36]

MacAdam's plans for publications in Irish were very ambitious and we do not know for certain if they were all implemented. He mentioned in the same letter to Philip Barron, on 20 June 1836:

> We intend to commence printing some small Irish pamphlets containing extracts from books, etc. to appear from time to time. These are intended for our Northern Schools and will be sold very cheap. As we have no Irish types here and the use of the h in printing in Roman type is such an abominable nuisance I propose to get the dotted letters in Irish type which I can mix with the plain Roman letters when required.

This is a completely accurate description of the publication which appeared in the following year, *Bolg an t-Soláir*, part I, which was printed in Belfast in 1837, showing that Barron must have sent him the Irish type which he requested in the same letter. As shown elsewhere in the present work, these stories were adapted from Scottish Gaelic versions published by the Rev. Norman McLeod. Furthermore, it is clear from his letters to Philip Barron and Thomas Swanton of Ballydehob, Co. Cork, that he intended to found a printing press in Belfast, so that he could publish the manuscripts that he had collected.[37]

From a very early age he took a deep interest in the culture and history of his country. When the Belfast Natural History and Philosophical Society was formed in 1821, he was present, a mere boy, at the age of 13.[38] On the formation of the Ulster Gaelic Society in 1828, he was made a co-secretary along with Dr Reuben Bryce. But MacAdam was the youngest of the officers and carried the brunt of the work. At the same time, with the help of Tomás Ó Fiannachtaigh, he made efforts to set up a school for teaching the reading of Irish in the parish of Ballynascreen, Co. Londonderry.[39] For the rest of his life he continued to implement the objectives of the Ulster Gaelic Society, even after it ceased to formally exist. His most significant contribution was to harvest as much written Irish literature as possible and the extensive manuscript collection at present housed in the Belfast Public Library, although only a fraction of the total which he originally collected, is a fitting monument to his diligence.

In 1835, while he was still a young man, he wrote an Irish grammar for use of the Irish classes in the Royal Belfast Academical Institution, his *alma mater*.[40] His knowledge of Irish and interest in antiquities brought him in contact with the great names of John O'Donovan, Sir William Wilde, Dr Hincks and Bishop William Reeves. It was MacAdam who introduced O'Donovan to the Belfast Irish-speakers when he visited the city in 1834. It was through him that O'Donovan got to know Dr James MacDonnell and Rev. Reuben J. Bryce. He had to do with a great spectrum of contemporary Irish language activities, and is recorded as having given advice to Nicholas O'Kearney, the last of the bards of Louth, to apply for a professorship in one of the newly formed University Colleges.[41] Robert had no secondary motivation when it came to promoting Irish. His behaviour and his words showed this clearly and in one publication he described his aim as '... the resuscitation of our long lost national literature'.[42] In addition, he was completely apolitical.

In 1852 the meeting of the British Association for the Advancement of Science was held in Belfast and he took a major role in organising an exhibition of Irish antiquities to be shown in the Belfast Museum, an institution in which he took a large part in promoting. This initiative led directly to the founding of the famous *Ulster Journal of Archaeology*, of which he was editor from the time when it first appeared, in January 1853, until 1862. The nine wonderful volumes are of great historical importance and show better than any other monument the purpose and results of his efforts to preserve Irish culture and language. One of his personal contributions was a collection of 600 Ulster Gaelic proverbs.

They were written down by himself from the mouths of Irish-speakers in the north. His collection surpassed that of any other, including John O'Donovan's, until the publication of *Sean-Fhocla Uladh* in 1907.[43] That book by Énrí Ó Muirgheasa included the 600 of MacAdam's proverbs, taken from the *Ulster Journal of Archaeology* (1858). He wrote a fascinating article entitled 'Is the Irish language spoken in Africa?'[44]

He encouraged scribes and scholars to provide him with manuscripts for which he provided patronage and paid them handsomely. By this he aimed to save some of the rich literary tradition in Irish still flourishing in the south Ulster and north Leinster areas. In contrast to John O'Donovan, who preferred to concern himself with ancient manuscripts and with the more fossilised kind of Irish, MacAdam was excited with the living, spoken and written tradition on his doorstep.[45] One of his helpers in the period 1842–1858 was Hugh McDonnell (Aodh Mac Domhnaill) from the Meath Gaeltacht. He was a Catholic but had worked with the Home Mission of the Presbyterian General Assembly for three years, as a teacher in one of the schools which taught Irish-speakers to read using the Irish Bible as a text. McDonnell was a considerable author in his own right. His great work was the *Fealsúnacht* (Philosophy), a treatise on natural history considered to be the most important original nineteenth-century prose work in Irish.[46] The work was published in 1967 by Colm Beckett.[47] It was around the year 1842 that MacDomhnaill started the transcribing and the tracing of old documents for MacAdam. These activities encouraged MacDomhnaill himself to start writing and composing. So Robert MacAdam can be given the credit for Aodh's subsequent success. Aodh later wrote lines praising MacAdam as follows:

> Is fear fearúil an MacAdhaimh sin thug grá mór don Ghaeilge, A bhíos cummanach dáimhiúil le bard an Eigse (which can be translated as: This MacAdam is a manly man who has a great love for Irish. He is the associate and friend of bard and poet).

The scribe, MacBennett, was jealous of the position held by Mac Domhnaill and he demonstrated great resentment. He compared McDonnell's post to that of a court poet in medieval Ireland, but Hugh continued to live in Belfast until 1856.[48] Another scribe who helped him was Peter Galligan from Nobber, Co. Meath, a man with a prolific output.[49] On hearing about this scribe for the first time, MacAdam sent for him with a *fáilte míosa* i.e. a welcome to stay for a month. After this visit Galligan wrote a commemorative eulogy partly in prose and partly in verse, called *The Adventures of Peter Galligan*. His visit to the Soho Foundry was described in Irish through the eyes of a rural dweller quite unused to the industrial scene. He likened the workers to black demons and their foreman, Joe English, to an arch-demon. However, Galligan's really important contribution was to transcribe for MacAdam many rare manuscripts in Irish, including the life of St Mogue (also called Maedoc and Aedh), the great saint of Drumlane, Co. Cavan. Because of the sad loss of many of the original MSS, such copies have now become our only sources of these valuable works. Galligan was largely responsible for copying and thus preserving a large corpus of the work of Séamus Dall Mac Cuarta, the famous South Armagh poet. Some of the MSS were actually transcribed by MacAdam himself. But the vast majority were executed by his many scribes, who looked up to him as a patron and an enlightened saviour of Irish literature. There is reason to believe that the payment of scribes and purchase of manuscripts were subsidised by the profits of the Soho Foundry.

With time, MacAdam had put together a large collection of manuscripts. After his death, they were scattered, but some are to be found today in the Belfast Central Library, and a smaller number in the Royal Irish Academy. Before his death MacAdam sold over 50 of his manuscripts to Dr Reeves, the Irish-speaking Protestant Bishop and on the death of the latter most of these MSS were purchased by the Royal Irish Academy.[50] There is no catalogue of his full collection, but some of his manuscripts were used or referred to by other authors. For example, O'Donovan in his grammar[51] published an extract '... from O'Hickey's medical manuscript, dated 1420; now in the possession of Mr Robert MacAdam, of Belfast, merchant'. This MS is now in the Royal Irish Academy, numbered 24P36.

MacAdam's income came from the Soho Foundry, situated next to the Presbyterian church, at numbers 28 and 30 Townsend Street in

Belfast. The business, jointly owned with his older brother James (1801–1861), was begun in 1838. In 1844, they sold the old shop and in 1846 they sold their family house in High Street. With this capital they bought out all the shares in the Soho Foundry.[52] The foundry produced a wide range of iron products: for example steam engines, gates, window frames, waterwheels, pumps and turbines. At its height more than 250 workers were employed. Orders came from many foreign countries particularly Egypt where a number of turbines were installed in 1840. The windows in the palace of the Pasha were moulded in the Soho Foundry. Because of its export trade this foundry was one of the most interesting businesses in Ireland. On account of his Egyptian connections Robert became very friendly with Ibrahim Pasha, the son of Mehemet Ali, who used to came to Belfast to visit him. They conversed in French, but Robert wrote an account of Ibrahim in Arabic in one of his Irish manuscripts, today to be found in the Royal Irish Academy (No. 23 0 58).[53] Ibrahim Pasha is referred to in Young's *Historical Notices*,[54] quoting an excerpt from the MacAdam MSS, as follows,

> When Ibrahim Pacha paid a visit to Belfast in 1846, he arrived on a Sunday morning, and put up at the Royal Hotel. Being desirous of making good use of his time, and not knowing that Sunday would make any difference, he forthwith sent out a messenger to seek a gentleman for whom he had a letter of introduction. This was the representative of the linen-house of Richardson Co., Mr Valentine, who at the time had just gone to church. The messenger followed him there in great haste, and told the sexton his errand, and that he must let Mr Valentine know at once. The sexton accordingly went in, and going forward to the pew, addressed him literally in these words,: 'Mr Valentine Sir, if you please, the King of Egypt's wanting you.'

When editor of *U.J.A.*, Robert wrote an interesting paper bringing together his knowledge of Irish and other languages to trace the history of watermills in Ireland.[55] He showed that the Irish learned from the Vikings, and not from the Romans, how to make and run watermills.

Although, apart from his many letters, he did not write much in Irish himself, he undertook to put together an English-Irish dictionary. The manuscript is today housed in Queen's University library, still awaiting publication. This prodigious work runs to 1388 pages and appears to have been ready to print in 1850.[56] In the introduction MacAdam said that the purposes for which he undertook the dictionary were, '... méad mo ghean ar mo thír dhúchais agus ... teasghrá don teangaidh ...', i.e. my loving attachment to my native land and ... my deep affection for the language.

He was associated with many of the cultural societies in Belfast. In 1828 he was elected a member of the Belfast Natural History and Philosophical Society (B.N.H.P.S.) and became a member of Council in 1831; a position he continued to hold till 1889, a period of 58 years – an official connection with the society altogether without parallel.[57] Before this society he read papers on tours to the West of Ireland and to Belgium, France and Switzerland. He read also a paper on *The Potato* and another on *The Natural Magic of the Ancients*.

Robert played a part in the early days of the Belfast Museum and on 30 January 1835 he placed an advertisement in the local newspaper about the recently acquired Egyptian Mummy.[58] In 1841 he was honorary secretary to the then newly-formed Belfast Harmonic Society.[59] He was President of the Belfast Literary Society in the periods 1846–7 and 1856–7, and read papers mostly on European countries, for example Belgium, Switzerland, France and Sweden.[60] In 1855 he published in the *Ulster Journal of Archaelogy* the first most comprehensive account of the Giant's Ring at Purdysburn, Belfast.

MacAdam's uncle, Robert MacAdam, was a member of the Irish Harp Society founded by Bunting and MacDonnell in 1808, with the purpose of '... primarily providing blind boys and girls with the means of earning a living by teaching them the harp; secondarily to promote the study of the Irish language, history and antiquities'.[61] So it is clear that the love of things Irish ran in the family. For example, young Robert's great passion was for the language, music and archaeology of Ireland.[62] He was influential in having a question on Irish included in the 1851 census of population.[63] The activities and objectives of the Belfast Harp Society inspired the young Robert to devote efforts towards the preservation and revival of the ancient music of Ireland.[64] He was as keen to collect Irish music as he was to collect poetry and folklore in Irish.

His brother James (1801–1861) was a great support to him in his efforts to help Irish. James himself attended the Irish classes in Inst. Born in January 1801 he was the elder and quieter of the two brothers and of delicate health. He was educated at Inst and then later at Trinity College, Dublin (B.A. 1836). Along with Robert, he managed to run the foundry business and yet, at the same time, he succeeded in pursuing his other interests in Natural History. His private collection of geological specimens ranked as one of the best in Ireland.[65] He was one of the founders of the Botanic Gardens. James was the first librarian to Queen's College Belfast, but held the post for just one year, resigning on 10 October 1850. He was described as '... an excellent example of a Belfast type in which the pursuit of business and devotion to learning were successfully combined'.[66]

Robert MacAdam had a knowledge of thirteen languages and it was said that he started learning Spanish when he was seventy years of age.[67] The editor of the *U.J.A.* described him as a man of wide culture and refined tastes and as a person who took a warm interest in all that concerned the welfare of his native town. He had collected, so far back as 1837, 'Notes on the History of Belfast Spinning etc.' referred to by Young (1896), and excerpts were published showing lists of flax spinning mills and of bleachers in the province of Ulster.[68] He collected stories about old Belfast, part of which Young published in his *Historical Notices*. This includes the information that the first steam engine erected at Belfast was at the Springfield Cotton Mill belonging to Messrs Stevenson, '... and was actually used for pumping up water to drive a water wheel'.

It has not been possible to obtain a photograph of Robert MacAdam, but in the Ulster Museum there is a silhouette of him which came from the Young family, probably made by Robert Young (1822–1917),[69] who also happened to be a nephew of Reuben John Bryce, the co-secretary with MacAdam in the Ulster Gaelic Society.

Robert MacAdam died unmarried on 3 January 1895 at 89 Great Victoria Street, Belfast.[70] He had recently changed his address from 18 College Square East where he and his brother James had lived since

1833. He is buried in Knockbreda graveyard. Over his grave, which is near the front side of the church, stands a large memorial with three panels, dedicated to the family of Shipboy, which was his mother's surname.

REUBEN JOHN BRYCE (1797–1888) M.A. 1817, LL.D 1831

The Rev. Dr R.J. Bryce, a minister of the Reformed or Covenanting Presbyterian Synod, was founder and co-secretary to the Ulster Gaelic Society (*Cuideachta Ghaeilge Uladh*) which came into existence in 1828.[71] He gave his name in Irish as R.E. Bríse in one of the publications of the Society.[72] The E. stands for Eoin (John). The other secretary was Robert S. MacAdam.

His interest in Irish was related to his progressive ideas on the theory of education. Atkinson in his history of Irish education described Bryce's contribution to Irish educational thought as '... by far the most important'.[73] He was also described as a highly intelligent, widely read man who held strong and original opinions on educational questions.[74] Bryce believed that educational success depended on the quality of the teaching profession and that even better teachers could be produced by modern scientific methods of training. He became friendly with Maria Edgeworth, the novelist, and agreed with her ideas on female education.[75, 76] Through their cooperation some of Maria Edgeworth's stories were translated into Irish and published by the Ulster Gaelic Society.[77]

Reuben John was born in 1797 in Wick, in the far north-east of Scotland and so might well have been a Gaelic speaker from an early age. His father was the Rev. James Bryce (1767–1857) of Airdrie and his mother Catherine Annan of Auchtermuchty (1782–1837). They had seven sons and four daughters.[78] The children were reared in a language-conscious, classical environment, both parents being classical scholars and teachers.[79]

In 1805, when Reuben was aged seven, the family moved to Ireland because the father had accepted a call from the Aghadowey congregation near Coleraine. During his ministry the name of the congregation was changed to Killaig.[80] In 1811 Mr Bryce withdrew himself and his congregation of Killaig from the Seccession Synod and refused to accept the *Regium Donum*, the royal annual grant received by each minister. He formed, in 1816, the Associate Presbytery of Ireland.[81] Such independent behaviour was typical of the whole Bryce family including Reuben John.

The Rev. James Bryce ran a classical school in Ballyclough. The Rev. Jonathan Simpson attended this school as child and said of it in later life:

> ... in the close of 1827, father took me off to enter me in the Classical School. There was one ... at a place called Ballyclough, and kept by the Rev. James Bryce of Killaig U.P. Church, father of the celebrated teacher and scholar, Rev. R.J. Bryce, LL.D ... In a room fitted up in his own house as schoolroom he had some two dozen pupils ...'.[82]

In his autobiography, the Rev. Thomas Witherow, the historian, recounted Bryce's Classical School:

> On Monday, 16 June, I made my first appearance before Mr Bryce at his residence at Ballyclough and received my first lesson in the Latin Grammar ... Mr Bryce was a painstaking and careful teacher ... .[83]

When Reuben John was growing up in Killaig, in the early 1800s, the language of this almost totally Presbyterian district was broad Scots. As Witherow said about nearby Aghadowey: 'I found that my new neighbours spoke as pure Scotch as a man might hear in any part of Ayreshire'.[84] In contrast Reuben Bryce recounted in a pamphlet that:

> In an adjoining district of nearly the same extent, which began about five miles from our house, a Protestant Episcopalian was the black swan and a Presbyterian was nowhere to be found. The inhabitants all spoke Irish and very few even understood English, or, as our people called it, 'Scotch'.[85]

So, in his youth Bryce lived only five miles away from a Gaeltacht. In the year 1812 he became a student at the University of Glasgow. During the vacations he helped his parents in the tuition of children in the Killaig area. One of these pupils was a little girl who was said to be backward and consequently difficult to manage. He soon came to the conclusion that she had been forced to learn from books that she did not understand and had reacted by non-cooperation, thus giving the impression of lack of intelligence. Instead of a book he handed her an orange and asked her did she know where this fruit had come from. She did not, but was curious. She was so anxious to find out about strange countries which produced such exotic fruits that she promised to learn to read, if Dr Bryce would reward her with geography lessons! The girl turned out to be a scholastic success and Dr Bryce had begun to formulate his principles of modern education, based on this and other cases.[86]

In his final year he was appointed as one of the four Stint-Masters in the University. These posts were filled by senior students who were granted powers to fix the fee to be paid by each M.A. graduate. Reuben graduated M.A. (then the primary degree) from Glasgow in 1817. It is presumed that he then returned to his parents' classical school to take part in the teaching programme. After two years, however, the matriculation records in Glasgow show that he entered the medical faculty as a student. In 1819–20 he attended classes in Anatomy, Surgery, Chemistry and Natural History. In the following academic year he continued with his Anatomy classes.[87, 88] In his own words he said that,

> I conceived a strong desire, in early boyhood, to acquire skill in teaching: and ... when my Medical Education was nearly finished, circumstances occurred which made it my duty to follow the early bent of my mind; so I gave up Medicine as a profession, devoted myself to the Christian ministry and the work of education ... .[89]

His first application for an academic post was in 1821, aged 24. It occurred as a result of the death of William Neilson on 27 April 1821. He was author of the Irish *Grammar* and taught Irish at Inst. After his death his post was divided into two parts, Head of the Classical School, and Professor of Greek, Latin and Hebrew. R.J. Bryce was one of the many who applied for the latter post. In this he was supported by the Rev. Henry Cooke, who became his ardent champion[90] and recounted in a later testimonial:

> My intimate knowledge of your literary and religious character induced me in 1821 to support, with all my heart, your claims to the Greek Chair in the Academical Institution, Belfast ... .[91]

However, the successful candidate turned out to be Rev. William

Bruce, who was a Non-Subscriber and well known for his Arian views. Cooke expressed disquiet at the prospect of orthodox students for the ministry being taught by persons who did not believe in the Trinity and started a campaign to oust Arian ministers from the Presbyterian Church. This incident began the second Non-Subscribing controversy in the Synod of Ulster.[92] Later Bryce defended Dr Cooke publicly against the charge that he was not in favour of Catholic Emancipation.[93] In 1831, Dr Cooke recommended to the Synod of Ulster Dr Bryce's proposal for reviving the College Department of the Belfast Academy, but the idea was turned down. The original aim of the Academy was to provide some instruction at third, or college, level carrying out some of the functions of a university. The goal of collegiate status was never achieved.

Bryce was President of Belfast (Royal) Academy from 1824, the year he was ordained,[94] to 1880, a period of 56 years. For some of this time he taught Irish and was assisted by Tomás Ó Fiannachtaigh.[95, 96] A.T.Q. Stewart noted that one interesting aspect of language teaching in the Academy was the teaching of Irish, and continued:

> There was, as it happened, some enthusiasm for the Irish language among the Presbyterians most closely associated with the founding of the Academy. This arose from two rather different motives. The liberal Presbyterians and especially the United Irishmen were genuinely anxious to revive the Gaelic language and culture as part of their attempt to establish a national identity. This fitted in with the whole trend of the Romantic movement, the taste for moonlight ruins and the poems of Ossian. They published a magazine in Irish, *Bolg an tSoláir*, in Belfast in 1795. In the same year the *Northern Star* ... commented favourably on the work of Patrick Lynch, who was teaching Irish in the Academy and in private houses. A few months later it mentioned that he was preparing to publish an Irish grammar.[97]

Apart from the publication of the above magazine and Thomas Russell learning Irish, both of which were apparently the work of Patrick Lynch, there is not much evidence that the United Irishmen as a body were particularly interested in the language. As far as Wolfe Tone was concerned, it hardly existed. Similarly, there is no evidence that Samuel Neilson, Henry Joy McCracken or William Drennan did anything specific to promote Irish. On the other hand, it is clear that few, if any, of those who fostered the language around these times were in the United Irishmen, or even had similar ideas. Examples are Dr James MacDonnell, Dr Samuel Bryson, Patrick Lynch, General Charles Vallencey, Miss Charlotte Brooke, Rev. William Neilson and many others, of whom Dr Reuben Bryce was a more recent example.

Many of these individuals are mentioned elsewhere in this work, but it is worth pointing out here that Charles Vallencey (1721–1812) was '... a prime mover in the important movement in the late eighteenth century to end the Anglo-Irish community's neglect of Irish antiquities and the Gaelic language'.[98] He wrote extensively about Irish and published a grammar of the language.[99] It also happened that as a military engineer he planned much of the counter attack on the United Irishmen's rebellion of 1798, including a detailed plan for the defence of Dublin city.[100]

A.T.Q. Stewart explained the second motive for Presbyterians being enthusiastic about the language:

> Not all those eager to learn Irish were United Irishmen. Some ministers thought that Irish might be useful in the work of attempting to convert Catholics in Irish-speaking areas. The Rev. Moses Neilson of Rademon in Co. Down, one of the most active of the Academy subscribers, gave Irish lessons in his school ... His son, the Rev. Dr William Neilson ... was an accomplished Irish scholar.

The implication above is that the Neilson's had evangelistic intentions in their use of Irish. Missionary zeal through Irish was not particularly strong in the Ireland of this period and, even if it were, the Neilsons would be the last to be involved. Moses taught pupils who became Roman Catholic priests and bishops and William's grammar shows a remarkable absence of any evangelistic approach.[101] Their use of Irish was entirely natural, considering the exceptional numbers of Irish people, including many Presbyterians, for whom Irish was the normal and everyday means of communication, at that time.

While Principal of the Belfast Academy (the epithet 'Royal' was not added until 1887), Reuben Bryce promulgated his theories of education and in 1828 he published his plan for a system of national education.[102]

He embarked on a series of lecture tours and spent so much time on promoting his educational theories, that, ironically, his own Academy sometimes suffered from neglect. His *alma mater*, the University of Glasgow, was very impressed with his work and, in January of 1831, agreed to confer on him the honorary degree of LL.D. This honour was reserved for eminent men as a mark of respect and was only rarely awarded.[103]

He much admired the works on education published by Maria Edgeworth and her father. She in turn supported his efforts to achieve some practical advances in education. He campaigned to have courses for teachers in which they would learn the Science and Art of Education. Having read his pamphlet, she wrote:

> I sat up late last night to finish it. I think it contains a great deal of truth and sense and wish it may produce the effect of convincing people that those who are to teach must learn how to teach.[104]

In a footnote to this letter Bryce recounted that he visited Miss Edgeworth in Edgeworthstown in Co. Longford. This appears to have been in the 1840s and there is another letter from her in 1847. Considering that they had corresponded in 1833, when she gave permission for the translation of two of her stories into Irish, they must have kept in contact over a very long period, perhaps until her death in 1849.

He also had correspondence with Dr Charles E.H. Orpen, a pioneering educationalist, who in 1816 had founded the National Institution for the Education of the Deaf and Dumb at Claremont, near Dublin. As a philanthropist, he was active in organisations such as the Anti-Slavery Society.[105] Orpen was eager for the spread of education in Ireland and became a keen supporter of the Irish Society for Promoting the Education of the Irish, through the medium of their own language. He himself was fluent in Irish and wrote a number of pamphlets on the subject. One was an analysis of the errors in the Irish translation of the Bible, in which many inaccuracies were found.[106] Another of Orpen's works was an appeal for a greater use of Irish in education. In it he combed all the statistical reports and quoted estimates of Irish-speaking for all the available parishes. He arrayed many facts to show that Irish is a sophisticated language with a respectable literature and countered many of the arguments against the use of Irish.[107]

Orpen, writing in 1838, said that he had attended different lecture courses given by Dr Bryce on the science and art of education[108] and was so impressed by his knowledge and lecturing skills that he had asked him to come and live in Dublin, because he would then be in a position to teach Orpen's six sons. (His only daughter had died in the previous year). The Rev. Bryce applied for the Professorship of Greek in the University of Glasgow, which had fallen vacant in 1838. On discovering that, if successful, he would be expected to become a member of the Established Church of Scotland, he withdrew his application.

In addition to his educational activities Reuben Bryce was involved in practical spirituality. He was the main founder of the Belfast Town Mission (later called the Belfast City Mission). He and a number of friends formed the organisation in February 1827, with the object of helping the poor people in Belfast who were not in contact with any church organisation. Although the purpose was to get people religiously involved and to encourage study of the Scriptures, the Mission was to be strictly non-denominational. He constantly supported the work of the Mission until 1843. It was then that a 'High Church member of less liberal ideas (than Rev. Dr. Bryce) broke up the old Mission and organised another on Episcopalian lines'.[109] The Presbyterians then formed their own Mission, but thenceforth Reuben Bryce, having failed to retain the non-denominational character of the Mission, retired from that scene. He was consistent in his tolerance of other religions. In 1845 he wrote to Thomas Wyse MP, who was a Waterford Catholic, about the Irish Colleges Bill, which proposed to set up University Colleges in Belfast, Galway, Dublin and Cork.[110] In the preface he said that, '... the sectarian character of our Educational Institutions inflicts the deepest injury on the community at large'. In his letter he said: 'I approve of the non-sectarian education which the Bill aims at, but in my opinion, does not attain. If ever the plan be reduced to practice, the Colleges will be not non-sectarian but non-christian'. These letters were discussed in the general context of the contemporary debate in a paper by Mac Eoinín.[111]

By 1860, Bryce now aged 63, had lost some of his earlier energy and enthusiasm and his health was not good.[112] However, on the credit side he could number among his pupils the Lord Chancellor of England, Cairns, and his own nephew, the Right Hon. James Bryce[113] who became Chief Secretary for Ireland and later Ambassador to the United States. Sir Samuel Ferguson was a pupil before he transferred to Inst. The young Samuel could easily have had Irish lessons from Bryce or Ó Fiannachtaigh. He was elected member of the Belfast Literary Society in 1864 and one of the papers he read was 'Specimens of unpublished poetry in the Scoto-Hibernian dialect of the North of Ireland, with notices of their author, the Rev. R. Magill, and of the character and habits of the people'. The Society elected him president for the period 1878–9.[114] In 1875, despite his age, now 77, he applied for the Professorship of Education in the University of Edinburgh. He was not successful.

In 1880 the Belfast Academy moved from its position in Academy Street, near St Anne's Cathedral, to its present position on the Cliftonville Road, formerly known as the Old Lodge Road. Dr Byrce took this opportunity to retire. This left him free to be more deeply involved with his ministry to his congregation at York Street.

When Dr R.J. Bryce died on 10 May 1888, his nephew, the Right Honourable James Bryce M.P., took charge of the funeral arrangements, and he asked the Rev. Dr. William Johnston, an old friend and former pupil of the deceased, to officiate at the graveside.[115] He was buried beside his father in the churchyard at Killaig.

BRYCE FAMILY

About this family it was said: 'For intellect, independence and longevity, the record of the Bryce family ... would be difficult to equal.'[116] Although the only member of the Bryce family whom we know for certain to be an Irish-speaker was Reuben John Bryce, it is not unreasonable to suppose that many of his ancestors, natives of Scotland, were proficient in the Gaelic language. The most remote ancestor, so far known, was Archibald Bryce of Dechmont Hill, Lanarkshire,[117] who would have been born around 1700. He was the father of John Bryce, who was born, perhaps in the 1730s, in New Monkland. John grew up to marry Robina Allan and she gave birth to James Bryce in Airdrie, Lanarkshire, on 5 December 1767.

James was ordained on 2 September 1795 at Wick, which was an Antiburgher congregation. It is interesting to note that his predecessor but one, Thomas Darg, was a Gaelic-speaker. It was stated that the fact that he had Gaelic was in his favour when he was called to Wick in 1771[118] indicating that the congregation spoke that language. James Bryce succeeded him just twenty years later, so it would be surprising if he in turn did not have at least some of the language. In a short time trouble arose between Mr Bryce and his congregation. He had liberal views on marriage and he himself, having failed to get a magistrate to marry him to a thirteen year old girl, arranged an irregular wedding service in the town of Auchtermuchty where she lived. His young bride, Catherine Annan, had been one of his pupils before he went to Wick. On account of this incident and for other reasons James was in habitual dispute with his church. After ten years in Wick, he accepted a call to Killaig, Co. Londonderry, where he was installed on 16 August 1805.

Their son Reuben has been discussed already in this work. He was the eldest child and had five brothers and three sisters, all but the two eldest, born and reared in Killaig. The second son, Robert (1806–1862) had a career in medicine; James (1806–1877) became a mathematics teacher and a geologist; Thomas Annan received an M.A. from Glasgow University and died in Toronto in 1875; David went to live in London; and the youngest son Archibald became Principal of the High School in Edinburgh. His sister Catherine married Robert Campbell Brown M.A. of Ballinacannon; Robina (1814–1887) married James Clarke of Gill's Cottage; and Jessie married James Fitzpatrick of Boveedy, Co. Londonderry.

The children were very influenced by their mother, who combined the roles of mother and teacher. Archbishop William Alexander, husband of Cecil Frances Alexander, the famous hymn writer, who translated *St Patrick's Breastplate* from the Irish, knew James Bryce and admired him deeply. He pointed out that because he refused to take the *Regium Donum*, '... there was often no bread in his house; his children, highly educated, went bare-headed and bare-footed'.[119] The Irish *Regium Donum* was originally a free and unconditional gift, out of Crown funds. Subsequently, it became a parliamentary grant, but still without conditions. A change came in 1800 when the Synod of Ulster received a large increase coupled with conditions. One was that every minister was to take an oath of allegiance before two magistrates.[120] Bryce strongly objected to all aspects of the bounty.

James had to support his family from his church income of £30 per year, and from whatever he could earn from running his classical school.[121] Elsewhere, his salary is stated to be £26 *per annum* and is contrasted with the salary of £730 earned by the Church of Ireland rector in the same parish, the Rev. Robert Alexander, a relation of Mary Jane Alexander who translated hymns into Irish. Even his co-religionist, the Rev. John Brown of Aghadowey, had a salary of £185, (£100 from *Regium Donum* and £85 stipend).[122]

Later in life his son, Reuben John, showed the same kind of other-worldliness and self-sacrifice in the interest of his spiritual beliefs and for the good of his fellow man. One of his biographers said about him,

> ... he made big sacrifices to enable [the Belfast Academy] to be carried on under public control, and he allowed his own interest to be passed over in favour of the interests of the school. In his later years, also, he did his work without any salary.[123]

Reuben John did not marry. His brother, James Bryce, married Margaret Young in 1836. Through his brother's marriage, he was related to R.M. Young the historian of Belfast. This James Bryce (1806–1877) was a fellow teacher with his brother Reuben in the Belfast Academy.

James had a son also called James who was the most distinguished of all the Bryces. This was James, Viscount Bryce (1838–1922), jurist, historian and statesman. He was born in Belfast and educated first at the Belfast Academy and then in Glasgow, Oxford and Heidelberg. After an academic career in law he went into politics and was Chief Secretary for Ireland from 1905 to 1907 and then Ambassador to the United States from 1907 to 1913. He was popular in Washington

because he had written a book about America and because of his '...
Presbyterian democratic directness'.[124] On his retirement he was
created Viscount Bryce.

He then devoted his time mainly to writing. He died in Sidmouth in
1922. His distinctions included honorary degrees from 31 universities.
Patrick Dinneen, the lexicographer, wrote articles in Irish on Bryce for
The Leader.[125, 126] One was an assessment of Bryce's suitability as Chief
Secretary for Ireland. Dinneen noted that many were saying that he was
an excellent choice because of his learning, being of Irish extraction and
because he was favourably disposed to Ireland. However, Dinneen had
no confidence in him. Firstly, being over 70 he was too old: nor did he
have enough experience of this kind of work. He felt that he had bad
advisers in the Castle. In another article Dinneen complained that Bryce
had made promises to help Irish but had not fulfilled them. Of course,
he was hardly long enough in the post to get much done. However, he
appeared to be serious, because, as reported in Celtia, Bryce's parting
words to Birrell, his successor in the Chief Secretaryship, were: 'Do all
you can for the Irish language!'[127]

JAMES MacKNIGHT (1801–1876)

James MacKnight, journalist and land reformer, was born near
Rathfriland, Co. Down on 27 February 1801 and died 8 June
1876.[128] Historically he is best remembered as a founder of the Ulster
Tenant Right Movement which, in time, led to legislation protecting
the rights of Irish tenant farmers. It has been said that in his day he was
'... perhaps the most influential layman in Ulster'.[129] He was also
described as '... an acute observer of the Presbyterian scene'.[130]

MacKnight was of firm Presbyterian stock and perhaps, from his
surname, descended from one of the many native Irish converts who
found an attraction to Scottish Presbyterianism through the common
language of Gaelic. Indeed, his father was a fluent Irish-speaker, who
also enjoyed other aspects of Irish culture, especially Irish music.[131]

James' father passed on to his son a love of the Irish language and
music, to the extent that when James grew up he was fluent in Irish and
could also read the language with ease. He studied Latin and Greek with

David Henderson of Newry.[132] At age 24 he became a student in Royal Belfast Academical Institution (Inst), with the intention of becoming a Presbyterian minister. Samuel Ferguson was his school-fellow there.[133] While attending college in 1826 he was made deputy librarian of the Linen Hall Library, in the absence of the librarian, Alexander Henderson.[134] Indeed, he was successful in his examinations, but apparently was not a good enough speaker to be a fluent preacher. Perhaps for this reason, or others, he changed his mind about becoming a minister and resolved instead to take up journalism. While still at Inst he had been contributing articles to the *Belfast News Letter*.

In 1827, at the invitation of the proprietor, Alexander Mackay, Senior (d. 1844) he became the editor of the *Belfast News Letter*, succeeding Dr James Stuart (1764–1840), the historian of Armagh and friend of the Gaelic scholar Samuel Bryson. Stuart had been editor of the *Belfast News Letter* since 1821. MacKnight continued as editor of the *News Letter* for 19 years.[135] During this time it will be noticed that the paper was very favourably disposed to the language. As editor, MacKnight was anxious to review publications in Irish as they came out and complained when the publishers failed to send him a review copy.

In politics he was a Unionist and opposed any move to repeal the Act of Union. Nevertheless, he was also a Liberal in his outlook and as such was often in conflict with Alexander Mackay, the conservative proprietor of the newspaper. There are many examples of his fondness for the language to be found in the *Belfast News Letter*. For example, in 1832 he reviewed John Reid's book, *Bibliotheca Scoto-Celtica*, which was an account of all the books printed in Scottish Gaelic up to then.[136] He expressed the wish that Reid would produce a similar bibliography for Irish Gaelic. He showed his appreciation of the wealth of manuscripts extant in the Irish language and wrote:

> The importance of these manuscripts is now beginning to be better understood than at former periods and it is hoped that this circumstance may lead to a more general cultivation of the language in which they are written – if the energy and the zeal which are too frequently in teaching Irishmen how to hate each other most effectually, were employed in doing for our native language – and for the millions who understand no other, what Scotsmen have done for their country, how different in a little time would be our national condition!

He appealed to the newly formed Ulster Gaelic Society to take more action and praised Lord George Hill for his patronage of Irish learning. He went on to say: 'Belfast rescued the Irish harp from oblivion, and to perfect its fame a revival of the Irish language and the Irish literature is only wanted'.

In 1832 he referred in an editorial to the motion put by Henry Cooke to the General Synod favouring the cultivation of the native language. Although this motion was adopted as Synod policy, MacKnight asserted that northern Presbyterians could have done more for the language.[137]

On 9 January 1835 MacKnight wrote an editorial comment in the *Belfast News Letter* welcoming the publication of the weekly magazine published by Philip Barron, *Ancient Ireland*. The very first issue had come out on 1 January. He had this to say:

> We observe from an advertisement in the Dublin Evening Post that Philip F Barron Esq, of Waterford, has commenced a weekly magazine, for the exclusive purpose of bringing before the public the neglected treasures of ancient Irish Literature. Mr. Barron is a gentleman of independent fortune, one whose national spirit is not inferior to his resources, and whose acquaintance with the history, the language and the antiquities of his country, is at once extensive and profound, and it is therefore with peculiar gratification that we have received the announcement of his having in good earnest applied himself to a task for which few are qualified, and for which even fewer have the requisite zeal. In addition to his Magazine, Mr Barron proposes to, publish, in numbers, an Irish Primer, a Grammar, Irish Sermons, an Irish Dictionary, and a collection of songs, under the denomination of the 'Irish Harp' – From all of these publications, politics and religious polemics are to be excluded ... Although Mr Barron has announced his intention of having his publications forwarded to all parts of Ireland, it is singular that not even a solitary copy of his Magazine has yet found its way to Belfast in which there are numbers of Irish Scholars, who would zealously and efficiently aid its circulation. We throw out this hint , because we have not been able to procure a sight of the Magazine in question, notwithstanding the interest which we confessedly feel in the ... *laoithe blasda agus dreuchta seanchais* (precisely told lays and poems of ancient lore) of our native country, and others, we are convinced, have experienced a similar disappointment.

Once more, MacKnight complained that publishers of material in Irish were not sending review copies to the *Belfast News Letter*. But having delivered his rebuke, he continues,

> As Mr Barron has avowed his intention of publishing an Irish Dictionary, we take leave to offer a suggestion on the subject. It is not a common school dictionary that is truly required in the present state of Irish literature – we want a general, comprehensive, dictionary which shall include the ancient as well as the modern Irish. For ordinary purposes O'Brien and O'Reilly are quite sufficient – the former is valuable chiefly on account of the curious genealogical information which his work contains; and the dictionary of the latter is what the Germans would call a 'word-book' – in other terms, a mere vocabulary; for the author was not capable of fulfilling the higher office of a Lexicographer. Still, however, these dictionaries are sufficient for every common purpose, and, in fact, of Irish elementary works there is no lack, in consequence of the labours of Thady Connellan and others; but what the Irish scholar, who has not access to MSS wants, is something to read, and if he has access to MSS he wants a Glossary to enable him to understand them. We wish to see that done for the Irish language which the Highland Society have done for the Scottish Gaelic in their splendid publication – the *Dictionarium Scoto Celticum* ... and unless something of this kind be done, there is reason to fear that many of our most ancient MSS will, in the course of another century, become in a great degree unintelligible. Next to the removal of this cardinal deficiency is the necessity of publishing the most valuable remains of ancient Irish learning – the Duke of Buckingham has liberally done something of this kind, by his publication of the *Rerum Hibernicarum Scriptores*, under the direction of the late Dr O'Connor; but still this act, munificent as it may be in itself, is only a green spot in a desert of almost limitless extent. Could a Society not be formed for the patriotic purposes to which we have thus hastily alluded?

This essay by MacKnight shows again how knowledgeable he was about the contemporary position of literature in Irish and it also demonstrates further his great concern for harvesting the extensive literature still existing only in manuscript form.

Later, in 1835, he reported on the recent meeting of the Synod of Ulster and drew attention to a resolution on the Irish class at the Royal Belfast Academical Institution.

Students of Divinity in connexion with the Synod will do well to attend to the following important resolution which has been agreed to respecting attendance upon the Irish class in the Royal Institution: In reference to the overture of last year, respecting the study of the Irish language, the Synod being informed that few students had attended the Class during last Session, express their regret at this circumstance, and declare that no Student will be received into the Divinity Class after this Session, who has not attended the Irish Class; and enjoin Presbyteries to direct their respective students to pay strict attention thereto. The Divinity Class Committee are instructed to inquire into the attendance of our Students on the Irish Class during the next Session and to report thereon to the Synod.

MacKnight then commented:

With the spirit of this resolution we entirely agree, as our readers have had frequent opportunities of knowing.

He, however, sounded a warning note and felt that it might not be practical to ask all students to study the language. Furthermore, the study of Irish for just one Session would be inadequate. He felt that it would take at least four Sessions to become proficient. In August 1835, he reviewed a book of hymns in Irish. This pocket-sized hymnal was titled *Cláirseach Naomhtha na hÉireann* i.e. the Sacred Harp of Ireland, and was edited by Miss Alexander, who called herself, in Irish, M.J. Alasdruin. MacKnight said: 'A copy of this interesting little publication, which has just made its appearance in Dublin, accidently (sic) fell into our hands a few days ago'. This is a gentle chide for not having been sent a review copy, his constant rebuke to Irish language publishers. He continues:

To our surprise we found it to contain faithful and even elegant translations into Irish verse of a number of the most popular devotional pieces of a similar kind in the English language. This collection is introduced with a preface adressed 'Chum dhaoineadh na hÉireann', 'To the people of Ireland', and subscribed 'M.J. Alexander', who, we have since learned, is a daughter of the Bishop of Meath. The whole is elegantly printed in the native character and the names of the principal contributors mentioned in the introduction are those of Owen Connellan and Peter O'Daly of Ardbreccan in Meath; but as the translations of these writers are distinguished by their initials, we may presume that the remainder have been furnished by the Lady herself, who has thus secured a lasting claim to the gratitude of every real lover of his country.

MacKnight complained that the Protestants had done little to provide metrical compositions in Irish even though these were much in demand by Irish-speakers. He was referring not only to hymns but also the metrical psalms. The Synod of Ulster had resolved to provide the Psalms of David in Irish, but that was a year ago. He pointed out that an excellent model was the Scottish *Gaelic Book of Metrical Psalms*, which could be easily adapted. That would be quite easy compared with the difficulties which Miss Alexander faced, having to start from the beginning. For this she deserves all the more praise.

> Of this Lady we happen to know nothing ... so that the favourable expression of our opinion is altogether the result of our strong convictions to the merits and importance of the cause to which she has devoted powers of no common order ... .

He then quoted some of the verses, without translation, and he quoted also some of the verses from Norman McLeod's *Leabhar nan Cnoc*. And finally he concluded:

> The real beauty as well as the literal closeness of these extracts need no elucidation ... Had the native population of this country been treated as rational beings two centuries ago, we should not now have had to lament the existence of evils which an opposite system of internal management has banished from these districts of the sister isle, which in respect to the language and general character of their inhabitants, were originally similar to a majority of the districts of Ireland.

Another example of his continued support for Irish and his interest in its literature was shown by the notice given of the death of a scribe in Cork. This appeared in 1837:

> Died on the 17th inst at Cnoc Buidhe, in the North Liberties of Cork, Micheál Óg Ó Longáin aged 72 years. From the early age of 18 he devoted himself in a particular manner to the study and culture of his native language. He composed several pieces and transcribed nearly 300 volumes of Irish manuscripts – thus rescuing from destruction several rare and curious specimens of the ancient literature of Ireland.

On 4 January 1841 MacKnight wrote an essay in the *News Letter* about the Irish origin of the Scottish Highlanders. He pointed out that all Scottish historians of any authority now admitted that the original Gael of the Highlands were a colony of the *Cine Scuit* (the tribe of the Scots), imported from Ireland. He produced interesting evidence that the Acts of the General Assemblies of the Church of Scotland showed that the Assemblies had never any doubts about the Irish origin of the Gaelic-speaking Highlanders. Examples were; the General Assembly held in 1643, enacted that 'Young students that have the Irish language be trained up at Colleges ... in order that being trained for the Ministry, they may be sent forth to preach the Gospel in these Highland parts'.

MacKnight quoted many subsequent Acts which described Scottish Gaelic as the Irish language and which also demonstrated how keen the Scottish Presbyterian Church was to make sure that the Gaelic-speakers were spoken to in their own language.

> These enactments ... prove the deep wisdom which guided the Church councils of our Presbyterian forefathers. In Ireland, Episcopalian statesmen insanely made it a crime to cultivate the language of the native population and the discouragement and opposition with which the good Bishop Bedell met, in his endeavours to impart religious instruction to the Irish through the medium of the only language they understood, are unhappily of facts indelible, and, we may add, of disgraceful record. It is delightful to think that at an early period of its history the Synod of Ulster had several Irish preachers, small as the body then was – we refer to the period immediately succeeding the Revolution of 1688, the MS records of which shew the anxiety then felt by the Synod on this important subject.

He pointed out that the majority of Scottish Highlanders were originally Papists, but that now they are mostly devoted Protestants. And why? 'The Ard-Eaglais na h-Alba (the Church of Scotland) treated them as rational beings, afforded them religious instruction in their own language ...'.

In the *Belfast News Letter* of 16 June 1843 there was a detailed account of the Repeal Demonstration at Mallow, where an estimated 400,000 had assembled to hear Daniel O'Connell. The commentator, clearly MacKnight, the editor of the paper, heavily criticised the whole affair on the grounds that O'Connell's speech was, '... atrocious, venomous and embittered ...', and anyway that it was delivered on the Sabbath. But he reserved his most sophisticated attack for the barbarity of the Irish language used.

The very Rev. Dr Collins, a R.C. Bishop, occupied the chair on the occasion and, after the viands had been consumed, a blessing was asked by the Rev. Mr Horgan, P.P. of Blarney, in the following terms both in English and in Irish:

'Beannaigh a Dhia an phroinn,
Is éist ár Righbhean óg
Go dtugadh ár Righbhean óg
Comhdháil Éireann dhuinn
Do bless, O Lord, this food
And hear our humble prayer;
O may our youthful Queen
Grant Erin the Repeal'

The Irish as reported is not very intelligible, while its attempted translation makes the matter still worse. Who that understands Irish ever translated 'Righbhean óg' – 'our humble prayer' as is done in the extract quoted? The literal meaning is 'king-woman young', or in English our 'young Queen', while the proper Irish term is not 'Righbhean', but 'beanrioghan', so that the Repeal reporter has been making a regular hash of both languages.

Despite the display of apparent indignation it must be concluded that MacKnight was only teasing, because the piece of Irish and its translation were really not all that incorrect. The word 'righbhean' is occasionally used as an alternative to 'beanrioghan', (now spelt banríon) and indeed is to be found in O'Reilly's dictionary which had been quite recently published (1821) and to which MacKnight had referred in an earlier article.

In 1844, the proprietor of the paper, Alexander Mackay sen., died, leaving the ownership to his widow and her three daughters. In 1845 the proprietorship devolved to the young, 21 year-old James Alexander Henderson, son of the proprietor of the *Newry Telegraph*. It is possible that the editor and the new proprietor did not see eye to eye, for shortly after the change in ownership MacKnight resigned his position to take up the editorship of the *Londonderry Standard*. With a break of five years he continued to be editor of the *Standard* until his death. On 28 June 1847, he wrote to Gavin Duffy, asking:

Is there anything doing in the way of Celtic literature? I have had no opportunity of adding to my small stock of Irish books and with the exception of Walsh's late, one half of which is a slavish reprint from Hardiman, the publishers do not send me works of this description – a neglect which, on their part, is very absurd. At one time you hinted something about the publication of a comprehensive Irish Dictionary – I wish something of this kind was undertaken by competent hands, in the plan of the great work published by the Highland Society of Scotland. Above all things the ancient dialects ought to be systematised and preserved, as their importance is incalculable for the purposes of comparative philology.[138]

It was shortly after leaving the *News Letter* that he began his active support for the rights of small farmers, and in 1850 he chaired the first Tenant Right meeting from which was founded the Tenant League. The final outcome was to be a better deal for tenant farmers.

At the age of 75, he became ill and had to take to his bed. Before long it was clear that he was not going to recover. On his death-bed, he asked his servant, a Roman Catholic, to recite for him the Lord's Prayer in Irish. She did as he requested, but at one point was interrupted by the dying MacKnight, who pointed out that she had mispronounced one of the words.[139] He died on 8 June 1876. His widow survived him many years, but they had no issue.

A copy of a devotional work in Irish[140] which belonged to him and which he appeared to read regularly was reported on by Séamus Ó Néill in the *Irish Times* where was also published a photograph of the title page and MacKnight's signature in both English and Irish (Seámas Mac Neachtain).[141] MacKnight was awarded the degree of LL.D. by the University of Aberdeen.

HENRY RIDDELL MONTGOMERY (1818–1904)

This individual was no relation of the Rev. Henry Montgomery, the great opponent of the Rev. Henry Cooke. Henry Riddell Montgomery was born at 2 Arthur Place, Belfast on 12 March 1818,[142] the youngest son of a family of eleven children.[143] Having travelled much throughout the world he died in London, 14 March 1904.

His *magnum opus* was a selection of Irish poetry, entitled, *Specimens of the Early Poetry of Ireland.* The full title continued. *In English metrical translations, by Miss Brooke, Sir Samuel Ferguson, Wm Leahy, J.C. Mangon, T. Furlong, J. D'Alton, H.G. Curran, E. Walsh and J. Anster, LL.D., etc.*[144] The book was dedicated to Her Excellency the Marchioness of Dufferin and Ava, British Embassy, Paris.

It is a collection of poems translated from the Irish, from the earliest times to the eighteenth century. The first edition appeared in 1846, the second in 1892. He said in the preface that the reason he did not include the original Irish language versions was that, '... however valuable in themselves, [they] would possess no interest to the mere English reader'. Ó Casaide, however, felt that the '... chief defect in this interesting book ... is the omission of the Irish originals'.[145] There can be no doubt that the absence of the originals takes away substantially from the publication. Montgomery's erudite comments show, however, that he had a good facility with Irish.

He published an anonymous pamphlet in 1840, entitled 'An Essay towards investigating the Causes that have retarded the Progress of Literature in Ireland ...' in which he recounted:

> In 1830 the Ulster Gaelic Society was instituted for the preservation of the remains of ancient Irish literature, maintaining teachers of the Irish language where it most prevails and publishing useful books in that tongue. The Marquis of Downshire is President.[146]

Like many contemporary writers, he pointed out that the great mass of the people were only accessible through the Irish language.[147] Education in their own language had been completely neglected and even the Irish Bible had not been available until '... the formation of that noble institution,the Irish Society, in 1818'. Montgomery was one of a number of authors who made translations from Irish, some apparently having been stimulated by the Belfast Irish classes.[148]

SIR SAMUEL FERGUSON, Q.C., LL.D (1810–1886)

Samuel, the youngest child of John Ferguson and his wife Agnes Knox, was born on 10 March 1810, in the home of his Knox grandparents, in Belfast. On the occasion of the centenary celebration of his birth it was stated that the house in which he was born was then occupied by John

S. Shaw, hatter, 21–23 High Street.[149] Ferguson was a forerunner of the Celtic Revival which in turn inspired W.B. Yeats and contemporaries. He has been called the 'Homer of the Gael'.

In later years, both he and his wife, who wrote his biography, were very coy about his religious affiliation. Yet, it seems highly likely that Ferguson was born into a Presbyterian family as evidenced by Lady Ferguson's own comment about the origins of her husband's antecedents: 'The Ferguson family came from Scotland early in the seventeeth century.' She then quotes evidence to support the Scottish origins.[150] Secondly, the vast majority of Donegore inhabitants are and were Presbyterian. Dr Henry Cooke's biographer, Josias Leslie Porter, had the following to say about Donegore: 'He was now on the 'holy ground' of Ulster Presbyterianism. The people of the parish were descendents of Scotch colonists, and many of them bore the well-known Ayrshire names of Shaw, Hunter, Ferguson, Stevenson and Blair.'[151]

Thirdly, Samuel had his education in the Royal Belfast Academical Institution,[152] which in his day was a college for training Presbyterian ministers. Before entering Inst in August 1823, he had spent some time at the Belfast Academy.[153] In his youth he dabbled in politics but gave it up to devote himself to scholarship and poetry, contributing significantly to the Gaelic Revival.

Much of his poetry was translated from the Irish, which language he learned in Belfast and which was perhaps introduced to him by his old teacher the Rev. Reuben Bryce, Principal of Belfast Academy, and co-secretary of the Ulster Gaelic Society, who ran Irish classes in the Academy. Later, in 1833, he belonged to a small group in Belfast who formed a private class to learn Irish. The other members were John MacLean, later to be a London millionaire, Thomas O'Hagan, ennobled in 1870 with the title of first Baron O'Hagan of Tullahogue[154] and George Fox. On 13 September of that year he wrote to Petrie, saying: 'Pray make my respects to O'Donovan and tell him I have begun Irish and have translated all I want of Hardiman ...'.[155] This study of Irish had a major influence on the subsequent career of Ferguson. The group made literal translations of Irish classics and he was delegated the task of expressing these translations in verse. They were published in the

Dublin University Magazine in 1834. These poems from the Irish retained much of the aroma of the originals.[156] He has been described, rather colourfully, as the inventor of the Celtic Twilight.

It is significant that Ian Adamson, a Unionist writer with regard for cultural traditions, has re-published much of Ferguson's work including the translation of *The Battle of Moyra*. He describes Ferguson as typifying '... the Ulster intellectual of his day – intensely proud of his 'Gaelic' heritage, but without the rancour of the xenophobe.'[157] His knowledge of the Irish language was put to the test when he undertook to make a critical evaluation of 'Irish Minstrelsy,' published by James Hardiman in 1831. But he enlisted the help of George Petrie and, through him, Eugene O'Curry and John O'Donovan. He found fault with Hardiman's translations from the Irish and in many cases provided superior versions himself. W.B. Yeats described him as the 'most Irish' of Irish writers and there is no doubt but that Yeats emulated him in many ways.[158]

About his facility with Irish there has been perennial debate. One author has stated about Ferguson: 'His profound knowledge of Irish helps him to succeed where Mangan has failed.'[159] But we have the following statement from Lady Ferguson herself, who wrote in her Introduction to his *Lays of the Red Branch*. 'In early youth he commenced for his own gratification the study of Irish. Although he never mastered the language, he knew enough to glean from Gaelic sources the material, which in after life, he made the ground-work for many of his poems'.[160]

Neither of these two authorities distinguish between knowing modern Irish and the ability to understand ancient texts, from which, presumably, many of Ferguson's translations were made. The unfortunate habit of not publishing the original texts alongside the translation makes it very difficult to draw appropriate conclusions. The verdict of Hodder seems to be closest to the truth. He points to the accuracy of Ferguson's literal verse translations and how they reproduce '... the rich idiomatic, syntactical and verbal texture of the Irish'. As far as old Irish was concerned he could enjoy a pun in that language, as shown in a letter to him from John O'Donovan. From the evidence, Hodder concludes that Ferguson was '... knowledgeable, but not proficient in Irish'. Armed with a grammar and dictionary, he would have little difficulty in deciphering and experiencing the original material for himself.[161]

All his career he maintained a scholarly interest in the Irish language, which sat quite easily beside his strong unionism. According to Hume, 'he loved the island of his birth with a devotion beyond mere nationalist separatism.'[162] Ó Dúill commented that Ferguson belonged to a group of upper-class cultural nationalists, which included figures such as Todd, Graves and Reeves. They were loyal to the state, which reciprocated with generous support for various projects. This group believed that native learning constituted no threat to the status quo, but, on the contrary, independent scientific investigation was supportive of the state.[163] For Bunting's work he furnished an essay on the antiquity of the harp and bagpipes in Ireland.

By the end of his life he had achieved an impressive literary output. Some of his works were, *Lays of the Western Gael, Congal, Poems, Remains of St Patrick, Ogham Inscriptions in Ireland, Wales and Scotland*, and *Lays of the Red Branch*.

J.C. Beckett, the prominent historian, holds that Ferguson's influence as a person, and presumably as a symbol, was of outstanding importance – '... more important, indeed, than his own writings'. The reason is his very great influence on W.B. Yeats, who described him as '... the greatest poet that Ireland has produced ...'.[164]

He died in Howth on 9 August 1886 aged 77 and he was buried, at his own request, in his native Donegore, Co. Antrim. His widow, and biographer, Mary Catherine, died in March 1905, aged 81 and was also buried there. The stone post at their burial plot is inscribed with a crest, which is identical with the old Highland Clan of Ferguson – a Scottish thistle with a bee, sucking honey. The motto is DULCIUS EX ASPERIS,[165] meaning *Sweeter after difficulties*.

WILLIAM HAMILTON DRUMMOND, D.D., M.R.I.A. (1778–1865)

Drummond, the eminent scholar, poet and divine, was well acquainted with the Irish language and made many translations from Irish literature into English. He was born in August 1778 at Larne, Co. Antrim, the second of three children of Rose Hare and Dr William Drummond, a surgeon in the Royal Navy who died young.[166] Another son of Surgeon Drummond was James Lawson Drummond (1783–1853), who became the first Professor of Anatomy at the Medical College of the Belfast Academical Institution.[167] The eldest child was Isabella (1776–1845), who married Andrew Marshall M.D. It is of interest that Margaret Marshall, their daughter, married the Rev. John Scott Porter,[168] who was a keen student of the Irish language. According to Shannon Millin,[169] '... his early youth was spent amid the romantic glens of Antrim ...', which would mean that he was in close contact with Irish, because, up until quite recently, this was an Irish-speaking area.

William was educated first at the Belfast Academy under Dr Crombie and Dr Bruce and then at age 16 he entered the University of Glasgow (November 1794). During his undergraduate career he continued to write poetry.[170] When he left the university in 1798 it was without taking his degree. It is suggested that he was needed at home to support the family which was in needy straits. On his return from Scotland he began to provide tuition, while at the same time studying for the ministry under the Presbytery of Armagh. In 1798 he became a tutor in a family at Ravensdale, Co. Louth,[171] then an Irish-speaking area. Considering that he did not return to Belfast until the next year, he would have had ample opportunity to become proficient in the language.

He was licensed by the Presbytery of Antrim on 9 April 1800 and in August of that year he was made minister to the Second Congregation in Belfast, where he served for 15 years. It was around 1801 that he married Barbara, daughter of David Tomb of Belfast. She was to die young. In 1805 he opened a school for boys at Mount Collier, which he ran until 1815.[172] During that period he lived in this house, which was situated on the northern outskirts of the town, and it was here that he wrote *The Battle of Trafalgar*, *Lucretius* and *The Giant's Causeway*.[173]

From this time forward it appeared that his importance as a writer and preacher continued to grow. One of his friends, Bishop Percy of Dromore, exerted his patronage to have the degree of D.D. conferred on him by Marischal College, Aberdeen, in 1810. He was one of the original members of the Belfast Literary Society, before which he read many papers.

In November 1815 he received a call from the Strand Street congregation in Dublin and thus he became a colleague of Mr Armstrong (1780–1840), who had been a minister in Strand Street since 1806.[174] His home was at 27 Lower Gardiner Street. It was in Dublin that he married his second wife, Catherine, daughter of Robert Blackley. Their two sons subsequently became ministers. The Rev. Blackley Drummond B.A., was incumbent of St Mark's, Edinburgh and the Rev. James Drummond, born in 1835, was Principal of Manchester College, Oxford.

Whilst of a poetic disposition, he published many religiously-motivated volumes, some controversial. He was also intensely patriotic, as were most of the persons of his social class and background at that time. The latter was shown clearly by his publication in 1852 of his book on Ancient Irish Minstrelsy,[175] which included over twenty translations from Irish into English of Ossianic poems relating to Fionn Mac Cumhail and his companions. These legendary tales were recited by Oisín (Ossian), son of Fionn, who had returned from Tír na nÓg (The Land of Youth) to find that all the Fianna were dead. In the course of his Ossianic research Drummond came across the original manuscripts and for this work he was awarded a prize by the Royal Irish Academy.

The Ossianic Society paid him a glowing tribute in the preface to the annual report for 1855,[176] when they traced the history of publications of Ossianic poetry. While manuscripts had existed since writing came to Ireland, the article said, the printing of Ossianic poetry began with Charles Wilson's collection in 1782. Later came Charlotte Brooke, Edward O Reilly, and then,

> ... the Rev. William Hamilton Drummond, D.D., whose name should be dear to every lover of Ossianic lore, wrote a very learned essay on the same subject (Ossianic literature), which is also printed in the same volume with O'Reilly's: both essays being written in refutation of Macpherson's theories, are highly deserving the attention of Irish scholars. In 1852, the latter gentleman (Dr Drummond), who, indeed, may be justly termed, 'Oisín a n-diaigh

na Féinne', published a volume of Ossianic poetry consisting of metrical translations into English from the original Irish, with an interesting critical dissertation on Fenian history, literature and lore.

This note of praise was written probably by John O'Daly, the Society's secretary. The words in Irish which he quoted mean, 'Ossian after the Fianna'.

In the second issue of *Ancient Ireland*, (10 January 1835),[177] which was a weekly magazine established to promote the Irish language and edited by Philip Barron, there was published an excerpt of a letter from Drummond. The editor, Philip Barron, described him as '... a dissenting clergymen of the highest respectability, a native of Belfast; distinguished alike for his controversial writings, and for some poems in the English language'. The editor then pointed out that Drummond had composed *The Giant's Causeway*,[178] and had translated poems from the Irish, including those which had appeared in Hardiman's Collection.[179] Some of his poems translated from the Irish also appeared in Montgomery's collection.[180]

In his letter to *Ancient Ireland*, Drummond said that it was with interest and satisfaction that he had read the first issue. He welcomed the exclusion of politics and polemics from its pages, because '... literature presents a green spot of neutral ground ... for those with different religious and political sentiments.' He went on to say: 'Your publication must be successful. – It is admirably calculated to bring about, effectually and expeditiously, the revival of the Irish literature and language, a consummation devoutly to be wished. Anxiously looking forward for this consummation, I beg to enrol myself among your subscribers ...'.

It is clear from these accounts that his facility with Irish was good and that he personally translated very many of the poems from the original Irish, Indeed he describes himself as 'the translator'. However there is other evidence suggesting that, for at least the more difficult texts, he had the help of others. In one of the copies of his *Irish Minstrelsy*, in the possession of this author, there is inscribed a note in the hand of a Stewart Blacker, saying, '... I assisted Dr Drummond in obtaining a careful literal yet spirited translation of the ancient Irish poem the *Chase of Glennasmol* (see page 61 of this Volume). It was prepared by Eugene Curry of the R. Irish Academy and was probably the last version made for this Volume by Dr Drummond as he presented it to me soon after in 1852. Stewart Blacker Adt., M.R.I.A.'.

Most of our evidence about his facility with Irish is indirect, yet reasonably conclusive, pointing to a sound understanding and a good ability to read the language, but falling short of an academic ability to read and understand all the ancient texts on his own. One further example of the evidence will suffice. On discussing the Battle of Gavra in *Ancient Irish Minstrelsy* (p. 103), he says about the copy taken from the Report of the Highland Society of Scotland. 'It is accompanied by the Gaelic original, the orthography of which will appear to the merest novice in the Irish language to be exceedingly corrupt'. This is obviously a personal comment based on his own knowlege and experience. One of his lesser known works was referred to by Paul Walsh,[181] who said that he published a metrical version of *Diombáigh triall ó thulcaibh Fáil* in 1831. It has not been possible to trace this.

He was elected a Member of the Royal Irish Academy, and frequently contributed to its *Transactions*. For many years he was Librarian to the R.I.A. Aged 87 years, Dr Drummond died in his home at Lower Gardiner Street, Dublin on the morning of Monday, 16 October 1865, and was buried in the Mount Jerome Cemetery, at Harold's Cross, Dublin on 20 October. About his personality it was said that '... his warm, genial, and sympathetic temperament secured for him in no ordinary degree the admiration and love of those who enjoyed the privilege of his friendship. A man of purer mind or more enlarged and comprehensive charity did not exist. Among his many theological opponents, he had not a single personal enemy'.[182]

JOHN SCOTT PORTER (1801–1880)

The Rev. Porter was very favourably disposed to Irish. Indeed, he was related by marriage to the Irish translator William Hamilton Drummond, being married to his niece, Margaret. W.H. Drummond's sister Isabella (1776–1845) had married Dr Andrew Marshall (1779–1868) and their daughter, Margaret, married John Scott Porter.[183]

'A.M.P.' in a biography described Porter's facility with various languages. With regard to Irish, Porter was said to be a student of the language, though not proficient.[184]

He was a friend of the Irish-speaking Dr William Reeves, Bishop of Down and Connor and he was on friendly terms with Robert MacAdam, through membership of the Belfast Literary Society. He was president of the society for six different terms, and read papers on the Brehon Laws, the life of St Patrick, the life of St Columba, and on the poetical works of William Hamilton Drummond, his wife's uncle.

John Scott Porter, as member of the Board of Visitors of the Royal Belfast Academical Institution, gave evidence on 17 July 1835 before the Select Committee on Education (Ireland). This evidence was summarised by Ó Casaide.[185] In response to questions Porter said,

> There are [students of Irish at present in the Institution] ... but I am unable to state the precise number, not having been furnished with any return ... The [Irish] class has been in operation I believe for three years; it is under the management of Mr. Feenachty, who is considered a competent teacher, and able, and has translated several English works into the Irish language; among others I remember having heard of some translations from Miss Edgeworth, I think, of some of her *Popular Tales* ... The English language has been acquired by a great number of the lower classes in Ireland, for the sake of the convenience it affords in the transaction of business; but I cannot say that they have acquired it for the sake of obtaining literary information ... I do not understand how a child can be well taught English without it [i.e., Irish], if Irish be the vernacular tongue ... The Irish class [in the Institution] was established that it might afford a facility of acquiring that language to persons, designing to settle in the south, whether as clergymen or as professional men, and also as a means of preserving such relics of Irish literature as are yet accessible to the learned from falling into decay, and elucidating the study of Irish antiquities ...
>
> The ... language is spoken as their vernacular and the beloved mother tongue by a great number of our population; and those who wish to influence their hearts and feelings, find it very often necessary to address them in Irish. I have been told, for instance, that in extensive districts of the south of Ireland, the clergy of the

Roman-catholic Church address their flocks in the Irish tongue, and that in that way they obtain an access to their feelings, and an influence over their hearts, that the same discourse, though it might be equally distinctly apprehended, would not produce if delivered in English. As they say themselves, the Irish comes warm to their hearts.

The Rev. Porter sought to explain to his interrogators that the Irish language was an important educational medium for a very large number of Irish children, that a great amount of native literature was available only through the language and that Irish, for hundreds of thousands of people, was the language of their emotions as well as their literature.

These valid pleas fell on barren ground and the commissioners of the National Schools decided to exclude from their curriculum any element of the Irish language. Barkley listed the National Schools as one of the major causes of the decline in the use of Irish; one other major factor being the influence of O'Connell and the Roman Catholic Church.[186]

V
PRESBYTERIAN PUBLICATIONS IN IRISH

Writing in the Irish language dates back to the fifth century, and there still survives a very extensive literature in manuscript form, dating from the eighth century, making it the oldest vernacular literature in Western Europe.[1] Of the Presbyterian contribution in transcribing and rescuing these valuable Irish manuscripts, the outstanding examples were Samuel Bryson and Robert Shipboy MacAdam.

The first book printed in Irish did not appear until 1567. In April of that year John Carswell's translation of John Knox's *Book of Common Order* was published in Edinburgh, only seven years after Knox founded the Presbyterian Church in Scotland.[2] Irish and Scottish Gaelic, especially in their written forms, were essentially the same language at that time and so this book is listed in the standard bibliography of books in Irish.[3]

It is very appropriate, therefore, in this account of Presbyterian publications in Irish, that the first-ever printed book in Irish was Presbyterian. The fact that this book was circulating in Ireland is said to have given rise to consternation in the English Court, because of the fear that Scottish Presbyterianism would get a major grip on Ireland. A constant fear in England at that time, and later, was that Presbyterians would form an alliance with Irish Catholics. Such an alliance would completely change the power structure in Ireland and so was one of the factors leading to the publication of Anglican material in Irish.

Carswell, in the preface, addressed his book to Irish-speakers and Gaelic-speakers alike. For example, he said the following (spelling modernised):

> Is mór an leatrom agus an uireasa atá riamh orainne Gaeil Alban agus Éireann, thar an chuid eile den domhain, gan ár gcanúint Gaeilge a chur i gcló riamh, mar atá á gcanúint agus a dteanga féin i gcló ag gach uile chineál dhaoine eile sa domhain ...'. (We Scottish and Irish Gaels have suffered great distress and deficiency

more than other parts of the world because our language has not been printed, in contrast to all other countries ...).

Later books continued to be written in the literary Gaelic common to both Scotland and Ireland. In 1631 an Irish/Gaelic translation of John Calvin's Catechism was published. R.L. Thomson described the language of this book as: 'Not Scottish Gaelic, but the literary Gaelic which was still the common property of Scotland and Ireland at the time.'[4] The first printed text to exhibit unmistakably Scottish Gaelic characteristics was the translation in 1653 of the *Shorter Catechism of the Westminster Assembly* (1648). The work of the ministerial members of the Synod of Argyll, it made a second edition in 1659.[5]

The missionary spirit which exhibited strong stirrings in the Presbyterian Church at the beginning of the eighteenth century, led to publications in Irish. The records of the General Synod of Ulster in 1710 tell us that there were then available translations into Irish of the Bible, *Confession of Faith*, and Catechism. A catechism was commissioned by the General Synod in 1716. The minutes record that it was ordered,

> ... that the Catechism in Irish, with a little short Irish grammar of a leaf or two subjoined to it, be printed in Dublin; that Mr Patrick Simpson oversee the press; and that each minister within this Synod be obliged to take and pay for thirty copies of the same, which will make an impression for above three thousand copies subscribed for on our part.[6]

At a meeting of the Synod in the following year (June, 1717), it was reported that the catechism had not yet been printed,

> ... because it was some time before it could be got well translated; but now Mr Simpson tells this Synod that, by the help of an Irish man, he has got it done; which translation we order to be laid before such members of the Irish Societies as are here, who are to meet this evening after the interlocution, to consider and report their judgement of the said translation.[7]

By the time of the meeting of the General Synod in 1719 the Catechism had been published and reprinted. At that time it was resolved:

> That care be taken that the Irish Catechisms now reprinted and in

Mr Simpson's hands, be distributed among the several Presbyteries, and that Mr Simpson be satisfied for his trouble and charges.

It was also agreed that,

> ... the defraying of the expenses of printing of the Irish catechism be referred to the Committee to meet at Dublin, and that the Society erected for improving themselves in the Irish tongue shall ... distribute the said Catechisms in such proportions as they shall judge most for edification.[8]

So it seems clear that this Presbyterian Catechism was published c.1718 and was reprinted shortly afterwards. But although 3,000–6,000 copies were produced, it appears that no example has survived.

In 1722 was published *The Church Catechism in Irish* compiled by Francis Hutchinson, Bishop of Down and Connor.[9] It was printed in Belfast by James Blow and was directed towards the people of Rathlin Island.[10] This has been described as the Presbyterian Catechism, but it is closely associated with the Church of Ireland and it may have been confused with the Presbyterian Catechism of c.1718.

In 1726 a small but fascinating and seminal work was published by Dr Caleb Threlkeld, a Protestant dissenter and Non-Conformist, i.e. a Presbyterian. It was entitled in Latin, but explained as *A Short Treatise of Native Plants, especially such as grow spontaneously in the vicinity of Dublin; with their Latin, English and Irish names* ... The Irish-Latin appendix at the end of the book gave a very informative glossary of Irish names for plants.[11]

The *Northern Star* began publication in January 1792. It was the Belfast organ of the United Irishmen and all of the twelve proprietors except one were Presbyterian.[12] Contributors included Samuel Neilson (editor), Counsellor Sampson, Rev. James Porter, Rev. Sinclair Kelburn and Rev. Steel Dickson. In April 1795 the paper published a notice advertising the Irish lessons given by Patrick Lynch in the Belfast Academy. In August the same year the *Northern Star* published *Bolg an tSoláir*, the first magazine in Irish. It was advertised as the:

> ... *Gaelic Magazine* containing *Laoi na Sealga* or the famous Fenian Poem, called the *Chase*, With a collection of choice Irish Songs Translated by Miss Brooke, to which is prefixed an abridgment of

Irish Grammar, a Vocabulary, and Familiar Dialogues. To be had
at all Booksellers, and at the Star office, Price: Thirteen Pence.[13]

Only one issue was published, yet it was a pioneering endeavour.
Included in the issue (120 pages), were a grammar, a dictionary, Ossianic
poems, phrases and dialogues, etc. all edited by Patrick Lynch. A facsimile
edition of *Bolg an tSoláir* was published by the Linen Hall Library in 1995.

In 1797 The *Northern Star* was suppressed, the troops used being the
Monaghan Militia (mainly Catholic). These events led Stothers to
comment:

> Thus, somewhat ironically, as history has gone since, there was a
> largely Presbyterian-backed Gaelic Magazine published in
> Presbyterian Belfast, with a Roman Catholic as compiler, and it
> was suppressed by Roman Catholics in the service of the Crown![14]

Stothers also says, '... what the 1790s do tell us is that not a few
Presbyterians were interested in, and actively involved in promoting,
native Irish culture, particularly Irish music and the Irish language,
and this because they believed that it would help to advance the cause
of unity among all Irishmen'. Neilson's *Grammar* was published in
1808.[15] In 1810 he published *Ceud Leabhar na Gaoidheilge* (A first
book in Irish).[16] A second edition of the *Grammar* was published in
1843, a third in1845 and a fourth in 1990.

In 1833 translations of Maria Edgeworth's moral stories, *Forgive and
Forget and Rosanna*, were published by the Ulster Gaelic Society,[17] an
organisation with a strong Presbyterian input. Both secretaries were of
that denomination. The book had two different forms. The more
common version gave the stories first in Irish and then at the end, the
original text in English. However, there was another version totally in
Irish except for two pages; these being the English version of the title
page and of the dedication page. Clearly the second version was aimed
at the many monoglot Irish-speakers for whom the English version
would have been superfluous. The book is dedicated to the third
Marquis of Downshire, the President of the Ulster Gaelic Society. His
brother, Lord George Hill was landlord of Gweedore in Co. Donegal,
and was himself an excellent Irish speaker, as well as an avid collector of
Irish language manuscripts. Robert MacAdam with the cooperation of

Tomás Ó Fiannachtaigh published a grammar in 1835, for use in the Royal Belfast Academical Institution (Inst).[18] This was associated with the classes which were started to teach Irish to student ministers.

A *magnum opus* of the Synod of Ulster was the long awaited *Psalms of David* in Irish, published in 1836.[19] This was the work of the renowned Rev. Norman McLeod D.D., minister of St Columba's

DEDICATED, BY PERMISSION, TO THE KING.

ᵽS2Iᒪᴀᑫᴀ ᴅ2Iᗷⁱ,

ᴚⁱᴳ JᔕᴚᴀᴇL.

THE

PSALMS OF DAVID

IN THE

IRISH LANGUAGE.

NOW FOR THE FIRST TIME RENDERED INTO METRE.

———

For the Use of the Native Irish.

· 2 LOᴎᴅᴜIᴎ:
AR NA CHUR NA GCLO RE RICHARD WATTS,
Crown Court, Temple Bar.
—
1836.

BY NORMAN MᶜLEOD, D.D.
MINISTER OF ST. COLUMBA'S PARISH, GLASGOW.

parish, Glasgow. In his native Gàidhlig he was nicknamed *Caraid nan Gaidheal* (Friend of the Gael). His son, also called Norman, was a great preacher and a favourite of Queen Victoria. He was helped by Thaddeus Connellan who is acknowledged in the preface to the first printing, but also David Murphy whose name does not appear. Shortly after the first printing Mrs Tonna (Charlotte Elizabeth), wrote a review in the journal of which she was editor, *The Christian Lady's Magazine*.[20] She commented diplomatically:

> One drawback there is on our satisfaction and in that we are very sure that Dr MacLeod participates. Justice has not been rendered according to his express wish, towards one whose peculiar fate it is

to do much, very, very much, in this cause and to get no credit for his exertions. We are not able to speak, altogether from our own personal knowledge and without the concurrence of the individual in question. David Murphy ... rendered such essential service to Dr McLeod in his work, that we boldly appeal to that most respected individual, to say whether it would now have been published without his assistance.'

She goes on to point out that although Dr McLeod was an excellent '... and profound Gaelic scholar ...' that he would be in difficulties with the 'vernacular Irish' so he would need help. She said that Mr Connellan only helped at the beginning and that McLeod was left in the lurch until Murphy came to help, corrected the whole manuscript, re-composed much of it and transcribed the whole and brought it through the printing. She pointed out that Dr McLeod had provided a title-page which showed Murphy as the main author of the work but this was not published, and in the acknowledgements Beamish and Connellan were mentioned but not Murphy.

The outcome of this criticism was that there was a new printing in the same year and in the *Advertisement* it was stated that, '... Dr McLeod was assisted ... in the first instance, by Mr Thaddeus Connellan ... and subsequently by Mr David Murphy, Scripture Reader under the Irish Society of London, and author of *Lays of Erin's Ancient Harp*'.

A journal came out in 1837, *Bolg an t-Soláir*, in two issues.[21, 22] This was part of a series of pamphlets in Irish intended for the use of the Irish Schools, connected with the Synod of Ulster's Home Mission. It was '... calculated to impart useful instruction to the long-neglected natives of Ireland.'[23] The title was borrowed directly from the magazine published in Belfast in 1795 by *The Northern Star*.

The first number, *An Ceud Rann*, has three stories printed with a most unusual type, being a mixture, throughout the text, of some Gaelic letters and some Roman letters. The first story, *Mar Fuaras a Mach America* (How America was discovered), describes the journey of Columbus to the New World. This is followed by a very short essay on the dangers of bad company. The last item, *Innseanach America*, is a story about an American Indian. These pieces are taken directly from the *Gaelic Miscellany*, called *Leabhar nan Cnoc*, of which Norman

McLeod was the editor.[24] With minor changes they were made
suitable for the Irish reader. The sketches are pleasantly readable, even

LEABHAR NAN CNOC	BOLG AN T-SOLÁIR
Mar fhuaradh a mach America	Mar fuaras a mach America

'An toiseach an fhoghair sa'
bhliadhna I492, chuir Columbus fa
sgaoil mu éirigh na gréine, ann an
làthair sluaigh mhòr, a thog an
ùrnuigh suas as a leth gu nèamh,
a' guidheadh gu dùrachdach gu'n
soirbhicheadh leis, ge nach robh
dùil sam bith aca gu'm buadhaich-
eadh e anns na bha 'na bheachd.
Cha robh aige ach tri loingeis,
agus cha robh iad sin féin ach
beag. Bha annta so ceithir fichead
pearsa 's a deich, a' chuid bu mhò
dhiubh 'nan seòladairibh; a bhàrr
air àireamh bheag eile a chaidh
leis air tòir na dh'fheudadh iad
a bhuannachd; agus cuid do uaislibh na Spàinne a chuir a' bhan-righ
a mach maille ris. Rinn e 'ghabhail
gu dìreach airson nan eileanaibh
sin ris an abrar na Canaries; 's
an déigh dhoibh an loingeas agus
gach acfhuinn a bhuineadh dhoibh
a cheartachadh, agus gach uidheam-
achadh eile bha feumail a dheanamh,
ghabh e 'chead deireannach do'n
àite sin, air an t-sèathamh là do
mhìos meadhonach an fhogharaidh.
'S ann a nis a thòisich e air an
turas fairge bha 'na bheachd: stiùr
e gu dìreach an iar: thréig e gach
àird, agus gach slighe fairge, air
an do sgaoileadh, gus a sin, seòl,
agus ghabh e'n cuan mòr fo 'cheann.

A d-toiseach an fhoghmhair
'sa m-bliadhain I492, do thóg
Columbus a sheólta timchioll
éirigh na gréine a lathair sluaigh mhóir, a thóg a n-urnaighthe
suas ann a leith go Neamh ag guidheadh go duthrachdach go soirbh-
eochadh leis,ge nach raibh súil
air bith aca go n-eirochadh leis
an rud bhí a n'intinn a chur a
g-crich. Ni raibh aige acht tri
loingis,7 ni raibh siad sin féin
acht beag. Bhi ionnta so deich 7
ceithre fithchid pearsa, an chuid
budh mho diobtha 'na seoladoiridh;
gan tracht air áireamh bheag eile
a chuaidh leis a n-doigh tairbhe
eigin; 7 cuid d'uaislibh na Spáinn
e a chuir an bhan-rioghan a mach
maille ris. Sheól se go direach
air son na n-eileán sin ris a n-
abarthar na Canarienses; 7 tar
éis iad na loingis 7 gach acfhuinn a bhaineadh dhóibh a chur a
n-eagar, 7 gach ullmhughadh eile
bhi feumamhuil a dheanamh, thug
se slan deighionach don áit sin,
air an t-seiseamh lá de mhios
mheadhonaigh an fhoghmhair. Is
ann sin a thoisigh se an turus
fairge bhi'n intinn: stiúr se go
direach gus an árd shiar: thréig
se gach áird 7 gach slighe fairge
air ar sgaoileadh seól go d-ti
sin, 7 d'imthigh se roimhe air an
muir mhóir.

A comparison of the Scottish Gaelic on the left and Irish on the right shows
conclusively that the texts in *Bolg an t-Soláir*, Part One (1837) were
translated from Norman McLeod's *Leabhar nan Cnoc*.

today. They tend to be moral in tone, but that was the general flavour of the age. They were meant to entertain as well as instruct and were designed to provide a stepping stone to more difficult texts. The person who put the Irish-Gaelic clothes on the Scottish-Gaelic essays is not known, but it is likely to have been Tomás Ó Fiannachtaigh. The second number, *An dara Roinn*, was more religious in character and quite brief. It was simply a selection of sentences taken from Bedell's Bible aimed to illustrate various theological points, such as characteristics of God, the contrasting imperfections of humans and how God has provided Salvation for fallen Man.

The approach in many ways mirrored that of the Anglican Irish Society, which took great pains not to offend Catholic susceptibilities.[25] There seemed to be a genuine desire to, first and foremost, educate Irish-speakers in their own language. If this should turn them to the Bible, well and good, but all major confrontation with the Roman Catholic clergy was to be avoided, as this would be completely counter-productive. Review of this work in the *Orthodox Presbyterian* explains the philosophy as follows: 'If a series of plain religious tracts were printed and circulated amongst them (i.e. Irish-speakers), such as would be precisely adapted to their situation and wants, we cannot but think that great good would result. We know that the London Tract Society have printed a great number of their English tracts in Irish ... but still, we believe that a collection of tracts might be composed and published, better suited to the taste and the condition of the people connected with our Home Mission operations – a collection which would embrace and briefly illustrate all the topics comprehended in the second part of *Bolg an tSoláir* ...'.[26]

In the same year, 1837, was also published an Irish language version of the Presbyterian Shorter Catechism, *An Teagasg Críosduigh*.[27] The Synod of Ulster, through its Home Mission, had commissioned George Field, its agent, to do this work. The reviewer in the *Orthodox Presbyterian*,[28] the journal of Henry Cooke's orthodox party, asserted that this was the first time that the Presbyterian Catechism had been translated into Irish. This is erroneous, because there are detailed accounts of the 1718 translation, recorded clearly in the Minutes of the General Synod of Ulster at the time.

In praising Field's translation, the critic had to say that it was '... now happily executed ...', and '... highly creditable to his attainments and his industry ...'. He said that Field had been sensitive to the great idiomatic differences between English and Irish, to the extent that the natural Irish phraseology in the translation would hardly reveal that this was a translation at all: 'It is evident that Mr Field is well acquainted with the grammatical forms and idiomatic peculiarities that distinguish the two languages.' This tells us quite a lot about the critic, who must himself have had a very good grasp on Irish to be able to make these comments. His only major criticism was that the title was much too long.

In June 1838 the Ladies' Gaelic Society published a tract, reviewed in the *Orthodox Presbyterian*,[29] entitled '*Leabhar na mBan Uasal Uladh, – an chéad mhíniuagh 'Sé spiorad Dé Ughdar na Sgriobtúir*' i.e. *The Ulster Ladies' Book – the First Essay, The Spirit of God is the Author of the Scriptures*. The reviewer said that it was the *Orthodox Presbyterian* which first suggested that there should be a translation into Irish of the book entitled 'Essays on some of the Principal Doctrines and Duties of the Gospel'. This tract was an Irish version of the first essay in that book. The reviewer welcomed this Irish contribution as a first step in translating the whole volume. The critic was of the opinion that this first offering of the translation was '... ably executed ...' and went on to explain:

> The idioms of the English are transfused into the Irish with sufficient perspicuity, and with a degree of literality throughout, as far as the two languages allow. The Rev. author need not therefore be ashamed of the dress in which his composition has been put.

The name of the reverend author is not mentioned. Nor do we know who were the individuals responsible for the actual work of translation. It appears that the critic in the *Orthodox Presbyterian* had a good knowledge of Irish, otherwise he would not have been able to make these remarks. This conclusion is supported by the last comments of the critic.

By way of appendix to the tract is given a 'short account of the Holy Scriptures', intended to be useful, but containing several errors and blunders from which it would have been well to have kept free.

The Ladies' Gaelic Society published a further work in the same year (1838), this time an Irish grammar with a section on religious instruction. It was titled *An Irish Primer Compiled and Published Under the Patronage of the Ladies' Gaelic Society*, Belfast'.[30] Ó Casaide suggested that Tomás Ó Fiannachtaigh, the Professor of Irish in the Royal Belfast Academical Institution, may have been the compiler.[31] It was printed by Goodwin, Son and Nethercott, Dublin and the type was that devised by Fry with both the Gothic and a new set of Irish capital letters.[32] There was a pictorial Irish alphabet, which later appeared in a grammar (1841) by George Field, the Agent to the Presbyterian Home Mission. Irish and English texts are laid out in parallel columns. A section at the end gives the Irish text with an English translation between each line, just as displayed in a book by Owen Connellan, published in 1830.

In 1841 was published the notable grammar of Irish by George Field,[33] who called himself in Irish Seorsa Ó Mhachaire, hence the author's initials 'S.Ó.Mh'. The full title was, *'Casán na Gaoidhilge: an Introduction to the Irish Language; compiled at the request of the Irish Teachers: under the patronage of the General Assembly in Ireland, and dedicated to them as a tribute of esteem for their zeal in preserving and extending the knowledge of our beloved Mother-tongue, By Their Friend and Countryman, S.Ó.Mh.'* The Irish title means 'The Path of Irish'. Ó Buachalla has pointed out that this Irish grammar was the third one published in Belfast over a period of six years and furthermore that it was the fifth Irish book to come out of Belfast since the Ulster Gaelic Society (*Cuideachta Gaoidheilge Uladh*) was formed in 1830 (sic).[34]

In the preface, Field made it clear that his grammar was intended for the use of those whose native language was Irish, but also for those '... who wish to acquire a knowledge of our sweet and venerable mother-tongue'. He went on to acknowledge the valuable contribution of previous grammarians, O'Brien, O'Reilly, Neilson, Halliday, Connellan and O'Feenachty, and also Stewart and Munroe. The latter two had written grammars of Scottish Gaelic. Field also acknowledged the assistance and instruction given by Michael McNulty, Hugh Gordon, Hugh McDonnell, Michael Brannigan, 'and other native Irishmen'. He ended his preface by challenging his critics to produce, '... that long expected gift – a perfect Grammar of the 'teanga bhinn mhilis na hÉirionn'. (Sweet melodious, language of Ireland).

Monoglot Irish-speakers may have found this grammar difficult to follow because the basic language used was English, but aids included the lithographed pictorial alphabet as a frontispiece and also individual sections being labelled bi-lingually, e.g. An Irish Grammar (*Graiméar na Gaoidhilge*), Orthography (*Toirleaghadh*), Etymology (*Forusfhocal*), Syntax (*Coimhréir*), and Prosody (*Ailbhlas*). Grammatical terms were consistently provided in their Irish equivalents, to convenience readers with little English. In the fourth part Field seems to have forgotten the learner and has given large chunks of Irish poetry without any translation whatever. Stothers has analysed this important work in detail and explains how it aimed to serve both the Irish-speaking monoglot and the English-speaker trying to learn Irish for the first time. The result is a very unusual publication, consisting of a mixture of English and Irish and a mixture of Roman and Gaelic script.

On page 6 there is an exceptionally modern comment about standard Irish spelling. Modern standard and simplified spelling and grammar were introduced about 1950 but Field, writing in 1841, had this to say: 'The poets, wishing to lengthen words, or multiply their syllables, frequently inserted a dotted consonant between the vowels, thus making two syllables out of one, as *tiarna* a lord, is written *tighearna*, having a dotted 'g' inserted.' The Irish print used in this book was the then popular Fry's type, also used in the translation of Maria Edgeworth's stories published by the Ulster Gaelic Society.

Casán na Gaoidhilge is mainly a secular publication, aimed at teaching Irish as an objective in itself. The Bible is not mentioned although extracts are given, as one of the available texts in Irish.

Stothers felt that the absence of much religious material was very significant, considering that this was a publication commissioned by the Assembly.[35] It is noteworthy that the lithographed pictorial alphabet facing the title page is the same as that which appeared in the *Irish Primer* (1838), published by the Ladies' Gaelic Society, demonstrating the interrelationship of these publications.

There are many everyday word lists, tables of declensions, tables showing the tenses of irregular verbs etc. An Appendix discusses the way that words in Irish can be built up from basic terms, 'primitive words'. This is followed by a section of explanatory notes. Towards the end are exercises in reading. The Irish text is given with an interlinear translation, just as in the *Irish Primer* (1838) and in *St John's Gospel in Irish* (1830). The texts come from Keating's *History of Ireland*, 'From an old Manuscript' and from the *Acts of the Apostles*. Finally, there is a text from Neilson's *Grammar*, (*Story of Bryan the Smith*). The second last item is a list of English Words, which '... seem capable of interpretation through the Celtic'. Examples are: Algebra, from eala-díbireac (hidden knowledge), Africa from ath-freach (great blackness), Copenhagen from Ceap an Aigéin, meaning headland of the sea. After a page of *errata*, the book ends with a list of '... contractions alphabetically arranged ...'.

Some publications in Irish, whilst not of Presbyterian origin, were, however, used in the Presbyterian Irish Schools. Two of these were the work of Miss Mary Jane Alexander, daughter of the Bishop of Down and Connor and later of the diocese of Meath. One was her translations was of *The Sinner's Friend* into Irish.[36] Henry McManus described in his *Sketches*,[37] the result of one of his first encounters with the Irish-speaking people of Connemara.

> Having procured an Irish copy of 'The Sinner's Friend', I called with it on a poor Roman Catholic widow, who lived on the seashore near Roundstone, (Cloch na Rón), and asked her permission to read a portion of it. This was freely granted; and so I read some passages, setting forth the atonement of Christ and the freedom of salvation. 'How do you like that?' said I, when I had done. Her reply was emphatic. '*Cá tuige nach dtaitneoch sé liom?*' 'Why should I not like it, for it has sense and reason with it?

Miss Alexander's other publication in Irish was *Cláirseach Naomhtha na hÉireann*.[38] (*The Sacred Harp of Ireland*), also used in classes and reviewed in the *Orthodox Presbyterian*. Her publications in Irish are referred to in the *Reports of the Home Mission*. For example, in the Fifth *Report* (1836), page 10, it is stated: 'As many of the Teachers and scholars are deriving much pleasure and, as is hoped, profit also, from singing the Irish hymns, which have been provided by Miss Alexander, we feel constrained to express our grateful acknowledgement of her liberal and zealous services in this good cause. *The Sinner's Friend*, a small book which has proved so extensively profitable to English readers, may shortly, through her Christian labours, become a useful companion to the Bible, for the reader of the Irish tongue ...'.

VI
TWENTIETH CENTURY
A
Gaelic Revival 1890–1915

GENERAL

The tail-end of the nineteenth century saw the foundation of the Gaelic League, a movement which had its roots in the Gaelic Society of Dublin (1808) and the Ulster Gaelic Society (1828). The latter was perhaps the only predecessor of the Gaelic League which placed the living language first. The League was instituted in 1893 by Eoin MacNeill (1867–1945), a native of the Glens of Antrim and Douglas Hyde (1860–1910), son of a Church of Ireland rector of Frenchpark, Co. Roscommon. The aim was '... to keep the language alive among the people'.[1] The League, four years after formation had still only 43 branches.[2] However, by 1902 the number had increased to 227. In 1903, December 31, there were 13,025 pupils attending Irish classes in Ulster, and in 1904 the number of branches of the League came to almost 600, with a total membership of around 50,000 people. In the same year *An Claidheamh Solais*, the organ of the Gaelic League, reached its highest ever circulation of 30,000 copies per week.

Robert MacAdam, the secretary of the Ulster Gaelic Society, lived until January 1895, long enough to see the formation of the League and to know that his life's work was not in vain. On 19 August 1895 the Belfast Branch of the Gaelic League was formed at a meeting in the house of P.T. MacGinley at 32 Beersbridge Road. At this time the President of the Belfast Gaelic League was Dr John St Clair Boyd, a Belfast Protestant and Unionist whose family had been long associated with the Blackstaff Linen Mill.[3] Indeed for many years the Irish language movement was not confined to any political or religious section of the community. However, the year 1915 brought a change in this relationship when the Gaelic League, through pressure from political activists, passed a resolution which added the political independence of Ireland to the aims of the organisation. It was because of this breaching of the non-political constitution that Douglas Hyde resigned from the Presidency of the League. It should be useful to give more details of some of the Presbyterians who were affected in one way or other by the Gaelic revival.

GEORGE RAPHAEL BUICK, M.A., L.LD., M.R.I.A. (1841–1904)

George Buick spent his entire ministry in Cullybackey, Co. Antrim, but for a while he was a Vice-President of the Belfast Gaelic League. A notice in the *Gaelic Journal* of 1 December 1895,[4] goes as follows:

> BELFAST GAELIC LEAGUE. – This Society has now fairly started on what we hope will be a long and useful and honourable career of work, and has started under the most favourable auspices. The following are the names of the patrons, that is practically of the Vice-Presidents of the Society, coming after the name of its President, Dr St Clair Boyd: Very Rev. Henry Boyle, President of St Malachy's College; Rev. Dr Buick, Moderator of the General Assembly; Francis Joseph Bigger, M.R.I.A.; Rev. Canon Crozier, D.D.; Henry Clarke, M.A., T.C.D.; Most Rev. Dr Henry, Bishop of Down and Connor; Rev. R.R. Kane, L.L.D.; Very Rev. A. McMullen, P.P., M.R.I.A.; Rev. James O' Laverty, P.P., M.R.I.A.; W.H. Patterson, M.R.I.A.; Mrs. W.J. Smythe; Rt. Rev. Dr Welland, Bishop of Down, Connor and Dromore; Francis D. Ward, J.P., M.R.I.A.; Robert Young, J.P., C.E. It would be difficult to compile a list more representative of education, culture, and advancememt in the Northern capital and its neighbourhood. The Committee have secured the commodious rooms of the Belfast Art Society, 49 Queen–St, Belfast, where classes are held every Wednesday from 7.30 to 9.30 p.m., by competent Irish teachers. The Hon. Secretary is Mr E. Morrissey.

A rough estimate of the denominational distribution of the above persons gives eight Protestants, of which three are Presbyterians. There are four Roman Catholics and three whose denomination is indeterminate.

The *Fasti*[5] show that George Raphael Buick was born on 27 May 1841, son of Rev. Frederick Buick (1811–1908) of Ahoghill and of a daughter of George Raphael of Galgorm. He was ordained at Cullybackey and spent his entire ministry at the Cunningham Memorial in that town. In 1895 he was Moderator of the General Assembly. Later in life he became the General Assembly's Jewish Mission Convenor and it was while on work for the Mission that he died in Damascus on 28 April 1904.

The publication entitled *Buick's Ahoghill*[6, 7] is supposed to have been written by him. The document, composed about 1901, is an account of the Ahoghill of his own father's time. The Rev. Frederick Buick had had a ministry of some 72 years in the town and many changes had taken place, such as the Seceder movement and the great Ulster religious Revival of 1859. In 1900 he had been a minister for 65 years in the town and the inhabitants marked the occasion by presenting him with a purse containing 200 sovereigns, along with an illuminated address, signed by over a hundred people. He was to continue to minister for another seven years until he died in 1908 at the age of 97. Indeed, he survived his son George by four years.

George Buick was a member of the Royal Irish Academy. He was made a member of the Royal Society of Antiquaries of Ireland in 1882, elected fellow in 1887 and was Vice-President 1892–97, and later 1898–1902.[8] It is not known how fluent George Buick was in Irish, but many culturally concerned people like himself were active members of the Gaelic League at that time, irrespective of their fluency in the language.

RICHARD LYTTLE (1866–1905)

There was a cluster of Irish-speakers in Moneyrea, near Comber, Co. Down in the 1911 census, amounting to over 1 per cent of the population of the District Electoral Division. Drawing attention to this, G.B. Adams suggested[9] that this relatively high prevalence was due to the previous activity of the Rev. Lyttle, a Non-Subscribing Presbyterian minister, who was very energetic in the teaching of Irish, organising classes and generally getting people interested in the language.

Son of a linen merchant, he was a native of Dromore, Co. Down. He studied for the ministry at the Theological College, Manchester. In about 1888 he was appointed to the congregation at Moneyrea, succeeding the Rev. G.W. Bannister and the Rev. Harold Rylett. He was listed as the Rev. R. Lyttle, the Manse, Moneyrea, Comber in the roll of members of the Belfast Naturalists' Field Club for the years 1896, 1897, and 1898[10] and so he appears to have been a member only for those three years. The Irish class started in 1892, so perhaps it was under the Club that he learned Irish.

The Belfast Gaelic League was begun in 1895 and the Rev. Lyttle was involved. He attended the important meeting held in the Ulster Hall, Belfast, on 10 April 1896. All shades of political and denominational orientation were represented and the Belfast press, without exception, referred in favourable terms to the work being done by the Gaelic League.[11]

The Rev. Lyttle was secretary to the Farmer and Labourers Union and through this he worked hard to improve the conditions of tenant farmers and agricultural labourers.[12]

He happened to be in Bristol when he died, on 22 October 1905, aged only 39 years.[13]

THE ABERDEENS

In 1906 a new Liberal Government was elected and one of the first appointments was Lord Aberdeen (1847–1934), a Presbyterian, as Vice-Roy (Lord-Lieutenant) of Ireland. This finally ended Presbyterian discontent about appointments, which up to then had not been in their favour.[14] By coincidence, it happened that his Chief Secretary for Ireland was also Presbyterian. This was James Bryce, nephew of the Rev. Reuben Bryce who, as we have seen, was once Secretary of the Ulster Gaelic Society. Aberdeen and Bryce, already personal friends, appear to have worked very well together.[15] The 7th Earl of Aberdeen, otherwise Sir John Campbell Hamilton-Gordon, was Lord High Commissioner to the General Assembly of the Church of Scotland from 1881 to 1885 and again in 1915.[16] He had two spells as Lord Lieutenant of Ireland; first from January to July 1886[17] and then from December 1905 to February 1915.

His wife was the Hon. Ishbel Maria Marjoribanks, daughter of the first Baron Tweedmouth. She had Irish connections on her mother's side. One of her uncles was Sir James MacNaghten McGarel-Hogg, of Magheramorne House, Larne, Co. Antrim. The Aberdeens were married in 1877. Lord and Lady Aberdeen arrived in Ireland with their four children, whom they dressed in Irish poplin.[18] In 1905 they visited Belfast to attend the Belfast Civic Union and to receive a presentation made by Sir Hugh Smiley on behalf of Irish Presbyterians.[19] Later in the year they made another visit to Belfast and attended a function in the Presbyterian Assembly Hall where Lady Aberdeen, on behalf of the Presbyterian Church of Ireland, made a presentation to Mr Alexander McDowell in recognition of his outstanding services to the Church.[20] Both Lord and Lady Aberdeen were clearly favourably disposed to the Irish language, and took every opportunity to put it to the fore. When they came to take another title they chose *Temair*, which is the original Irish version of Tara.

Lady Aberdeen edited a journal of health promotion which she had entitled *Sláinte* i.e. Health. Another one of her projects was a travelling caravan which visited the rural areas bringing health information directly to the people. The writing on one side was in English and on the other side in Irish. The medical lecturer, Dr J. O'Connor, was able to give talks in both Irish and in English.

Lord Aberdeen played an important part in having Irish included as an integral part of the intermediate school curriculum. In May 1906, the House of Commons passed a resolution demanding that the Commissioners of Irish Intermediate Education should place Irish on a par with French and German. Yet the Commissioners grimly refused to comply with this direction, on the grounds that it was not '... in the interests of education ...'. Lord Aberdeen, thereupon sent a letter to the Commissioners reminding them '... that their action in passing the resolution of 31st May was inconsistent with the constitutional duty imposed upon them by the Act which estabished the Board'.

He threatened to use his powers of appointment and dismissal. Nevertheless, the Commissioners would not yield. In one of the letters they indicated that, whatever the cost, they would not give in. It was a sharp and long correspondence but, because of the decisiveness and persistence of Lord Aberdeen, the Commissioners finally reconsidered their position and framed rules which reflected the will of the House of Commons, which indeed coincided with the will of the Irish people.[21]

On 18 January 1907, the correspondence was made public and was looked on generally as another victory for the Celtic Revival.

SIR JOHN BYERS (1853–1920)

John William Byers was the son of Rev. John Byers, a Presbyterian missionary. His mother, Margaret Byers (1832–1912), was the Founder and Principal of Victoria College.[22] The young John was born in Shanghai in 1853. For 27 years (1893–1920) he held the Chair of Midwifery at Queen's University, Belfast. He was noted for being a successful practitioner and teacher of his subject, as well as for the numerous papers which he published. He also carried on a long-standing tradition of the Belfast Medical School, in being deeply involved in a wide range of interests outside his own profession. Byers was twice President of the Belfast Literary Society and he was a very interested student of Irish folklife, language and Belfast archaeology.[23] He fought very hard to get the Irish language accepted as a matriculation subject in the medical faculty.[24] In these efforts he was assisted by Samuel Dill, Professor of Greek, and others. Samuel S. McCurry published a collection of local verses[25] and Sir John wrote an extended introduction to it. This consisted mainly of a short treatise of the Ulster dialect, in which he showed a fine knowledge of the subject, including the Irish elements.

He made use of his knowledge of Irish in a pamphlet, entitled, *The Characteristics of the Ulsterman*.[26] First, tracing the early history and legends of the country, he indicated how a great mixture of races resulted from invasion after invasion. He said that even the very name of Ulster was of mixed linguistic origin, because when the Norsemen came they added the termination 'ster' to *Uladh*, the Irish for Ulster and created a name pronounced *Ulla-ster*, later contracted to Ulster. He gave examples of derivation of some surnames and placenames from the Irish language.

In his interest and writings about Ulster speech, Byers had an ear for characteristically unusual means of expression.[27] An example of one of his stories is: A patient said to me at Hospital, in presence of my students, 'I can't stan' on my feet with my head' (i.e., with the severity of a headache). When the time came to celebrate the centenary of the

Rose Young
(Róis Ní Ógáin)
1865–1947

Robert Lynd
1879–1949

Aoidhmín Mac Gréagóir (1884–1950) on left,
next to Seosamh Mac Grianna (1900–1990), the writer,
in Ranafast, Co. Donegal, 1936.
COURTESY OF AN tULTACH AND PÁDRAIG Ó CNÁIMHSÍ

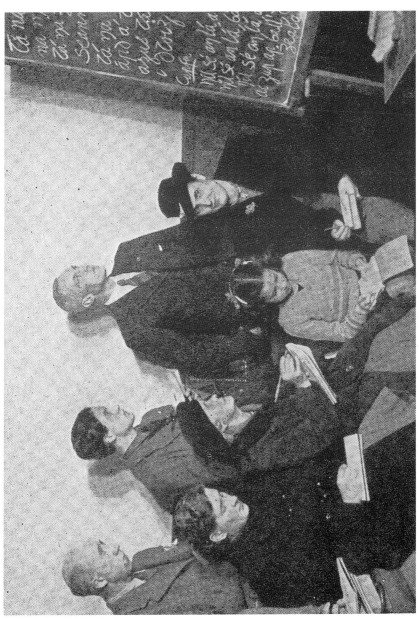

Seán Pasker
taking an Irish
class at the
Y.M.C.A Gaelic
Fellowship.
Behind him
Barry Kinghan and
Liam MacIlherran

Unveiling a plaque to Róis Ní Ógáin, 4 Dec. 1995, Galgorm Castle, Ballymena
LEFT TO RIGHT: Micheál Ó Muircheartaigh, Chairman of Bord na Gaeilge;
Rosemary Lady Brookborough, grand-neice of Róis Ní Ógáin;
Diarmaid Ó Doibhlin and Christopher Brooke

Rev. Patricia McBride, Irish-speaking Presbyterian, and Mr Risteard Ó Glaisne, Methodist preacher, after the first Irish language interdenominational service, St Anne's Cathedral Belfast, 17 November 1995

birth of Sir Samuel Ferguson, Byers took a leading part in the Belfast activities.[28] He died in Belfast on 20 September 1920.

THOMAS WILSON DOUGAN (1852–1907)

Thomas Dougan, son of a Presbyterian minister, was a fluent Irish-speaker.[29] His father, Rev. Mr John Dougan (1817–1861), had the distinction of being the very first minister to Loughmourne, Co. Monaghan, where he was ordained in 1847.[30] His son Thomas, born in 1852, became Professor of Latin in Queen's College, Belfast in 1882 and died in office on 3 June 1907.[31] R.M. Henry, also an Irish-speaker, was in his Department. The latter was a son of the Rev. R.M. Henry, a Baptist minister who later joined the Plymouth Brethern.[32] For many years Dougan's home was at Salernum, No.12, Croft Road, Holywood, where he lived with his wife, Mary Elisabeth (b.c.1863) and mother Sarah Jane Grant (b.c.1835).

THOMAS HAMILTON (1842–1925) B.A.1863, M.A.1864, L.LD 1891.

The Rev. Hamilton, author of a history of Presbyterianisn in Ireland,[33] was very favourably disposed to Irish and supported the Gaelic Revival. Born in Belfast on 28 August 1842, he was a son of the Rev. David Hamilton (1805–1860),[34] the first minister to the York Street Church, and of Eliza Weir of Banbridge. Their son Thomas, who was ordained in 1865,[35] became the third minister in 1874 to serve that church.[36] In 1889 he was appointed President of Queen's College, Belfast and in 1908 he became Vice-Chancellor of the new Queen's University.

In *Celtia* 5, we read that he spoke on the occasion of the first public assembly of the Belfast Queen's College Gaelic Society (Feb. 1908) and that he expressed himself warmly in favour of the Gaelic Revival. Professor R.M. Henry chaired the meeting, attended by a large crowd of graduates and undergraduates, in the Examination Hall. Hamilton, as President of the College,

> ... spoke in keen appreciation of the literary value of the Irish language, expressed regret for the lapse of the Chair of Celtic in the College, hoped that it would now be revived under more auspicious conditions, and assured the Gaelic Society of sympathetic treatment.[37]

The Gaelic Society at Queen's (*Cumann Gaedhealach an Choláiste*), had been formed in January 1906,

> ... with the avowed object of re-establishing Irish as the language of Ireland. It was launched with great enthusiasm, under the patronage of the President of the College, Hamilton, and with a membership of fifty, [was] a good example of that fervent patriotism which T.M. Johnstone observed among the students of his time.[38]

It must be pointed out that, at that time, patriotism for Ireland was perfectly compatible with Unionism and being British and indeed the Rev. Thomas Hamilton was a Unionist in politics.

The minutes of the Gaelic Society, dated 5 November 1913, record that the Rev. Thomas Hamilton, now Vice-Chancellor of the newly formed Queen's University, was elected a patron of the Society along with Lord Castletown; and so it can be seen that his interest in Irish was consistent and enduring. We must assume, however, that like many Unionists, his enthusiasm may have grown cold after the Ard-Fheis (A.G.M.) of the Gaelic League held at Dundalk in July 1915, at which a resolution was passed saying that Irish independence was an aim of the organisation.

Hamilton was the author of *Irish Worthies* (1875), of *History of the Irish Presbyterian Church* (1886), and of *Beyond the Stars* (1888). An interesting photograph of him was published in Fisher and Robb's history of Inst.[39] The Rev. Thomas Hamilton died on the 18 May 1925. The family burying place is at Clifton Street Graveyard, Belfast.[40]

VI B

POST 1915

Despite the Gaelic League's change of policy in 1915 whereby they adopted the political aim of working for Irish independence and despite the Rebellion of 1916 and the eventual partition of Ireland, respect for cultural nationality continued to be a significant, if immeasureable, ingredient of Irish Presbyterianism. This quality was referred to by Eoin Mac Neill is an essay written some time after 1907, in which he said:

> I never knew any native of the Ballymena district or any district in County Antrim to style himself Scotch or to identify himself in any way with Scotch nationality, though in the Braid and north from Ballymena to Cullybackey and the Bush valley the old people speak a purer Scotch dialect than any Scot I have met ... It is a curious thing that the old Irish place-names are better preserved by the Ulster Presbyterians than by many Catholic districts in the country. I never saw any desire in the countryfolk of County Antrim to abandon the old names and invent new ones. The last Irish poet in County Antrim was a Protestant, an uncle of Sir Daniel Dixon.[41]

The poet referred to was John McCambridge, the composer of the beautiful Antrim song *Ard Í Cuain*. His uncle, Sir Daniel Dixon (1844–1907), was Unionist M.P. for North Belfast and Lord Mayor of Belfast.

Apart from the abiding sense of cultural nationality among the people, it is difficult to be more specific about actual numbers of Presbyterians who learned Irish or spoke or otherwise used it. The individuals who are known about come to attention because they were mainly persons of public importance, through their occupation, their writings, or their membership of organisations.

Therefore, the individuals now to be described must, of necessity, be only a fraction of Presbyterians involved with the Irish language. They represent an enduring tradition in their Church of regard for the cultural inheritance of the country.

SIR WILLIAM PORTER MacARTHUR (1884–1964)

D.S.O. (1916), O.B.E. (1919), C.B. (1938), K.C.B. (1939), M.B.,B.Ch. B.A.O. (1908), D.P.H. Oxon (1910), M.D. Belf. (1911), D.T.M&H. Cantab. (1920), Hon D.Sc. Oxon. (1949), M.R.C.P.I. (1911), F.R.C.P.I. (1913), F.R.C.P.(1937).

Sir William MacArthur was a man of many gifts and wide knowledge, a scholar in history and literature, a good teacher and a remarkable lecturer. He was one of the most distinguished medical graduates that Queen's University, Belfast has ever produced.[42] He was born into a Presbyterian family in Belmont, east Belfast. Some time later the family moved to Bangor, where the young William attended Dr Connolly's Intermediate School which, after 1900–1901, became Bangor Grammar School.[43] His father, John Porter MacArthur, a native of Burt, Co. Donegal and later a partner with tea importers in Belfast, died on 28 November 1930. His mother was Margaret Rainey Baird, daughter of Dr William Baird of Donemana, Co. Donegal. She died on 17 November 1936.

On his mother's side (she was called after Margaret Rainey Cooke, the youngest daughter of the Rev. Henry Cooke), William MacArthur was a grand-nephew of the Rev. Josias Leslie Porter, the son-in-law and biographer of the same Dr Henry Cooke (subject of 'The Black Man' statue). The Rev. Porter was President of Queen's College, Belfast from 1879 to 1889[44] and there is a portrait of him in the Great Hall at Queen's University.

The fact that the MacArthurs and the Porters were of Highland descent in Scotland attracted him from his earliest days. He found the opportunity of developing the Gaelic connection on the long summer holidays which his parents spent in Marble Hill, Co. Donegal. There were several pockets of Irish-speakers there and he set out to acquire the language with the persistence which was characteristic of him.[45] The result was that William became proficient in Irish from a very young age. In his teens he spent a long period in Irish-speaking Tory Island. He also made frequent visits, along with his wife and children, to the Cloghaneely Gaeltacht. He spoke and wrote Irish with a strong flavour of that area.

There is a reference to him competing for a prize in Irish proficiency in the Belfast *Feis* of 1902. He was 18 years old at the time and the competition was titled 'Conversation in Irish for students who have studied Books IV and V of O'Growney'. This was the standard and popular grammar at the time. The prize was the Feis Uladh Silver Medal and there were also a number of book prizes.[46] We do not know if he won a prize. It would be surprising if he did not. William, aged 19, entered the Belfast Medical School in October 1903. As a medical student at Queen's, he was already a fluent speaker of the language.[47] He was anxious to get Irish recognised in the College. After Professor John O'Donovan died in 1861, the chair of Celtic was suppressed,[48] and nothing had been done about the language since then. MacArthur knew that part of the problem related to elements in the College who were hostile to the language and so he tried a gradual recruitment of support, in order to get Irish classes started. R.M. Henry, reader in Classics at that time, was one of his staunchest allies. Eventually he and some friends met with the President of the College, the Rev. Thomas Hamilton, in the Michaelmas term of 1905. They found the President most friendly and helpful. He gave them a special room, with a fire which could be lit when needed and furthermore he provided the use of a porter to service the room.[49]

At first there was only one Irish class, but before long there were two, MacArthur teaching the higher level students and a young graduate called Ferran taking the beginners class. The membership of these classes would be mainly Protestant because there were very few Catholics at Queen's at that time, the number being for 1905–06 only 25 out of a total of 403 students.[50] There were even fewer Catholics among the teaching and other staff.

For those who had learned Irish at the classes, and for those who had it already, an outlet was required. This was the basis of the formation of the College Gaelic Society (Cumann Gaedhealach an Choláiste). Although others were involved, William MacArthur is credited with founding the Society. At its first meeting on 30 January 1906, he gave an address which formed the basis for the society's aims.

> ... to assist in the preservation of the Irish Language and its ultimate re-establishment as the language of the country, as Welsh

is of Wales ... . The Society is strictly non-political and non-sectarian. Any member introducing a religious or political subject at any of its meetings shall cease to be a member ... .[51]

There were more than fifty members present, from whom the following officers and committee were elected,

Patron: Rev. Dr Thomas Hamilton, President of the College
President: William MacArthur
Vice-President: Mr.F.P.Ferran, B.A.
Secretary: Charles Dickson
Committee: Miss D. Lynd, B.A., J.L. Lynd, B.A., J.Ferguson, B.A.

The secretary, Charles Dickson, was also a medical student fluent in Irish and in addition a Presbyterian, albeit Non-Subscriber.[52] They became very close friends while students, and continued to correspond in later life.

The Society flourished after that. Nearly two years afterwards it was reported that the number of its members had been steadily growing. The classes in connection with the Society had been very successful and a team sent to the recent Feis at Toome succeeded in winning one of the Language Shields presented for proficiency in Irish.[53] William MacArthur was still the President.

It was decided to hold a public meeting. This took place on 31 January 1908, in the Great Hall. William MacArthur spoke in Irish, as did also T.P. McGinley ('Cú Uladh'). There were speeches in English from Lord Castletown, the Rev. J.O. Hannay (George Bermingham), from Captain Otway-Cuffe and from R.M. Henry, who was now Professor of Latin. On behalf of the Gaelic Society a memorial address was presented to Lord Castletown, who had consented to be a patron.[54] The work of the Gaelic Society in creating a positive atmosphere for Irish at Queen's, apart from direct representation, must have had some influence on the decision to create a lectureship in Celtic. The post was created and filled in the following year.

In 1908 William qualified in medicine from Queen's, which was still, until the following year, a College of the Royal University of Ireland. He continued to be associated with the Gaelic Society, as a Vice-President. However, it is unlikely that he could have attended very often, because he was now launched into a very busy medical career. In 1909, on 30 January, he was commissioned into the Royal Army Medical Corps as a lieutenant and he was seconded for a year in a hospital appointment. He passed the Oxford Diploma in Public Health in 1910 and the M.D. from Queen's, Belfast in 1911. On 30 July of the following year he was promoted Captain.

He served in Mauritius from 1911 to 1914. In 1915 he was posted to the British Expeditionary Force in France where he was on active service until he was wounded in the stomach at the Somme and invalided home in 1916.[55] He was the subject of notable mention at a meeting of the Queen's University Gaelic Society, which took place 5 December 1916. It was recorded in the minutes:

> The Founder of the Society, Captain W.P. MacArthur, R.A.M.C. is to be congratulated upon having had the D.S.O. conferred upon him. He was also mentioned in General French's last despatch.

It was while in Mauritius that he met his wife-to-be, Marie Eugénie Thérèse, third daughter of Louis Ferdinande Antelme, M.D., of Mauritius. They were married in 1914. With special dispensation, the marriage ceremony was conducted by the minister in their own home at Windsor Park, Belfast.[56] They had two sons, Colán, who became a director of the Rank organisation and a writer. Ian, the younger son, was elected a Member of Parliament for Perth in 1959.

The two young boys, growing up in the 1920s, were reared through Irish. Their father, all through his life, retained a deep affection for all things Gaelic and especially the Irish language. He was very aggrieved that it was frequently made something of a political football. Despite the obvious difficulties, MacArthur did everything he could to make sure that his children had Irish as a first language. Mrs MacArthur, who was French-speaking, acquired quite an understanding of and proficiency in Irish after her marriage; and her household in Bedford Park, W.4, always had a couple of Cloghaneely or Rosses girls who were under command to speak nothing but Irish to any member of the family. It was fortunate that William was never too far away from his family while the children were growing up, because, most unusually in the army, he was based during all of this period in London.[57]

However, as Professor of Tropical Medicine with the Royal Army Medical College, a position he held from 1922 to 1929 and again from 1932 to 1934 he had many travelling commitments. The most gruelling one was in 1927 when he did a round-the-world journey for the Army which lasted from May to November. About once a month, he wrote a card to his son Colán, then seven years old. His brother, Ian, was two years old at that time. There were six postcards in all, still extant and they were all completely in Irish. They illustrate both his deep affection for his son and his fondness for Irish. One example may illustrate these points. On 23 July 1927, he wrote from Wei-Hai-Wei, 'via Siberia';

> Seo cuan iontach deas, sléibhte móra thart fá dtaobh dó, cosúil le sléibhte na hÉireann, agus oileán beag amuigh ins an fhairrge go díreach mar bhéadh Innis Bó Finne ann! Tá sé iontach te anseo, ach tá an t-aer tirim, agus cha bhím ag cur alluis i dtolamh, an dóigh a mbím in Shanghai! Daddaí.

In English this means:

> This is a wonderfully nice harbour, circled by great mountains, just like the mountains of Ireland, and there is a little island out in the ocean, just as if it were Innishbofin. It is very hot here, but the air is dry, and I am not always sweating, as I would be in Shanghai! Daddy.

In the twenties, when the children were young, all the holidays were spent in the Cloghaneely Gaeltacht. The young Colán would know immediately the reference to Innishbofin, because he would have seen the island very frequently. He did much thinking about an appropriate name for his first son. What he wanted was a name which would be genuinely Irish, but which would not give too much trouble to English-speakers. So he took advice from the Rev. Fredrick O' Connell, the Church of Ireland canon who from 1909 to 1925 was the lecturer in Celtic at Queen's.[58] O'Connell wrote to him, on 21 April 1920, discussing all the versions of Colin which are recorded in ancient manuscripts, such as the Dean of Lismore's Book, *Annals of Ulster*, *Annals of Tighearnach*, etc. This was how the choice of 'Colán' was made.

All during the twenties MacArthur kept regular contact with Ireland but particularly the Gaeltacht. He had developed the habit of jotting down information in his notebook. One of these, in possession of his son, was being used in the twenties and perhaps earlier. The material is varied. There are children's rhymes, for example the Irish versions of 'Humpty Dumpty', 'The House that Jack Built', 'This Little Pig'. There are numerous notes giving the names of plants and flowers in Irish. There are verses of songs and lists of words and phrases. Of course, he had a special interest in the Irish names for various diseases and complaints, and these are included. He had an ear for the racy and unusual. He has recorded, cúlóg, a pillion passenger; geiseadh, tiny cracks in wood, pottery, etc; teine thona, a phosphorescent light on water, in bogs, etc. There are terms for birds and insects. Two of his informants are mentioned, 'Kate', and 'Canon K'.

There must have been other notebooks because not included in this one are the terms he collected and used for his medical analysis of the diseases prevalent during the Great Famine.[59] In his youth he spoke to many of the Irish-speaking survivors of the Great Famine. One in particular who provided him with many terms was Myles Ferry of Gortahork.[60] His contribution on the medical history of the Irish Famine has not been superseded and it has been said that this great work owed as much to his scrupulous scholarship and mastery of the Irish language as to his incomparable knowledge of the diseases concerned.[61]

The culmination of his busy and successful medical career was in 1939 when he was appointed Director-General of the Army Medical Services, with the rank of lieutenant-general. In the same year he was knighted. He retired from the Army in 1941. He was now aged 57, but he returned to lecturing and doing medical history research. He frequently visited Scotland, Argyll in particular, where he found the Gaelic dialect very similar to his own Donegal Irish. So he was able to converse freely with the country people and to hear their folklore.[62]

In the spring of 1943 the Nuffield Provincial Hospitals Trust appointed Sir William, along with two others (Dr Stanley Barnes and Dr Duncan Leys), as surveyors to make a report on the Hospitals in Northern Ireland. The Report was presented to the Northern Ireland Regional Hospitals Council in the following year[63] and was described as '… the first comprehensive report made on the Northern Hospitals'.[64]

The Queen's University Gaelic Society (Cumann Gaelach) celebrated its golden jubilee in 1956 by publishing a volume titled *Fearsaid*. It was edited by Seán Mac Airt, then lecturer in Celtic and pride of place was given to Sir William as founder of the Society. He himself wrote a valedictory address, in his expressive Donegal Irish, in which he indicated great delight ('– is í ar chuir maise ar mo chroí –') about the progress of the Society. He also, in recounting its history, gave very interesting glimpses into the attitudes and atmosphere of the university fifty years previously. Other articles now provide us with a valuable account of the history and the then current situation of Irish in Belfast.[65] Also in 1956, in October, Sir William presented prizes at Bangor Grammar School, his *alma mater*, on the occasion of the celebration of the School's centenary.[66]

He died at his home in Chiswick on 30 July 1964 and is buried in the Balmoral Graveyard,[67] not far from the tomb of the Rev. Henry Cooke, to whom he was related through his mother.

CHARLES DICKSON (1886–1978)

M.C. (1917), M.D. (1911), D.P.H.(1910), F.R.C.P.I. (1922)

In addition to making a distinguished medical career, Charles Dickson was a notable writer and historian. He belonged to a Non-Subscribing Presbyterian family which had been associated for many years with Dromore, Co. Down.[68] It was there he was born on 20 January 1886, son of John Mitchel Dickson,[69] a linen merchant, who later moved to Holywood, Co. Down.[70] It seems clear that it was his ancestral connections that caused his abiding fascination with history, for his paternal grandmother, Matilda, was a sister of the famous John Mitchel (1815–1875), the Young Irelander.

His grandmother moved to 91 Wilmont Terrace, Belfast, after the death of her husband, Robert Dickson M.D. of Tullycairne, on 17 July 1862, aged only 57. It was in Wilmont Terrace that she died on 3 June 1897.[71] Her grandson Charles was eleven years old at that time, so he would have remembered her quite well. It must be stated, however, that in his historical works, mostly about the 1798 Rebellion, Charles Dickson set himself the task of being completely objective. He fought against the idea that history was a method of reinforcing one's prejudices.[72]

The young Charles was educated locally in Dromore and then in 1897 he went to the Royal Belfast Academical Institution for his second level education.[73] In October 1903 he entered the Belfast Medical School. It was now that he began to be intensely interested in the Irish language.[74] He had become friendly with his fellow medical student, William P. MacArthur, who was already fluent in Irish and this might have been an influence, even though William was an orthodox Presbyterian, while he was heterodox. However, at this time many people were enjoying the glow of the Celtic (Gaelic) Revival. This was not the property of any particular political viewpoint and even the Viceroy of Ireland and his wife, the Aberdeens, were very enthusiastic for all things Gaelic/Celtic.[75]

For whatever reason, it was then that Charles began his many visits to the Donegal Gaeltacht in order to learn and perfect his Irish. He had found friends in the Glenveagh area and every available holiday was spent there. He learned the language rapidly by going out every day with the postman on his rounds and it was agreed that no English whatever would be spoken between them. This process of total immersion meant that before long he was a wholly competent Irish-speaker. Later he went to the Kerry Gaeltacht and, despite some apprehension, found he was well understood.[76]

As a student at Queen's, he was involved, along with William MacArthur, in founding the Gaelic Society. At its first meeting on 30 January 1906 he was elected secretary.[77] In subsequent years he was treasurer. Based on a letter from Dickson, Pádraig Ó Snodaigh suggested that MacArthur, Dickson, and two others were equally responsible for founding the Gaelic Society,[78] but there seems little doubt that MacArthur was the leading light.

Dickson was a brilliant student and when he qualified M.B. in 1908 it was with first class honours and an Exhibition, in addition to coming first in the examination.[79] He was a house officer in the Royal Victoria Hospital during 1900–1910 and then for two years carried out research in the Department of Pathology at Queen's. For this work he was awarded the M.D. in 1911 and he published a paper on the subject in the same year.[80]

Surprisingly, however, he turned his back on laboratory medicine and in 1912 joined the civil service in Dublin. From then until 1923 he was Medical Officer with the National Health Insurance Commissioners, except for an interlude during 1915–1919, when he was a Captain in the Royal Army Medical Corps. He served in France and Belgium[81] and in 1917 was awarded the Military Cross for gallantry. The occasion was when he was in charge of an advanced dressing-station which came under intense bombardment from gas-shells and high explosives. The building was wrecked and his patients in extreme danger from gas and bombs. He took command of the situation and, while out in the open, under heavy fire, he organised a working party to replace the anti-gas screens. While disregarding his own safety, he saved the lives of many of his wounded patients.[82]

On his return to civil life he took up employment once more with National Health Insurance. In 1922 he became a Fellow of the Royal College of Physicians of Ireland and the following year became Chief Medical Officer to the Civil Service.[83] His daughter recounts that he always wore his fáinne (the Irish language badge) at work and that much more Irish than English was spoken in his office.[84] He continued to go back to the Donegal Gaeltacht from time to time.

In 1944 he published his first work on the 1798 Rebellion,[85] and after he retired from the Civil Service in 1954 at the age of 68, he began a new writing career. His second book on 1798 came out in 1955,[86] and the third work in 1960.[87] In 1962 he became editor of the *Irish Journal of Medical Science*. In recognition of his achievements, a rare honour was conferred on him in 1972, the Honorary Fellowship of the Royal Academy of Medicine of Ireland.[88] He had been secretary to that organisation since 1954. He had also been Registrar to the Royal College of Physicians of Ireland since his retirement in 1954.

His wife was Maeve, daughter of Packenham Erskine and they had two daughters Wendy Mary Mitchel[89] who married Norman Odlum, and Barbara. Charles Dickson died on 1 January 1978 at the age of 91. It was said of him in his obituary:

Charles Dickson, in his blending of the best of North and South, in his personality and his courage, in his scholarship and erudition, his military bearing as upright as his character, epitomised what most Irishmen would like to think was typical of the very best our country can produce.[90]

ROSE YOUNG (1865–1947)

Rose Maud Young was known in Irish as Róis Ní Ógáin. She made her reputation in that language with her three-volume set of Irish poetry. She was born on 30 October 1865 in Galgorm Castle, Ballymena, Co. Antrim.[91] Her father, the Right Honourable John Young, P.C. and his wife, Grace Charlotte Savage, had thirteen children, of which Rose was the eighth.[92]

Dr C.F. D'Arcy, Bishop of Armagh, knew her father as a prominent and influential Presbyterian, of whom he said:

> He owed this position (i.e. of influence) largely to a fine dominance of character and also to his handsome and impressive appearance. It was strengthened by the possession of a large family of tall sons and beautiful daughters, all of whom inherited something of their father's gifts.[93]

Killen included the earlier Youngs of Galgorm Castle in his *Biographical Notices of eminent Presbyterian Ministers and Laymen*.

Rose's grand-uncle, James Young, was very active as an elder and in fund-raising for the church. Killen described him as most orthodox in his leanings and a great admirer of Dr Henry Cooke. Her grand-grandfather, William Young (1760–1832) was also an elder. Killen mentioned these Youngs again in his autobiography, indicating that he had a high regard for the family. His own father was a fellow worshipper, with a grand-uncle of Rose's father, called Alexander Brown. At that time there was only one congregation in Ballymena.[94]

Apparently, it was Bishop William Reeves who stimulated Rose to study Irish.[95] She became friendly afterwards with other Protestant women who were interested in the language, such as Margaret Hutton, Ada McNeill and Margaret Dobbs.

She lived in Dublin for a while and got to know many who were active in Irish language circles, such as Osborn Bergin, Thomas O'Rahilly, Patrick Dineen and Douglas Hyde. It seems to be the latter two who encouraged

her to compile and edit her great collection of Irish poetry[96] the first
volume of which was published in 1921.[97] It had the secondary title of
Cnuasacht de na Sean-Amhránaibh is áilne agus is mó Clú (i.e. A Collection
of the most beautiful and most famous old Songs). Douglas Hyde wrote
the preface. He praised her industry and her choice of songs. In her
acknowledgements section, where her address was given as Cushendun
(Bun Abhann Duinne), she thanked Douglas Hyde for reading the
manuscript. Her notes to the songs are copious and interesting. In the song
'Thugamar féin an Samhradh linn' ('We ourselves brought summer with
us'), she had added the second verse, which she had herself taken down
from old Mrs Hamilton in Cushendun, Co. Antrim. In other words, she
had set out to save at least some Ulster Irish by noting down songs and
poems, at a time when the language was still spoken widely in the Glens of
Antrim. She had a number of references to Co.Tyrone Irish, as well.

The second volume came out in 1924,[98] with the supplementary
title of *Amhráin agus Dánta do scríobh Filidhe do mhair idir 1600 agus
1800.* (*Songs and Poems written by Poets who lived between 1600 and
1800*). In the preface, Douglas Hyde commended the way the editor
leads the reader through the years. He applauded the fact that every
single poem out of the 58 in this book was given a commentary with
biographical details of the poet. In addition he pointed out that she
had provided a most useful vocabulary.

Certainly, her notes reflect extensive research and are a great help in
reading her poems. For poem number eight, she explains that a mother
asked the great poet Eoghan Ruadh Ó Súilleabháin (1748–1784) to
baby-sit her infant. He composed an *extempore* lullaby to soothe her
baby to sleep. Rose Young in her commentary said:

> In this poem, (i.e. An Seóthó), Eoghan soothes his child with the
> promise of every precious thing belonging to his noble ancestry and
> the Gaelic race: Cuchullainn's magic spear which slew Feardia and
> Conlaoch; Naoise's white shield, Oscar's helmet, and the spear Angus
> Óg gave to Diarmaid when he fled with Gráinne from the Fianna ... .

Considering her Protestant background, she must have had
particular interest in editing the poem called *An Bonnaire Fiadh-
phuic Fáin* (*The Sturdy Runner*), which refers to the flight of King

James after the Battle of the Boyne. She commented:

> ... it speaks with bitter contempt of the King, the wandering stag', the sturdy runner', that 'leapt the boundary with a rush,' that forsook his haunt, refused the fight, and cleared out of his enemy's path, leaving the herd to its fate.

The third volume was subtitled (here translated) *Historic Poems, Religious Poems, the Lays of Ossian, the Three Sorrows of Storytelling, and others*.[99] This last volume was published in 1930.[100] This time each of the 53 poems was accompanied by an English translation. It is quite clear how many of these were translated by herself, for in each case the name of the translator is given. Those with no name, 39 all together, were done by Rose. There is no doubt about her excellent proficiency in the language. Many of these poems add a unique dimension in the full understanding of the history of Ireland and Rose noted that some had been used by Curtis in his History of the country.

She dwelt at length on poem number eight, *Brian na Múrtha* (*Brian of the Razings*). This was Brian Ó Ruairc who was a nobleman and Lord of Breifny O'Rorke (South Leitrim and North Cavan). He was knighted by Sidney in 1567, but he persisted in opposing English control and was brought to London on 3 November 1591. The use of an interpreter was necessary, because he understood not a word of the English language. Nevertheless, he was hanged at Tyburn. Miss Young describes the scene of the trial as reported by Standish O'Grady:

> He stood erect with his hat on and spoke in Latin. 'Why don't you kneel?' asked one of the Council. 'I am not so used.' 'Are you not used to kneel before pictures?' 'Yes, of God's saints, between whom and you there is much difference.

Miss Young continued: 'Sir Henry Sidney said of him he was the proudest man with whom he had to do in his time'.

This third volume of Irish poetry shows Miss Young to be in very assured control of her material and it is clear from this source alone that she was not only completely comfortable in modern Irish, but that she was an authority in the old texts and in the interpretation of older manuscripts.

It was said by one critic: no better work in the way of anthology has been done and the minor faults inseparable from a work of this kind must be forgiven.[101]

Fr Larry Murray, writing in *An tUltach*, also praised her anthology (here translated):Ever since the first volume of this verse anthology was published, the whole work has been praised, not surprisingly.[102]

According to Liam McGrattan, the writer and broadcaster who knew Rose well, she continued with her anthology, but nothing further was published.[103] A new edition of her poetry collection, edited by Diarmaid Ó Doibhlin, was launched at Galgorm Castle, Ballymena, by Rosemary, Lady Brookeborough on 5 December 1995. Rose had an interest in the Irish of Rathlin Island and wrote an article in which she analysed the surnames, placenames and the type of Irish spoken. Her conclusion was that there was a strong Scottish influence on the island. The article was mostly in English and she signed herself, 'Rose M. Young, Galgorm Castle, Co. Antrim'.[104] Rose also wrote an article on how Irish piety is demonstrated in the everyday spoken language.[105]

For the last sixteen years of her life she lived with her friend Margaret Dobbs, also an Irish-speaker, at Portnagolan, Cushendun, where she died on 28 May 1947. She is buried in the family burial ground at Ahoghill.[106] The Youngs of Galgorm Castle were a strongly Unionist family. Rose's eldest brother, William Robert Young (1856–1933), by occupation a linen merchant, was made a Privy Councillor by King George V, when he came to open the first Parliament for Northern Ireland.[107] He was a Chairman of the Mid-Antrim Unionist Association. He was grandfather of Rosemary, Lady Brookeborough.

Another brother of Rose's, Henry George Young, had a distinguished career as a soldier, retiring with the rank of Colonel and Honorary Brigadier-General in 1921. For the next thirty years he was Sergeant-at-Arms for the Parliament of Northern Ireland.[108] Her youngest brother, George Charles Gillespie Young, was a Unionist M.P. at Stormont and declared his recreational interests in *Who's Who* as '... Politics, Orangeism and the Special Constabulary'.[109]

Rose Young can be counted among the many young women of her class, at the end of the last century, who found that Irish language and culture was a way of asserting their own independence and of resisting the mould that had been made for them as women. Her friend Margaret Dobbs is another example.

ROBERT LYND (1879–1949)

Robert Wilson Lynd, the famous essayist, son of a Belfast Presbyterian clergyman, was devoted to the Irish language. Indeed, in September 1904, he first met his wife-to-be, Sylvia Dryhurst, a Dublin girl then aged sixteen, when they both were members of the Gaelic League in London and went to the Irish classes in Oxford Street.[110] They married in 1909 and their children, Sighle, born 1910, and Máire, born 1912, were reared speaking Irish.[111] Robert's sisters were also members of the London Gaelic League and were friendly with fellow member Mabel McConnell, daughter of John McConnell, Managing Director of Dunville's Whiskey and associate of James Craig.

Mabel McConnell had been a member of the Gaelic Society at Queen's in Belfast. It was at the Gaelic League in London that she met Desmond Fitzgerald, her future husband. One of their children is Garret Fitzgerald, former Taoiseach of the Irish Republic. He, in his autobiography, speaks with great respect of the close friendship of his mother with the Lynd girls.[112] One of these girls married Alec Foster, headmaster of Belfast Royal Academy, and another, Ina, married Bill Lowry, father of Chief Justice Lowry. Laura married Dr R.M. Jones, head of Inst.[113]

Robert's father, the Rev. Robert John Lynd (1833–1906), born in Greenfield near Coleraine,[114] was a pupil of the Rev. Reuben John Bryce co-secretary to the Ulster Gaelic Society and President of the Belfast Royal Academy. Dr Lynd was a strong believer in the Union with Great Britain and turned against Gladstone when the Home Rule Bill was introduced.

This Rev. Lynd took a major part in organising the commemoration of the centenary of the birth of Henry Cooke. His speech on 11 May 1888 was printed in the centenary volume, and ended with the verse,

'Stand together! work and pray;
Soon will break the glorious day!
Great Cooke's memory would say –
Ulstermen, be true!'[115]

His son Robert Lynd, although taking a very different course in life, was not all that different in temperament. Despite having achieved great fame in London as an essayist, his heart was always at home in his native Ireland.

He was born on 20 April 1879, in the Berry Street manse in Brookvale Avenue, the second of seven children of Dr Lynd and Sarah Rentoul. At the age of nine he won a prize for an essay which he submitted to *The Witness*. He was educated at the Royal Belfast Academical Institution (Inst) and Queen's College (later Queen's University), Belfast, where he graduated B.A. in 1899. In 1901 he went to London where he began a career as a journalist and essayist. For a time he shared a studio with Paul Henry the painter.

He sometimes wrote under the pseudonym of 'Brian Donn' (Brown Brian) and he published an essay under this name in *Guth na nGaedheal*, an occasional bi-lingual magazine published by the Gaelic League in London, in the March 1906 issue.[116] He compared Ireland to a kind of Cinderella with her garb (nationality) in tatters. He defined nationality as the personality and enduring soul of a nation. He said that Ireland's nationality was in semi-permanent eclipse. Her problem was denationalisation or, in other words, Anglicisation. His solution was the Irish language.

> Some people say that we are reviving the Irish language out of hatred of England. They might as well accuse a man who was trying to save his soul of doing it so to spite a neighbour ... Ireland may either become an imitation county of England – 'Irelandshire' in the bitterly significant phrase of Dr Hyde – or she may enter into the family of nations with a distinctive literature and music and industrial life of her own.

As we are now entering more fully into the life of a greater Europe, Lynd's words sound as though they are addressed specifically to that debate. He went on to say:

> In the former eventuality, (i.e. 'Irelandshire'), we shall go from worse to worse, becoming even more stagnant than we are and shall make an inglorious exit from existence, like the Red Indians, in presence of a more determined race ... If we aim, on the other hand, at taking our place among the nations, we must before all else, set to restoring the Irish language as the universal speech of the people. A national

language is like a wall of defence, strong to keep out foreign influences that are evil and containing plenty of openings through which may pass all such influences which are healthy and useful to the garrison within. Only behind such a wall can we develop our national capacities, the soul which makes us beautifully distinct from the other nations. In other words, the national language is the first condition that makes what we may call the 'home life' of a nation possible. Only by leading such a home life can we become noble sons and daughters of Ireland and, afterwards, useful citizens of the large world.

In an article in *Uladh*, September 1905, he signed himself as Riobárd Ó Fhloinn. In this essay he made a plea for Ulster people to speak out and express their views.[117] He had this to say about moderation:

Moderation is a very fine thing in its way and so is common sense ... Moderation in Ulster, however, too often spells moral and intellectual anaemia ... The moderate Ulsterman is supposed to be he who never so much as budges towards any patriotic goal at all, but sits in his chair and sneers or sniggers at all who believe in ideals and break through custom.

He went on to explain this parodox:

Your ideals are all very fine and noble', says your practical hard-headed Ulsterman, 'but to accomplish them is out of the question. Give them up and marry a decent, homely girl, and you may one day become an elder, and have a house in Windsor Avenue. ...' In reality it means, 'Let the community go to the devil, so long as you get plenty of plums from the pie and are guaranteed thoroughly respectable by your jealous neighbours.

Lynd clearly held his views very strongly, and further explained his analysis:

These people have resolved to laugh at the puerile notion of reviving the Irish language, to fling witty sneers at old men who paint their names on their carts in Irish and are willing to go to gaol for it and to express their disgust at the behaviour of Gaelic Leaguers who worry shopkeepers by insisting upon having Irish goods and who embarrass the Post Office by addressing their letters and parcels in the national tongue ... . Your moderate men have no passions except for peace and respectability ... . I prefer a thousand times the furious bigotries of Sandy Row and Smithfield ... . Here you have passion and for passionate men there is always a door of hope.

Among the essays he has written under his own name, there are many references to Irish and even snatches of the language here and there. In *The Driver*,[118] he and a friend had visited an Irish-speaking small town in the West. The driver of their side car brought them to hear a fiddler and Lynd spoke to him in Irish, starting off with 'Is dócha go bhfuil Gaedhilg agat?' (I suppose you speak Irish); then the conversation continued on in that language.

In his *Ireland a Nation*, Lynd devoted a section to literature in Irish, which began: The wealth of literature which Ireland has produced in Gaelic is as amazing almost as the poverty of the literature she had produced in English until last century.[119]

His *Home Life in Ireland*, was a social commentary on all aspects of the country. As we would expect, the Irish language received much attention. In the Preface he criticised those who suggest that Irish belongs only to a section of the Irish people.

> Just as Broadbent, in *John Bull's Other Island*, speaks of the Bible as an essential Protestant document, so a number of people talk of Gaelic as though it were a peculiarly Catholic possession. As a matter of fact, Irish is a national possession which the Protestant and Presbyterian inhabitants of the country inherit through their ancestors as surely as they inherit their share of Irish air and soil. Irish is a part of the traditional atmosphere of Ireland. In support of this view, Dr Douglas Hyde, Professor of Irish in the National University, referred some time ago to the language 'as it was spoken one hundred years ago, right up to the gates of Dublin; and in fact by all Ireland, even the descendants of the Elizabethans and Cromwellians, including even the Lowland Scotchmen in North-East Ulster, who I may mention in passing, were habitual Gaelic speakers, though the bulk of them came from Galloway and Ayreshire.' Indeed, he added, 'almost the only non-Irish-speaking population in Ireland were the children of a small body of planters who came from England, and settled in South Ulster, in parts of Armagh, Tyrone, and, perhaps in spots of Fermanagh'. An exaggeration, perhaps, but we know that in one Presbyterian church, within a short distance of Belfast, sermons in Irish used frequently to be delivered towards the close of the eighteenth century ... . Had the Protestant Church of Ireland lived in the spirit of the great Bishop Bedell, who had the Bible translated into Irish in the seventeenth century and had the Presbyterians realised the

truth of the Rev. Norman McLeod of Campsie's remarks about Irish two hundred years later, non-Catholic Ireland might have been Irish-speaking today. 'I am more convinced than ever', wrote Dr McLeod in The Orthodox Presbyterian for November 1833, 'that the Irish language is the key, the very key, to the Irish heart.'[120]

In the section on 'Schools and Children', Lynd was very critical of the National Schools system, with its policy of ignoring everything Irish, especially the language. Even in districts where Irish was the only language spoken, the children were taught that English and not Irish was their native language.

> In many places, teacher, priest and parent combined with the authorities in stamping out all knowledge of the native language from the minds of the children. The children were forbidden to speak any Irish in the schools and they carried little tally-sticks hung round their necks so that, every time they lapsed into Irish in their homes, their parents might cut a notch in these and the teacher might award as many strokes of the cane as he found notches in the tally-stick on the next morning. It is difficult to forgive a generation of parents, priests, politicians and teachers who thus flogged the children of the country out of the knowledge of their natural speech.[121]

However, he saw signs of hope. He noted that the number of bi-lingual schools, which were only in the Gaeltacht areas, had increased to 174, from 126 in the previous year (1908). St Enda's School in Dublin had started recently and taught partly in Irish and partly in English. He had visited this school recently and found that all the staff were Irish-speaking except the cook.[122]

In his discussion about the Catholic clergy (p. 136), he praised those patriotic priests who were courageous enough to oppose their bishops when the bishops opposed the interest of Ireland.

> During the present year, for instance, the Standing Committee of the Bishops declared publicly against making Irish an essential subject for matriculation and the first year's examination in the new National University. Some of them even forbade the clergy in their dioceses to do, speak, or write anything in favour of giving the Irish language this prominence in the University curriculum. Where ever the discipline of the Church permitted them, priests have none the less been found to come forward side by side with Catholic and Protestant laymen to

insist that Irish be given its due place in the University, or that the University must get no help or sanction from the Irish people. Father Ó Ciaráin, P.P., for instance, told the people of Castleblayney Feis that 'the Bishops of Ireland had as good a right to come into his garden and tell him to dibble his cabbage-plants head downwards as they had to tell the whole Irish nation that they would not tolerate any essential Irish in the new University.[123]

At the same time, Lynd pointed out that many of the priests were not enlightened either and he quoted the instance of a priest in a midland county who,

... denounced the Gaelic League for holding mixed classes of boys and girls. His insults to the Gaelic Leaguers from the altar outraged the sense of decency of one of them to such a degree that he rose in the chapel during the service and challenged the truth of the priest's words. Of course, there was a great scandal. But the sympathies of all that was best in Catholic Ireland were with the Gaelic Leaguer and the priest's 'Damn the Gaelic League!' has become historic.

In the same book he had praise for those of the gentry who had supported Irish, and he named examples.

All intelligent Irishmen know of the splendid work done in Kilkenny by Captain Otway Cuffe, brother of the Earl of Desart. Kilkenny has now a woollen mill, a furniture industry and a little national theatre, and Captain Cuffe has lately been standing on Gaelic League platforms, speaking in support of essential Irish in the National University ... Lord Castletown passionately advocates the revival of the Irish language ... . The Bishop of Clogher has urged the people of his church to establish a kind of Protestant Gaelic League.[124]

So it is quite clear that Lynd was a very strong supporter of the revival and use of Irish, but was he himself fluent in the language? He had begun to learn Irish at the Gaelic League classes in London, in 1904. Five years later he said of himself in *Home Life in Ireland*,

Irish literature in the Irish language is a subject which I will not discuss at length, because Irish is unfortunately a language of which I can as yet make but a limping and stammering use.[125]

Yet he seems, at this time, to have understood the language very well, as shown in *The Driver*. His speech in Irish was probably halting; but, although his ability to write was probably limited, anything he wrote in Irish was always very correct. His facility with Irish must have subsequently improved and have been quite adequate to be able to raise his children in the language. His daughter, Mrs Máire Gaster, who was interviewed on the occasion of the centenary of her father's birth, said that her father started his interest in Irish when he was still in Belfast, where there was a thriving branch of the Gaelic League. She said that later on Lynd taught Irish at Gaelic League classes in St Andrew's Hall in London. Apparently one of his pupils was Aodh de Blacam. Máire also informed Patrick Scott:

> My father attended the Irish summer schools at Gortahork, Donegal, and taught his friend Roger Casement, who admired his spoken fluent Irish ... Irish was spoken in our home, and our birth names were registered in Irish, and until we were three years old, we understood only Irish.[126]

Lynd died on 6 October 1949 and was buried in his native Belfast, at the City Cemetery. The funeral service was conducted by the Right Rev. Dr Wylie Blue of May Street Presbyterian Church, the Rev. Frazer Hurst and the Rev. Professor James Haire.[127]

HUGH WALTER GASTON MACMILLAN (1884–1950) (ALIAS AOIDHMÍN MAC GRÉAGÓIR)

In a letter to the Irish language monthly journal *An tUltach*[128] Maurice Drinan, the Irish scholar, wrote the following (here translated into English):

> Twenty five years ago I knew a Presbyterian here in Belfast ... He was a fluent Irish-speaker and had a special interest in Co. Antrim and in Scottish Gaelic. He spent many long years jotting down stories in Irish. A friend of his told me that he had a great amount of filled copy books but that when he died his relations got rid of them all! No doubt they felt that only someone who was odd would be interested in the like of this.

He was referring to Hugh Walter Gaston MacMillan, who was known publicly and to Irish-language society only by the name of Aoidhmín Mac Gréagóir (*anglice* Eamon Mac Gregor). Indeed his private name and full account of his life has only recently come to light through the diligent research of Dr Kieran Devine, computer science lecturer in Queen's University.[129]

His father, Hugh Wallace MacMillan M.D. was born c. 1850, son of John MacMillan, farmer of a 36 acre holding in Ballyrainey, parish of Dundonald, Co. Down. The father qualified M.D. from the Queen's University of Ireland and first practised medicine in Macclesfield, England until about 1877. From around 1883 he lived at Penistone, Sheffield.[130] Thereafter, he lived in Barnsley, Yorkshire[131] and that is how Hugh junior (Aoidhmín) came to be born in that town. The date was 16 February 1884. The family came back to Ireland about 1889,[132] and Dr MacMillan practised at 218 Newtownards Road, until his accidental death on 22 October 1890.

It is not known for certain how Aoidhmín learned Irish and Gaelic, but there is some evidence to indicate that after his father's death, when he was only six years old, he was fostered by a native speaker who was one of the seannachies providing material for Aoidhmín's book *Sgealtan X Rachreann* referred to later.[133]

By 1900, Aoidhmín was back in Belfast and he was recorded as teaching Irish in Ballymacarrett.[134] The 1901 census return[135] shows Aodhmhín living with his mother and sister at 243 Albertbridge Road, Belfast. He was described as 'a scholar who could speak both Irish and English.' After his mother died in 1903,[136] he moved into lodgings with a Mrs Sarah Megarry of 5 Harrow Street, whose husband Thomas was a stone-cutter. By now Aoidhmín was a medical student at Queen's College, Belfast. His mother left a substantial sum of money in her will but he did not come into his inheritance until 1908.[137] He left the Harrow Street digs, discontinued his unsuccessful career as a medical student and took up residence as 24 Legann Street, where in 1911 he is described as a writer and a gentleman.[138]

His first publication was in 1906, *Fréamhacha na hÉireann* (*Irish Roots*).[139] Included was a poem of his own and eight stories he had collected from different story tellers on Inis Meáin, the middle of the three Aran Islands. Each story is accompanied by an illustration made by Seaghan Mac Cathmhaoil (John P. Campbell), the Celtic Revival artist, who also designed the title page.

Aoidhmín's next book was in 1910 when he published his stories from Rathlin (*Sgéaltan X Rachreann*).[140] According to O'Rahilly,[141] the language of Rathlin is essentially a dialect of Scottish Gaelic and Holmer, who made a special study of the language,[142] said that it is a characteristic specimen of Gaelic of the Scottish type.

A second edition of the Rathlin stories has been recently published[143] and the text, which remains unaltered, except for the use of Roman instead of Gaelic script, is once more available for study of this unique form of Irish. Furthermore these stories have now been translated into English.[144] Mac Gréagóir's ability to handle this material faithfully shows his great facility with Scottish Gaelic as well as Irish. If, as previously suggested, he had spent much of his youth on Rathlin, this would go some way to explaining his proficiency. Devine[145] suggests that Aoidhmín learned Scottish Gaelic in Glasgow, in the course of his many visits to Scotland.

In the succeeding years Aoidhmín published much of the Irish language poems and songs that he had collected in the Irish-speaking areas (Gaeltachtaí). Many of these and his letters in Irish were published in *An Claidheamh Solais*. He also published a lot of his collected material in *An tUltach*, the Ulster Irish language monthly which began in January 1924, and is still regularly published.

Dinneen's *Dictionary*, first published in 1927[146] includes many words from Antrim and Rathlin. Practically all of these were taken from a list provided by Aoidhmín. For example, on p.107, we find the entry 'boillsceannach, a. middle; An Bóthar Boillsceananach, name of middle road running down Glenariff (Antr.)'. On p.170 it is stated that in Antrim 'cathair', can mean a cathedral and on p.169 it is recorded that 'cathail' in Rathlin means a gap. By diligent searching it would be possible to reconstruct Aoidhmín's list.

For most of his life (1908–1950) his residence was 24 Legann Street, in Ballysillan. He led a dual existence, once under the pseudonym of Aoidhmín Mac Gréagóir, who was personally well known in the Gaeltacht and in Irish language circles[147] and through his publications as a poet in Irish and a collector of Irish lore and verse. He regularly visited the Rosses in Co. Donegal and a photograph published recently[148] shows him in Ranafast, sitting next to Seosamh Mac Grianna, one of the finest of modern Irish writers.

His other existence was as Hugh Mac Millan, resident of Ballysillan, and regarded as a mildly eccentric neighbour. Those living in the same street called him 'the millionaire', because he had no gainful occupation, yet always seemed to be able to cope. Aoidhmín's talents were many and diverse. He was an accomplished artist and provided a lively drawing of a leaping fish for a book of fishing stories in Irish written by P.T. MacGinley (Cú Uladh).[149] Indeed, he was an excellent angler himself and the *Ireland's Saturday Night* of 18 April 1914 published a picture of him on the occasion of his winning the Pickwick Silver Cup and the first prize of trout fishing at Rathkenny, Cloughwater.

He died in the Royal Victoria Hospital on 14 March 1950. His death entry described him as a person of independent means, aged 66 years. He was buried in the Dundonald Cemetery, in section F3, under a stone marked Lecky.

ERNEST BLYTHE (1889–1975)

Earnán de Blaghd, as he was called in Irish, was born of a Church of Ireland father and a Presbyterian mother in Magheragall near Lisburn. His life-long interest in Irish began as a boy when he discovered that the first language of servant girls on their farm was Irish and not English. The homes of these girls were in Newry and South Armagh.[150]

He also discovered that he had Presbyterian relatives in the Castlewellan area who were native Irish-speakers. In his autobiography, he gives this account. (Here translated).

> My mother increased the interest in Irish that Mary O'Hanlon had awakened in me. She told me that, when she was a young girl, there was a custom, when the Presbyterians were having a party in the school, of putting up the words 'Céad Míle Fáilte', written ornately, somewhere on the wall. Everybody knew what it meant. In addition, my mother told me a story which she heard from her grandmother. One of my mother's male relatives came from a place near Castlewellan on a visit, around the beginning of the nineteenth century. He spoke broken English, because his normal language in the southern home was Irish, and as my mother heard, they would mock him behind his back, because of the strange sentences he spoke. He was a Presbyterian, just like his northern relations.'[151]

Having learned Irish in Dublin from Sinéad Flanagan, later to marry Eamon De Valera, and from Sean O'Casey, the playwright, he became completely fluent in the language after a sojourn in the Kerry Gaeltacht. He later evolved as a significant writer in Irish.

The Irish language was his first love and his other activities, as an important politician, including being a cabinet minister in the Cosgrave government, and as theatre manager, were secondary. Many, especially politicans, find Irish useful for other ends, but for Blythe Irish was an end in itself. One of his monumental achievements, as a cabinet minister, was the foundation of *An Gúm*, the government publishing house for the printing of hundreds of books in Irish, many of them translations from English and other languages including German, French and Russian. The first books came out in 1928.

For 26 years he was the managing director of the Abbey Theatre in Dublin. He was accused of hiring players more for their knowledge of Irish than their acting ability,[152] but his achievements in drama were later better appreciated.[153] Always on his agenda was the promotion of plays in Irish. He encouraged Mac Liammóir and Edwards to found *Taibhdhearc na Gaillimhe*, the Galway Irish-language theatre, which opened in 1928.

He was very keen on making sure that Irish was suitable for contemporary life. Tomás Mac Anna recounted:

> I first heard of him when a dedicated Christian Brother in Dundalk, striving valiantly to have us write Irish in the Roman rather than the ornate Elizabethan print, told us that a certain Earnán de Blaghd had introduced all those 'h's to modernise the language, the only man, he insisted, who had ever done anything for Irish, even though he was a Protestant, and an Ulster one to boot.[154]

He wrote his autobiography in Irish, three volumes in all.[155] He also wrote a book in Irish about Partition. True to his political philosophy, in the Preface he said (here translated):

> Partition exists because the Protestants of the country have demanded it, especially the Northern Protestants. Never will England, or any other power, exert violence on Northern Unionists to force them to join the Republic against their will. If it is not possible to persuade a few hundred thousand Protestants that they should vote for a reunified Ireland, the Border will never go. We will never change the

attitude of Unionists by threat, by derision or by harassment. Protestants demanded Partition on their own accord, not because Englishmen asked for it or advised it, or for the sake of England. At the beginning of this century, they were all, except perhaps one in a thousand, against Home Rule for Ireland; and this was because the Catholics of Ireland had led them to believe, by the way that they had deserted the Irish language and their ancestral traditions, that it was not for a national objective that they strived to relax the grip of England, but solely in the interests of the Roman Catholic Church.[156]

Blythe was highly critical of Daniel O'Connell, who was seen by him as someone only concerned with a sectional interest and who by discarding cultural Irish traditions, aligned himself with such as Cardinal Cullen who, in so far as he was interested in the subject, defined Irishness simply as Roman Catholicism with a strong Italian slant. Blythe, being a Northern Protestant himself, understood perfectly the Unionist position. No Unionist could have put his position more succinctly than the above.

Ernest Blythe wrote a regular column in the weekly newspaper *Inniu*, until almost before his death, under the appropriate pen-name of *Beann Mhadagáin* i.e. Cave Hill. His regularly recurrent theme was that, to persuade Unionists that they should re-join with the rest of Ireland, it was essential that they should be offered a common Irish identity, demonstrated principally through the Irish language, a proof that culture and not religion was the distinguishing feature of an Irish person.

He married Annie McHugh in 1919 and they had one child, Earnán.[157] Ernest Blythe died on 23 February 1975. A film about his life, *The Man from Magheragall*, was broadcast from Northern Ireland B.B.C. Television in the following June.

THE GAELIC FELLOWSHIP (CITY Y.M.C.A.)

The Fellowship was founded in the late 1940s by John (Seán) Pasker (1903–1965), a Presbyterian civil servant, of 15 Indiana Avenue, Belfast, with the object of, '... studying the Gaelic, music, etc., and to provide a means whereby the Protestants who are interested in these subjects may became acquainted'.

The prospectus also stated that the Fellowship was strictly non-political, and '... membership is limited to persons who are in agreement with the ideals of the Y.M.C.A. and who know, or would like to learn, Gaelic.'[158]

Meetings of *An Caidreamh Gaelach*, as it was called in Irish, were held every Thursday evening from 7.00 to 10.00 in the Committee Room, Third Floor, of the Y.M.C.A. Building at 12 Wellington Place in Belfast. Among the members from time to time were Isabel MacWilliams (née Rolleston) of 86 Wynchurch Park, who was secretary to the group, Bertha Ellison, Barry Kinghan, Bertha Geddis, Liam MacIlherran, Drew Donaldson, the railway enthusiast of 116 Lisburn Road and two daughters of John Sloan, after whom Sloan Street in Lurgan is named. These were Winnie and Florence Sloan. Their brother George, who was a doctor in Airedale, Yorkshire, called his house 'Tieve Tara'. His daughter Angela qualified in medicine from Queen's University. Most of the members were Presbyterian, but other Protestants were also welcome. For example, Pasker wrote a letter to the *Church of Ireland Gazette* to make this point, and he also reminded the readers that thousands of Protestants in Scotland were Gaelic-speaking.[159]

In an historical account of the Belfast Y.M.C.A., there is a photograph of some of the members of the Fellowship taking part in an Irish class, led by Seán Pasker.[160] In 1965 there were ten students in the beginners class and four in the advanced class.[161] In addition there were music and dancing classes. Although a Dubliner by birth, (b. 26 July 1903) Seán Pasker learned Irish while a civil servant in London. He came to Belfast in 1935 and two years later started an Irish class at Clarence Place Hall and afterwards in the Hall of the National Society for the Prevention of Cruelty to Children. At the outbreak of the Second World War he was transferred to Cookstown where he began an Irish class. At the end of the war he came back to Belfast and again started an Irish class, this time in the Presbyterian Hostel. The beginning of the Y.M.C.A. class at 12 Wellington Place was when he, as a member of the Y.M.C.A. choir, asked for a room to teach Irish. This was given and he set out with missionary zeal to speak to his fellow Protestants, reminding them that the language and the culture of Ireland were their's also. He distinguished between cultural nationality and political nationalism. He himself was an excellent singer and good violinist.[162]

Every year he went on holidays to the Donegal Gaeltacht, cycling, fishing and improving his Irish vocabulary.[163] His fellow Protestant, Risteárd Ó Glaisne, gave a picture of him as (here translated):

> ... a man in a well-cut tweed coat, a pipe in his mouth, with an attractive smile, good-looking, with a high forehead and a well covered head of silver grey hair, and an athletic figure.

His ambition was to help towards healing ancient wounds and if he had been a part of a more understanding society, his efforts would doubtlessly have been recognised by official honours. The Irish language community, however, was very appreciative of his courage and of the importance of his valuable work.

On 19 September 1965, he was out fishing in Gweedore when he suffered a heart attack. He was taken home and died in hospital in Belfast. The funeral service took place in the Presbyterian Church in Blackrock and he was buried in the Mount Jerome Cemetery. His death was sorely lamented by lovers of the language everywhere.

His work in the Fellowship was carried on by Isabel MacWilliams, until the next year, when it came to a close.[164] Ó Glaisne summaried the events as follows (Translated):

> Seán Pasker and the Gaelic Fellowship proved, during some twenty years, how much a group of Northern Protestants could do about Irish on their own, without feeling uncomfortable with Irish-speaking Roman Catholics.[165]

Eibhlín Ní Bhriain was told by a friend of Pasker's that he had done the work of a hundred men in giving back to Ulster Protestants their heritage.[166]

ANDREW VICTOR HENDERSON (d. 1980)

For over thirty years the Rev. Victor Henderson was a faithful and highly-regarded pastor in Rostrevor, Co. Down. Licensed in Cavan in 1940, he was ordained on 21 April 1942.[167]

He died on 19 January 1980. He had been attending local Irish classes right up to the time of his death. Indeed, along with others interested in Irish in the town, he appeared on 'Scene around Six', the B.B.C. television programme, and made a big impression with his sincerity. Rostrevor Presbyterian Meeting-house was overflowing at his funeral service. The whole town, which is 90 per cent Catholic, turned out to mourn him and it was said that there were more priests present than ministers.[168]

VI C

THE PRESENT DAY

Results of the 1991 census are now available showing that 142,000 persons in Northern Ireland have a facility with Irish.[169] The second of two reports, referred to later in the Appendix, shows a breakdown at this figure by religion and other factors. The total number of Irish-speaking Presbyterians, 1,614, is not very large but it nevertheless includes many individuals well known for their involvement with the language.

Dr Ian Adamson, born in Bangor in 1944, is a Unionist on the Belfast Council and has written extensively on the Ulster identity. He sees the Irish language as an important constituent of this identity and he is one of the original trustees of the ULTACH Trust which, with government help, was set up to promote the language among all sections of the Northern Ireland population.

In a television film, about Protestants and the Irish Language,[170] he mentioned that his medical specialty was with children and he compared Irish to a child needing to be nurtured and protected. He is a keen admirer of Sir Samuel Ferguson and edited and republished one of Ferguson's epic poems.[171]

He would like Irish to be taken out of the political arena and put back among the people, where it belongs. He points out that Irish is the mother tongue of Ulster and links Ulster with West Scotland. He believes that everyone in Ulster should know about the language. They should not think of Gaelic as alien.

The Rev. T.P. McCaughey, a Presbyterian minister, holds since 1964 the post of Senior Lecturer in Irish in the School of Irish and Celtic Studies in Trinity College Dublin. He is a fluent speaker of Ulster Irish and is married to a native speaker of Scottish Gaelic. Unlike most of his Irish-speaking clerical predecessors the Rev. McCaughey has a nationalist outlook. In a lecture, entitled 'Presbyterianism and the Radical Tradition', which he delivered to the Friends of the Kilmainham Society in 1981,[172] he argued that the rejection of an independent Ireland by Presbyterians in 1920 was a political mistake and a betrayal of their religious mission.

In March 1992 he gave a talk about the receptivity to reformed ideals amongst Gaelic-speaking people, in a Symposium, *The Culture and Cultures of Europe* held at Derry.

Dr Christopher McGimpsey, previously honorary secretary of the Ulster Unionist Party, believes that Irish is the common heritage of all the people of Ireland and that it could be built on as a source of togetherness.[173] He is descended from the family of Mac Díomasaigh (The proud one) who came to the Newtownards area, Co. Down long before the Scots arrived in the sixteenth century. They turned to be Presbyterian very early on. By the nineteenth century they had lost the Irish language, but it was by studying the history of his family and trying to understand them that Christopher developed a personal interest in the language.[174] He published an article in the June 1984 issue of the Irish language magazine *Comhar* in which he regretted the conclusions of the New Ireland Forum. His view of the Irish language in the future is that it will be part of 'bi-lingualism with choice'.[175]

He is a staunch Unionist and the case which he and his brother Michael took in the Dublin Supreme Court in March 1990 about the constitutionality of the Anglo-Irish Agreement was an embarrassment to the southern government. The decision by the Court was that the Accord was indeed constitutional and furthermore that Articles 2 and 3 imposed what Michael McGimpsey termed a constitutional imperative on the Republic's government to seek a United Ireland.[176]

Dr McGimpsey is a trustee of the ULTACH Trust which was established to promote Irish among all sections of the Northern Ireland population and he is keen to make his fellow Unionists aware that the Irish language belongs to them in a very special way.

Dr Seosamh Watson, a writer in Irish and lecturer in the Department of Irish in University College, Dublin, was raised as a Unionist and Presbyterian in Belfast.[177] He is the Cultural Director of a Summer College, called *Oideas Gael*, in Glencolmcille, Co. Donegal. Courses in Irish language and culture are aimed at teaching adults at all learning levels, and an interesting element is the high proportion of students who are from other countries throughout the world, even so far away as Japan. Although of Presbyterian background Dr Watson later became a member of the Bahai Faith.[178]

Many of the apparently small group of Presbyterians who are current Irish-speakers were pupils of Seán Pasker who ran the Gaelic Fellowship and Irish classes in the Y.M.C.A. They live mainly in Belfast and North Down and meet from time to time to talk in Irish.

Apparently, after the formation of the Irish Free State some presbyteries in that jurisdiction showed some opposition to the gradual extension of the Irish language programme in primary education. However, many others did not object, especially those that were situated in or near the Irish-speaking areas. MacArthur points out that many of the members of Presbyterian congregations in or near Gaeltacht areas must have been bilingual. In 1976, two Sunday school members in his little Donegal congregation in Dunfanaghy chose Irish dictionaries as their prizes.[179]

The Irish Mission of the Presbyterian Church still aims at having an Irish-speaker on its staff and the Colporteurs still carry copies of the Bible in Irish. Also, there has always been a number, albeit small, of ministers in the Presbyterian Church who can speak Irish. As a national church the Presbyterian Church in Ireland has shown in the past a concern and interest in all aspects of national culture and still continues to do so.[180]

For Presbyterians in the south the Presbytery of Dublin is the oldest and the premier organisation. At the 1978 meeting of the Synod there was a resolution about Irish. A sub-committee called for revision of Article 8 of the Irish Constitution which deals with the national language. It is significant that in their report they expressly stated that they had no hostility to the Irish language. However, they thought that English and Irish should be given equal status.[181] This position is not so far removed from that of language activists who would recommend the same circumstance, so long as Irish-speakers, in return, could have equal rights with English-speakers. This would include the right to have the same services from the State as those enjoyed by non Irish-speakers.

Another Presbyterian is a regular writer in Irish and frequently contributes historical biographies to Irish language journals, including *An tUltach*. The Irish Language Officer to one of the District Councils is the son of a Presbyterian minister. He reads, writes and speaks the language to perfection.

In keeping with the recent rise of interest in the language, the ULTACH Trust was founded in November 1989 with the object of cultivating the study and use of Irish among all of the people of Northern Ireland. Among the eleven trustees were five Presbyterians, three of whom were fluent speakers and two of whom were Official Unionists. The Trust expressly aims to widen access to Irish, irrespective of politics or religion.[182] Because of the tendency for some to stereotype the opposing groupings in Northern Ireland, the accomplishment of ULTACH's aims will require special efforts.

Perhaps only a minority of Presbyterians will actually be aware of the work of their ancestors in nurturing the language, or that the association of Irish with nationalism is something quite recent in history. In a sense, Protestants in general have allowed the separatists to commandeer the language. Yet, a recent survey found that 23 per cent of Protestants agreed that the study of Irish language and culture should be necessary for all secondary school pupils.[183]

Learning the language is a great problem for Protestants, because the classes are situated mainly in Catholic/Nationalist areas, where Protestants may not feel safe, particularly during 'The Troubles'. Even classes run in relatively neutral areas can make Unionists feel uncomfortable, because Irish-speakers, who, as a whole, genuinely and positively believe that the language belongs to all classes and creeds, often unwittingly assume that those Protestants learning Irish are on the way to becoming nationalists. This is because of the historic Protestant nationalist tradition. This assumption can make the Protestant Unionist feel apprehensive about the language.

The most compelling fact about Irish for Presbyterians is that the sister language, Scottish Gaelic, is the everyday medium for thousands of Presbyterian Scots, in the Highlands and Islands. In many cases the ancestors of the Ulster Presbyterians were Gaelic-speaking Scots. These elements are an integral part of the Scots-Irish heritage.

APPENDIX
THE PRESENT DAY POSITION
OF THE IRISH LANGUAGE

The number of persons in the Republic declaring themselves to be Irish-speakers was recorded as 1,043,000 in the 1986 census (31.1 per cent of persons aged 3 years and over). The closest estimate of the number of people who use Irish as everyday speech would be the number of Irish-speakers in the true Gaeltacht (Irish-speaking) areas. This came to 58,500 in the 1986 census.

The corresponding figures for Northern Ireland were first published in October 1992.[1] The last census to ask the question before 1991 was in 1911, when 29,423 persons described themselves as Irish-speaking. The question was asked in 1991 to determine the numbers who could read or write or speak Irish. The results show that persons who had one or more of these skills numbered 142,003, constituting 9.5 per cent of the population. The number who have all three skills combined is 79,012, being 5.3 per cent of the population. It has been argued that these figures are much higher than expected, yet previous estimates had been either as high or even higher.

In a letter to the Department of Education, the Northern Ireland Branch of the European Bureau for Lesser Used Languages calculated that there are about 60,000 Irish-speakers in Northern Ireland, of whom approximately half have a high level of competence in the language. They went on to say: 'Early indications of the results of the 1991 census ... are that more than 100,000 people will be returned as Irish-speakers of varying levels of proficiency. The last Scottish census returned about 80,000 speakers of Gaelic'.[2]

In the previous few years a number of social surveys had addressed the extent of Irish-speaking in Northern Ireland. In 1985 Ulster Television, in response to queries about the potential for Irish language television programmes, commissioned a marketing survey to measure knowledge of Irish among the Northern Ireland population.[3] Of the

1,119 interviewed, two per cent were fluent in Irish, another two per cent were learning or intending to learn. Altogether seven per cent would watch educational programmes in Irish. For Catholics this proportion was 16 per cent and for Protestants two per cent. It was calculated from these percentages that '…in aggregate, the existing potential for television programmes in Irish comprises approximately 20,000 fluent speakers, with a further 20,000 expressing a desire to become fluent'. It was further concluded that '… Educational programmes, however, have a potential audience of up to 70,000 (not all of whom could be expected to develop fluency ultimately)'.

The Policy and Planning Research Unit of the Northern Ireland Government[4] found that of the 5,111 persons interviewed, 11 per cent had a knowledge of Irish. For Catholics the proportion was 26 per cent and for Protestants 2 per cent. The latter figure is by no means insignificant and if applied to the total Protestant population comes to roughly 20,000 people. We do not know in this study how many of the Protestants were Presbyterian. Also in this study the results showed that Irish-speakers were more likely to use the language as a living medium in the home (16 per cent), compared with persons who know French (10 per cent), or German (7 per cent).

Then in 1988, the BBC conducted a survey to find out how many persons listened to the regular Irish language radio programme *Rud Eile*.[5] It was found that 11 per cent of those interviewed had heard the programme at some time. It is most interesting that this percentage is exactly the same as the proportion who had a knowledge of Irish in the PPRU study. The researchers calculated, on the basis of a total Northern Ireland population of 1,572,000, that 172,920 people had heard the programme since it started. In the same survey, 49 per cent of people interviewed said that having Irish language programmes on radio was 'a good idea'.

On 24 September 1991 Ulster Television broadcast an Irish language documentary called 'Iascairí Ghaoth Dobhair' ('Gweedore Fishermen'). A subsequent survey discovered that 44 per cent of viewers had seen it. This means that approximately 200,000 people in Northern Ireland had been looking at this programme, and that these were from both Northern traditions, The survey indicated that there were about 50,000 more than the normal number looking at this programme than at the usual programmes at this time of the evening.[6]

Whether indicating minimal or maximum estimates of Irish-speaking, these studies show that the extent that Irish is spoken and used in Northern Ireland is significant, and that the Irish language is still very much alive. The central presence and importance of the language as part of the identity of Northern Ireland is acknowledged by such thoughtful commentators as Ian Adamson.[7]

The final relevant statistic is the number of Presbyterians who know Irish today. The detailed Irish language report of the most recent census was published in 1993.[8] It revealed that 1,614 Presbyterians in Northern Ireland had some knowledge of Irish and that about half of these, 757 were fluent, i.e. could speak, read and write in the language. Although constituting only 0.5 per cent of all Presbyterians aged three years and over, this group was 10.5 per cent of the 13,577 non-Roman Catholic Irish-speakers and 29.1 per cent of those Irish-speakers who belonged to a named Protestant denomination.

Despite their small numbers, many of the present-day Presbyterians with Irish would be very conscious of being part of a long-standing and significant tradition stretching back over many hundreds of years.

REFERENCES

PREFACE

1 Ó BUACHALLA, Breandán, *I mBéal Feirste Cois Cuain* (Dublin 1968).

2 Ó SNODAIGH, Pádraig, *Hidden Ulster: The other hidden Ireland* (Dublin 1977).

3 STOTHERS, Thomas James, 'The Use of the Irish Language by Irish Presbyterians with particular reference to Evangelican Approaches to Roman Catholics' (Q.U.B., M. Theo. dissertation 1981).

4 HEMPTON, David and HILL, Myrtle, *Evangelical Protestantism in Ulster Society, 1740–1890* (Routledge 1992) p. 13.

5 British and Irish Communist Organisation, *Hidden Ireland Explored* (Belfast 1973).

6 HESLINGA, M.W., *The Irish Border as a Cultural Divide* (Assen 1962).

INTRODUCTION

1 *Bunreacht na hÉireann* (Constitution of Ireland). Article Eight. Section 1, 2.

2 STOTHERS, op. cit., p. 1.

3 ibid., p. 2.

4 BRADY, Anne M. and CLEEVE, Brian, *A Biographical Dictionary of Irish Writers* (Lilliput Press, 1985) p. 287.

5 BECKETT, J.C., *The Making of Modern Ireland, 1603–1923* (Glasgow 1973) p. 25.

6 Ó CUIV, Brian, *Irish Dialects and Irish-speaking Districts* (Dublin 1967) pp 19–20.

7 ANDERSON, Christopher, *Historical Sketches of the Native Irish and their Descendants* (Edinburgh 1830) pp 206–231.

8 STOTHERS, op. cit., p. 141.

9 Ó CUIV, op. cit., p. 22.

10 HOLMES, R.F.G., *Our Irish Presbyterian Heritage* (Belfast 1985) pp 25–26.

11 ibid., p. 26.

12 MULLIN, T.H., *Aghadowey: A Parish and its Linen Industry* (Belfast 1972) p. 44.

13 MOODY, T.W., MARTIN, F.X. and BYRNE, F.J. (eds), *A New History of Ireland, Vol VIII: A Chronology of Irish History to 1976* (Oxford 1982) p. 279.

14 HOLMES, op. cit., p. 57.

15 ANDERSON, A.C., *The Story of the Presbyterian Church in Ireland* (Belfast 1965) p. 60.

16 HAMILTON, Thomas, *History of the Irish Presbyterian Church* (Edinburgh 1886) p. 108.

17 MOODY, et al., op. cit., p. 318.

18 HOLMES, op. cit., p. 75.

19 STOTHERS, op. cit., p. 5.

20 ibid.

CHAPTER II

1 STOTHERS, op. cit., p. 22.

2 ibid.

3 REID, James Seaton, *History of the Presbyterian Church in Ireland*, Killen, W.D. (ed.), (Belfast 1867) Vol. 1. p. 51.

4 WARE, Sir James, *The Annals of Ireland of the Reign of Queen*

Elizabeth (1571) (Dublin 1705) p. 15.

5   MASON, Henry J. Monck, *The Life of William Bedell, D.D.* (London 1843) p. 106.

6   McGUINNE, Dermot, *Irish Type Design: A History of Printing Types in Irish Character* (Blackrock 1992) p. 18.

7   REID, op. cit., p. 63ff.

8   STOTHERS, op. cit., p. 24.

9   ibid.

10 ibid., p. 26

11 ibid.

12 ibid.

13 REID, op. cit., Appendix to Vol. 1, p. 409.

14 STOTHERS, op. cit., p. 27.

15 ibid.

16 ibid., p. 28.

17 ibid., p. 33.

18 ibid., p. 34.

19 REID, op. cit., Vol. II, p. 43.

20 STOTHERS, op. cit., Appendix II, p. 146.

21 ibid., p. 38.

22 BAILIE, W. Desmond, CROMIE, Howard, Carson, John T. and SCOTT, Alfred R., *A History of Congregations in the Presbyterian Church in Ireland, 1610–1982* (Belfast 1986) p. 104.

23 McCONNELL, James and McCONNELL, S.G., *Fasti of the Irish Presbyterian Church* (Presbyterian Historical Society, 1951) p. 8.

24 *Records of the General Synod of Ulster from 1691 to 1820* (1890), Vol. I, p. 211.

25 BAILIE, et al., op. cit., p. 105.

26 McCONNELL, *Fasti*, p. 9.

27 BAILIE, et al., op. cit., p. 291.

28 BARKLEY, John 'Josias Welsh' in

Bulletin of the Presbyterian Historical Society of Ireland, No. 2 (January 1972) p. 4.

29 REID, op. cit., Vol. II, p. 129.

30 McCONNELL, *Fasti*, p. 46.

31 BAILIE, et al., op. cit., p. 255.

32 McCONNELL, *Fasti*, p. 46.

33 *Records of the General Synod of Ulster*, Vol. I, p. 211.

34 REID, op. cit., p. 320.

35 MULLIN, Julia., *A History of Dunluce Presbyterian Church* (Bushmills 1995) p. 12.

36 STOTHERS, op. cit., p. 35.

37 McCONNELL, *Fasti*, p. 51.

38 BAILIE, et al., op. cit., p. 793.

39 ibid.

40 McCONNELL, *Fasti,* p. 51.

41 STOTHERS, op. cit., p. 19.

42 WILLIAMS, Ronald, *The Lords of the Isles: The Clan Donald and the early Kingdom of the Scots* (London 1984) p. 11.

43 ibid., pp 57–58.

44 THOMSON, Derick, S. (ed.), *The Companion to Gaelic Scotland* (BasilBlackwood Ltd, 1983) p. 232.

45 ibid., p. 89.

46 MacKINNON, Kenneth, *The Lion's Tongue* (Inverness 1974) p. 15.

47 THOMSON, op. cit., p. 109.

48 BARKLEY, John. 'The Presbyterian Minister in Eighteenth Century Ireland', in J.L.M. HAIRE (ed.) *Challenge and Conflict* (Belfast 1981) p. 46.

49 SCOTT, Maolcholaim. 'Ballymascanlon and Irish links with Gaelic Scotland' (unpublished, 1991).

50 PATTESON, W.M. 'Dundalk Presbyterian Church' in *Tempest's*

Centenary Dundalk Annual
(Dundalk 1959) pp 81–82.

51 D'ALTON, John and
O'FLANAGAN, J.R., *The History
of Dundalk* (Dundalk 1864)
pp 310–11.

52 SCOTT, op. cit.

53 RICHARDSON, John, *A Proposal
for the Conversion of the Popish
Natives of Ireland to the Established
Religion* (Dublin 1711).

54 ibid., pp 13–15.

55 STOTHERS, op. cit., p. 44.

56 RICHARDSON, op. cit., p. 16.

57 STOTHERS, op. cit., p. 45.

58 ibid., p. 17.

59 HESLINGA, op. cit., p. 159.

60 O'RAHILLY, T.F., *Irish Dialects
Past and Present* (Dublin 1972)
p. 117.

61 ADAMS, G.B., 'Aspects of
Monoglottism in Ulster' in *Ulster
Folklife* Vol. 22 (1976) p. 85.

62 De BLACAM, A., 'The Other
Hidden Ireland' in *Studies* Vol. 23
(Dublin 1934) p. 443.

63 Ó SNODAIGH, op. cit., p. 8.

64 RUSHE, D.C., *The History of
Monaghan for Two Hundred Years*
(Dundalk 1921) pp 25–26.

65 British and Irish Communist
Organisation, *The Irish Language:
Revivalism and the Gaeltacht, Policy
statement, No. 5* (Belfast 1972)
p. 14.

66 LORIMER, W.L., 'Gaelic in
Galloway and Carrick' in *Scottish
Gaelic Studies* Vol. VII (1953) p. 42.

67 ADAMS, G.B., 'The Dialects of
Ulster', in D. Ó MUIRITHE (ed).
The English Language in Ireland
(Dublin and Cork 1977) p. 57.

68 HESLINGA, op. cit.

69 STOTHERS, op. cit., p. 20.

70 LATIMER, William T., 'The Old
Session-book of Templepatrick
Presbyterian Church, Co. Antrim'
in *The Journal of the Royal Society
of Antiquaries of Ireland*, Vol. 31
Consecutive Series (1901) p. 165.

71 MacLYSAGHT, Edward, *The
Surnames of Ireland* (Shannon
1969) et passim.

72 ADAMS, op. cit., p. 84.

73 ROBINSON, Philip, 'The Scots
Language in Seventeenth-Century
Ulster in *Ulster Folklife* Vol. 35
(1989) p. 87.

74 ADAMS, op. cit., p. 84.

75 ibid.

76 BAILIE, et al., pp 450–51.

CHAPTER IIIA

1 BARKLEY, John M., *A Short
History of the Presbyterian Church
in Ireland* (Belfast 1959) p. 24.

2 STOTHERS, op. cit., p. 148.

3 *Records of the General Synod ...*
Vol. 1, p. 148.

4 ibid., p. 38.

5 McCONNELL, *Fasti*, p. 116.

6 *Records of the General Synod ...*
Vol. 1, p. 211.

7 STOTHERS, op. cit., p. 42.

8 *Records of the General Synod ...*
Vol. 1, p. 211.

9 ibid., p. 379.

10 STOTHERS, op. cit., p. 45.

11 RICHARDSON, op. cit., p. 16.

12 *Records of the General Synod ...*
Vol. 1, p. 402.

13 ibid., p. 403.

14 ibid., p. 422.

15 ibid., pp 439–40.

16 ibid., p. 457.

17 ibid., p. 461.

18 ibid., p. 497.

19 ibid., p. 498.

20 ibid., p. 521.

21 ibid., p. 527.

22 ibid., p. 534.

23 ibid., p. 541.

24 STOTHERS, op. cit., p. 54.

25 DAVEY, J. Ernest, *The Story of a Hundred Years, 1840–1940* (Belfast 1940) p. 54.

26 STOTHERS, op. cit., p. 55.

27 ibid., p. 54.

28 *Dictionary of National Biography* (London 1908) Vol. I, p. 48. Hereafter, *D.N.B.*

29 MULLIN, Julia, E., *New Row: The History of New Row Presbyterian Church, Coleraine 1727–1977* (Antrim 1976) p. 17.

30 *D.N.B.*, op. cit., p.48.

31 McCONNELL, *Fasti*, Part IV, p. 89.

32 REID, op. cit., Vol. III, p. 235.

33 ABERNETHY, John, *Religious obedience founded on personal persuasion* (Belfast 1720) p. 43.

34 *D.N.B.*, pp 48–49.

35 REID, op. cit., p. 209.

36 STOTHERS, op. cit., p. 51.

37 *Records of the General Synod ...* Vol. I, p. 461.

38 ibid., p. 474.

39 STOTHERS, op. cit., p. 52.

40 *Records of the General Synod ...* Vol. I, p. 429.

41 STOTHERS, op. cit., p. 52.

42 ibid., p. 148.

43 McCONNELL, *Fasti*, p. 90.

44 BAILIE, et al., op. cit., p. 620.

45 McLYSAGHT, op. cit., p. 144.

46 STOTHERS, op. cit., p. 148.

47 McCONNELL, *Fasti*, p. 95.

48 *Records of the General Synod ...* Vol. I, p. 128.

49 ibid., p. 223

50 STOTHERS, op. cit., p. 148.

51 *Records of the General Synod ...* Vol. I, p. 211.

52 MacLYSAGHT, op. cit., p. 144.

53 WITHEROW, T., *Historical and Literary Memorials of Presbyterianism in Ireland, 1731–1800* (Belfast 1880) pp 38–39.

54 ibid., p. 39.

55 BAILIE, et al., op. cit., p. 585.

56 WITHEROW, op. cit., p. 43.

57 ibid., p. 39.

58 MULLIN, Julia E., *The Presbytery of Coleraine* (Belfast 1979) p. 51.

59 McCONNELL, *Fasti*, p. 105.

60 *Records of the General Synod ...* Vol. I, p. 211.

61 WITHEROW, op. cit., (1879) Vol. 1, p. 318.

62 McCONNELL, *Fasti*, p. 105.

63 DUNDAS, W.H., *Enniskillen: Parish and Town* (Dundalk 1913) p. 79.

64 STOTHERS, op. cit., p. 48.

65 REID, op. cit., Vol. III, pp 384–85.

66 MULLIN, Julia E., *New Row*, p. 24.

67 ibid., p. 22.

68 BAILIE, et al., op. cit., p. 599.

69 STOTHERS, op. cit., p. 148.

70 McCONNELL, *Fasti*, p. 106.

71 STOTHERS, op. cit.

72 McCONNELL, *Fasti*, p. 114.

73 *Records of the General Synod ...* Vol. 1, p. 404.

74 WITHEROW, op. cit., p. 323.

75 McCONNELL, *Fasti*, p. 114.

76 MULLIN, Julia E., *New Row*, p. 30.

77 BAILIE, et al., op. cit., p. 324.

78 MULLIN, Julia E., *New Row*, p. 31.

79 BAILIE, et al., op. cit., p. 324.

80 MULLIN, Julia E., *The Presbytery of Coleraine*, p. 59.

81 ANDERSON, John, *History of the Belfast Library and Society for*

Promoting knowledge (Belfast 1888) p. 24.

82 McCONNELL, *Fasti*, p. 116.

83 ibid.

84 *Records of the General Synod ...* Vol. I, p. 211.

85 BAILIE, et al., op. cit., p. 635.

86 ibid.

87 WITHEROW, op. cit., p. 323.

88 RUSHE, *History of Monaghan*, p. 26.

89 BAILIE, et al., op. cit., p. 108.

90 MULLIN, T.H., *Aghadowey*, p. 136.

91 PARKER, Rev. E.L., *History of Londonderry* (New Hampshire 1851).

92 MULLIN, Julia E., *Presbytery of Coleraine*, p. 137.

93 *Records of the General Synod ...* Vol. I, pp 212, 402–03, 440.

94 MULLIN, Julia E., *The Presbytery of Coleraine*, pp 47, 136, 145.

95 WITHEROW, op. cit., p. 2.

96 WOODBURN, James Barkley, *The Ulster Scot: His History and Religion* (London 1915) 2nd edition, p. 215.

97 McCONNELL, *Fasti*, p. 115.

98 MULLIN, Julia E., *Presbytery of Coleraine*, p. 139.

99 *Records of the General Synod ...* Vol. 1, p. 211.

100 HAMILTON, *History of the Irish Presbyterian Church*, p. 114.

101 McCONNELL, *Fasti*, p. 119.

102 BAILIE, et al., op. cit., p. 506.

103 McCONNELL, *Fasti*, p. 119.

104 BAILIE, et al, op. cit., p. 471.

105 McCONNELL, *Fasti*, p. 119.

106 D'ALTON and O'FLANAGAN, *The History of Dundalk*, p. 309.

107 RUSHE, *History of Monaghan*, p. 26.

108 BURKE, Sir Bernard, *A Genealogical and Heraldic Dictionary of the Peerage and Baronetage* (London 1882) p. 1,033.

109 McCONNELL, *Fasti*, p. 119.

110 BAILIE, et al., op. cit., p. 451.

111 McCONNELL, *Fasti*, p. 121.

112 STOTHERS, op. cit., p. 148.

113 BAILIE, et al., op. cit., p.451.

114 McCONNELL, *Fasti*, p. 121.

115 *Records of the General Synod ...* Vol 1, p. 403.

116 D'ALTON and O'FLANAGAN, *History of Dundalk*, pp 310–11.

117 *Records of the General Synod ...* Vol 1, p. 422.

118 PATTESON, 'Dundalk Presbyterian Church', p. 81.

119 McCONNELL, *Fasti*, p. 121.

120 STOTHERS, op. cit., p. 148.

121 McCONNELL, *Fasti*, p. 175.

122 ibid.

123 STOTHERS, op. cit., p. 148.

124 BAILIE, et al., op. cit., p. 270.

125 McCONNELL, *Fasti*, p. 176.

126 STOTHERS, op. cit., p. 148.

127 ibid..

128 McCONNELL, *Fasti*, p. 122.

129 BAILIE, et al., op. cit., p. 618.

130 ibid., p. 363.

131 RICHARDSON, *A Proposal for the Conversion of the Popish Natives*, p. 15.

132 BAILIE, et al., op. cit., p. 53.

133 McCONNELL, *Fasti*, p. 122.

134 BAILIE, et al., op. cit., p. 534.

135 *Records of the General Synod ...* Vol. 1, pp 43, 45.

136 McIVOR, John, *Extracts from a Ballybay Scrapbook* (Ballybay 1974) p. 19.

137 McCONNELL, *Fasti*, p. 122.

138 SHIRLEY, E., Philip, *The History of the County of Monaghan* (London 1879, re–printed by Patrick Fox, 1988) p. 348.

139 *Records of the General Synod ...* Vol. II, p. 83.

140 McCONNELL, *Fasti*, p. 122.

141 *Records of the General Synod ...* Vol. II, p. 295.

142 STOTHERS, op. cit., p. 148.

143 McCONNELL, *Fasti*, p. 123.

144 BAILIE, et al., op. cit., p. 231.

145 McCONNELL, *Fasti*, p. 123.

146 ibid., p. 124.

147 IRWIN, Clarke H., *A History of Presbyterianism in Dublin and the South and West of Ireland* (London 1890) pp 305, 308.

148 BAILIE, et al., op. cit., p. 267.

149 NELSON, Charles, *Shamrock: Botany and History of an Irish Myth* (Aberystwyth 1991) p. 41.

150 THRELKELD, Caleb, *Synopsis Stirpium Hibernicarum* (Dublin 1726).

151 NELSON, op. cit., p. 42.

CHAPTER IIIB

1 STOTHERS, op. cit., p. 59.

2 TONE, W.T.W. (ed.), *Life of Theobald Wolfe Tone, Founder of the United Irishmen* (Washington 1826) Vol. 1, p. 157.

3 ELLIOTT, Marianne, *Wolfe Tone: Prophet of Irish Independence* (New Haven 1989) p. 173.

4 KENNEDY, David, 'James MacDonnell, 1762–1845' in *Capuchin Annual 1945–46* (Dublin 1945) p. 357.

5 YEATS, Gráinne, *The Belfast Harpers Festival 1792. Féile na gCruitirí, Béal Feirste* (Dublin 1980).

6 Mac GIOLLA EASPAIG, S. N., *Tomás Ruiséil* (Dublin 1957) p. 90.

7 STOTHERS, op. cit., p. 60.

8 Ó BUACHALLA, *I mBéal Feirste* ..., p. 14.

9 YOUNG, Robert M., *Historical Notices of Old Belfast* (Belfast 1886) p. 278.

10 Ó BUACHALLA, op. cit., p. 14.

11 Ó CASAIDE, Séamus, *The Irish Language in Belfast and County Down* (1930) p. 27.

12 STOTHERS, op. cit., p. 60.

13 Ó CASAIDE, op. cit., p. 27,

14 FOX, Charlotte Milligan, *Annals of the Irish Harpers* (London 1917) p. 227.

15 YEATS, op. cit., p. 19.

16 Ó BUACHALLA, op. cit., p. 24.

17 McNEILL, Mary, *The Life and Times of Mary Ann McCracken* (Dublin 1960) p. 84.

18 Ó CASAIDE, op. cit., p. 32.

19 BECKETT, et al., *Belfast: the Making of the City* (Appletree 1988) p. 71.

20 JOHNSTONE, Robert, *Belfast: Portraits of a city* (London 1990) p. 87.

21 VANE, Charles, *Memoirs and Correspondence of Viscount Castlereagh, Second Marquess of Londonderry* (London 1848) Vol. 1, pp 77–78.

22 Ó BUACHALLA, *I mBéal Feirste* ..., p. 30

23 ibid., p. 38.

24 ibid., p. 33.

25 BAILIE, et al., op. cit., p. 461.

26 McCONNELL, *Fasti*, p. 133.

27 *Matriculation Albums of the University of Glasgow, 1728–1858* (1779).

28 YOUNG, op. cit., p. 278.

29 FOX, Charlotte Milligan, pp 99, 133–34, 287.

30 Ó TUATHAIL, E., *Scéalta Mhuintir Luinigh* (Dublin 1933) p. viii.

31 Ó CASAIDE, et passim, p. 27.

32 Ó BUACHALLA, Breandán, *Clár na Lámhscríbhinní Gaeilge i Leabharlann Phoiblí Bhéal Feirste* (Dublin 1962) p. 43.

33 PATTESON, *Dundalk Presbyterian Church*, p. 81.

34 CLINT, J. and BLANEY, R, 'The Family of Dr Samuel Bryson of Holywood, Co. Down': in *The Irish Ancestor* Vol. XVI, No. 1 (1984) pp 32–34.

35 Ó SNODAIGH, op. cit., p. 10.

36 ibid. p. 17.

37 FOX, Charlotte Milligan, p. 134.

38 MORRIS, Henry 'Two Belfast Gaels' in *The Irish Book Lover*, Vol. XIII (Aug.–Sept. 1921) pp 3–6.

39 BIGGER, F.J., 'Samuel Bryson – a Belfast Gaelic Scholar' in *County Louth Archaelogical Journal*, Vol. V, No. 1 (December 1921) pp 61–62.

40 BIGGER, F.J., 'Memoir of Samuel Bryson' in *Centenary Volume 1821–1921. Belfast Natural History and Philosophical Society* (Belfast 1924) pp 66–67.

41 Ó CASAIDE, op. cit., et passim.

42 SIMMS, S. 'Sketches of Authors of Belfast Birth', in N. McNEILLY (ed.), *Selection from 150 Years of Proceedings of the Belfast Natural History and Philosophical Society, 1831–1981*, (Belfast 1981), p. 214.

43 MacAIRT, Seán, 'Filidheacht Aoidh Mhic Dhomhnaill' in *An tUltach* (December 1951) pp 4–5.

44 MORTÚN, Deirdre, 'Saol Cultúrtha Bhéal Feirste roimh 1850' in *Fearsaid 1906–1956* (Queen's University Gaelic Society, Belfast, 1956) p. 40.

45 Ó BUACHALLA, *I mBéal Feirste ...*, pp 53–57, et passim.

46 Ó BUACHALLA, *Clár na Lámhscríbhinní ...*, pp 40–44.

47 BAILIE, et al., op. cit., p. 451.

48 An MS footnote in a copy of Millin's, *History of the Second Congregation*, held in the Library of the Presbyterian Historical Society reads, 'The following is recorded on a flyleaf of the Rev. James Bryson's Sermons (1778), in MS by William Finlay, at Belfast, on 9 March 1826; (as told to him by Dr Bryson) – "Samuel Bryson, Esq. M.D. of Belfast, 21st son of the Author of these Sermons, was born 9 March 1776 (six). His mother bore 24, viz: 21 males & 3 females" (Note by Isaac W. Ward) The preceding Dr Samuel Bryson commenced business at No. 9 High Street, opposite St. George's Church [but not then built] on 3 August 1806, and after his death, it was continued by his sons, Drs Joseph W. and Samuel Bryson, Surgeons and Apothecaries. About 1850 Dr Joseph W. removed to 16 York Street, and his son Samuel, now (1900) resides in Holywood.'

49 CLINT and BLANEY, 'The Family of Dr Samuel Bryson ...' .

50 *Returns Relating to Apothecaries Licensed in Dublin* (1829) p. 99.

51 BIGGER, 'Samuel Bryson – a Belfast Gaelic Scholar', p. 61.

52 MALCOLM, A.G., *History of the Belfast General Hospital and other Medical Institutions in the Town* (Belfast 1851), Appendices vii and xxxi.

53 *Annual Report of the Belfast District Hospital for 1836*, p. 6.

54 *Belfast News Letter*, August 1806. Advertisement by Samuel Bryson.

55 Public Record Office of Northern Ireland. Copy of a mortgage dated 12 June 1834, D.1905/2/145.

56 *Belfast News Letter*, Friday 4 March 1853. Obituary of Dr Samuel Bryson.

57 Mac TIGHEARNÁIN, Eoghan, 'Gaeilgeoirí i mBéal Feirste san Naomhadh Aois Déag in *Glór Uladh* (Béal Feirste 1943).

58 Personal communication from Miss Alice Bryson.

59 DRUMMOND, William Hamilton, *The Giant's Causeway – a Poem*, (Belfast 1811).

60 ibid., p. 106.

61 ibid., p. 146.

62 STUART, James, *Historical Memoirs of the City of Armagh* (Newry 1819).

63 JOYCE, P.W., *Irish Names of Places* (Dublin, N.D., [c. 1913]) Vol. I, p. 525.

64 COLEMAN, Ambrose, *Historical Memoirs of the City of Armagh by James Stuart* (Dublin 1900) p. xxiv.

65 MERRICK, A.C.W. and CLARKE, R.S.J., *Old Belfast Families and The New Burying Ground* (U.H.F., Belfast 1991) p. 281.

66 NEILSON, Rev. William, *An Introduction to the Irish Language: In three parts. I. An Original and Comprehensive Grammar. II. Familiar Phrases, and Dialogues. III. Extracts from Irish Books, and Manuscripts, in the original character*. With copious Tables of the Contractions (Dublin 1808) p. v. 2nd and 3rd Edition (Achill 1843, 1845). Reprinted (Belfast 1990).

67 O'REILLY, Edward, *An English-Irish Dictionary* (Dublin 1821).

68 BUTLER, Rev. Richard, (ed.), *The Annals of Ireland by Friar John Clyn ... and Thady Dowling, ... together with the Annals of Ross* (Dublin 1849). Appended Report, p. 9.

69 CONNELLAN, Owen, *The Gospel According to St John, in Irish ...* (Dublin 1830) p. ix.

70 O'SHEA, P.J. 'Irish Manuscripts in the Museum, College Square, Belfast' in *Ulster Journal of Archaeology*, Vol. I (1895) pp 106–10.

71 HYDE, Douglas, 'An Irish Funeral Oration over Owen O'Neill, of the House of Clanaboy' in *Ulster Journal of Archaeology*, Vol. III (1897) p. 258 and Vol. IV (1897) p. 50.

72 MORRIS, 'Two Belfast Gaels'.

73 HUGHES, A.J. and McDANIEL, Eilis, 'A Nineteenth-century Translation of the Deirdre story', in *Emania* No. 5 (Autumn 1985) pp 41–47; No. 6 (Spring 1989) pp 43–47; No. 7 (1990) pp 54–58.

74 Ó MORDHA, Séamus P. ' Simon Macken: Fermanagh Scribe and Schoolmaster' in *Clogher Record* Vol. II (1959) pp 432–44.

75 ESLAR, Robert, 'Early History of Medicine in Belfast' in *Transactions of the Ulster Medical Society. Session 1884–85* (Printed Dublin 1885) p. 24.

76 *Northern Whig*, 5 January 1835, p. 3.

77 Young and MacKenzie Papers, PRONI, D.2194/23.

78 SALMON, John,'The Irish Harp Society' in *Ulster Journal of Archaeology* Vol. I (1859) pp 302–03.

79 Ó BUACHALLA, *I mBéal Feirste ...*, 'Moladh an Dr Brís', pp 56–57.

80 Ó MUIRGHEASA, Énrí, *Dhá Chéad de Cheoltaibh Uladh*, (Oifig Díolta Foillseacháin Rialtais, Baile átha Cliath 1934). 'Beirt Bhéal Feirsteach', pp 225–26.

81 LAOIDE, Seosamh, *Duanaire na Midhe* (Dublin 1914) p. 48.

82 Central Library, Belfast. Handout about Irish Collection, dated Sept., 1990.

83 SIMMS, 'Sketches of Authors of Belfast Birth'.

84 *D.N.B.* Entry for James Bryson.

85 McLYSAGHT, op. cit., pp 35, 37.

86 CLINT and BLANEY, *The Family of Dr Samuel Bryson* ..., p. 32.

87 McCONNELL, *Fasti*, p. 133.

88 *Belfast News Letter*, 25 November 1788.

89 O' BYRNE, Cathal, *As I Roved Out: A Book of the North* (Facsimile edition, Blackstaff Press 1982) p. 171.

90 Ó CASAIDE, op. cit., p. 27.

91 Ó SNODAIGH, op. cit., pp 14, 39.

92 BIGGER, F.J. 'Samuel Bryson–A Belfast Gaelic Scholar', p. 61.

93 CRAIG, W.I., *Presbyterianism in Lisburn from the Seventeenth Century* (Belfast n. d.[1960]).

94 MILLIN, S. Shannon, *History of the Second Congregation of Protestant Dissenters in Belfast* (Belfast 1900) p. 33.

95 MOODY, et al., op. cit., p. 279.

96 MILLIN. S. Shannon, *Sidelights on Belfast History* (1932) p. 169.

97 WITHEROW, op. cit., p.141.

98 McCONNELL, *Fasti*, p. 133.

99 *D.N.B.*, Vol. 3, p. 170.

100 ibid. Entry for William Bryson.

101 BAILIE, et al., op. cit., p. 635.

102 McCONNELL, *Fasti*., p. 116.

103 *Belfast News Letter*, 25 November, 1872. A letter written by 'Holywood', because of interest in longevity, gave details of the Bryson gravestone in 'the ancient churchyard of Holywood', as follows, 'John Bryson, died 23 November 1788, aged 103; Ann Bryson died 1704 (recte 1804), aged 106; Alicia Bryson, died April 17, 1840, aged 73; Samuel Bryson died Feb. 28, 1830, (recte 1853), aged 77'. The second named person, Ann, was clearly John's wife, who was 13 years his junior. Alicia (née Stanfield) was Dr Samuel Bryson's wife, and the stone shows conclusively that the famous scribe and Irish language scholar was buried in Holywood, his native town.

104 Personal communication from Miss Alice Bryson, dated 20 November 1980.

105 NEILSON, Rev. William, *An Introduction to the Irish Language* ... .

106 D'ALTON and O'FLANAGAN, *The History of Dundalk*, p. 340.

107 McCONNELL, *Fasti*, p. 225.

108 [ANON.] 'Lest We Forget' in *Irish Book Lover*, Vol. XIII (December 1921) pp 78–79.

109 KILLEN,W.D., *Reminiscences of a Long Life* (London 1901) p. 192.

110 BAILIE., et al., op. cit., p. 451.

111 MAGEE, J., 'The Neilsons of Rademon and Down: Educators and Gaelic Scholars' in *Familia: Ulster Genealogical Review*, Vol. 2 (1988) No. 4, pp 63–77.

112 SEERY, J., 'Dr Neilson's Irish Grammar' in *The Bulletin of the Presbyterian Society of Ireland* Vol. 20 (March 1991) pp 5–11.

113 O'LAVERTY, Rev. James, *The Bishops of Down and Connor, being*

the Fifth Volume of an Historical
Account of Down and Connor
(Dublin 1895) p. 568.

114 Belfast News Letter, 1 May 1821.
Obituary of Dr Neilson.

115 D'ALTON and O'FLANAGAN,
op. cit., p. 341.

116 BAILIE, et al, op. cit., p. 451.

117 JAMIESON, John, The History of
the Royal Belfast Academical
Institution, 1810–1960 (Belfast
1959) p. 40.

118 Belfast News Letter, 1 May 1821.

119 D'ALTON and O'FLANAGAN,
op. cit., p. 344.

120 BOYLAN, Henry, A Dictionary of
Irish Biography (Dublin 1988) p. 48.

121 D.N.B. Entry under William
Neilson, p. 187.

122 D'ALTON and O'FLANNAGAN,
op. cit., pp 343–44.

123 NELSON, J., Memoir of William
Neilson, D.D., M.R.I.A. in Belfast
Literary Society, 1801–1901 (1902)
p. 57.

124 Hibernian Magazine, 13 July 1805.

125 Walker's Hibernian Magazine,
September 1805, p. 575.

126 Ó SNODAIGH, op. cit., p.15.

127 Newry Telegraph, 1 June 1813.

128 Ó CASAIDE, op. cit., p. 39.

129 SEERY, op. cit., p. 7.

130 ibid., p. 5.

131 MOODY, T.W., MARTIN, F.X.,
BYRNE, F.J. (eds), A New History
of Ireland (Oxford 1984) Vol. IX,
p. 498.

132 O'RAHILLY, op. cit., p. 265.

133 Mac PÓILIN, Aodán, Background
Information on Dr William
Neilson (Unpublished report,
dated 5 November 1990).

134 O'LAVERTY, Bishops of Down
and Connor, p. 568.

135 DE hÍDE, Dubhghlas, Mise agus
an Connradh (Dublin 1905) p. 11.

136 'H', 'Review of Neilson's Irish
Grammar', in Belfast Monthly
Magazine, Vol. 2, No. 8 (March
1809) pp 215–18.

137 NEILSON, Wm, 'Letter to editor'
in Belfast Monthly Magazine, Vol. 2,
No. 10, (May 1809) pp 351–52.

138 SCURRY, James, 'Remarks on the
Irish Language, with a Review of
its Grammars ...' in Transactions of
the Royal Irish Academy, Vol. XV
(Dublin 1828) p. 35.

139 O'DONOVAN, John, A
Grammar of the Irish Language ...
(Dublin 1845) p. lx.

140 Ó BUACHALLA, I mBéal Feirste
..., p. 239.

141 [Neilson, Dr] Céad Leabhar na
Gaoidheilge. Air Na Chur A gCló,
Chum Maitheas Puiblidhe Na
hÉirin, Air Iartas Agus Costas Na
Cuideachta Éirionaighe, 1810
(Shacklewell: Printed by T. Rutt,
1810).

142 Ó BUACHALLA, I mBéal Feirste
..., p. 64.

143 Ó SAOTHRAÍ, Séamas, William
Neilson, D.D., M.R.I.A.,
1774–1831 in Meascra Uladh
(Coiste an tUltach, Belfast 1974)
p. 83.

144 O'KEARNEY, Nicholas, The
Prophecies of Sts Colum-Cille,
Maeltamlacht, Ultan ... (James
Duffy, Dublin 1925) pp 770–71.

145 O'REILLY, Edward, A
Chronological Account of nearly
Four Hundred Irish Writers
(Irish University Press, Shannon
1970) p. v.

146 Records of the General Synod ...
Vol. III, p. 305.

147 CROZIER, John, A., *The Life of the Rev. Henry Montgomery, LL.D.* (London 1875) p. 76.

148 Ó BUACHALLA, *I mBéal Feirste* ..., p. 60.

149 McCONNELL, *Fasti*, p. 225.

150 STOTHERS, op. cit., p. 71.

151 Ó BUACHALLA, *I mBéal Feirste* ..., p. 64.

152 STOTHERS, op. cit., p. 70.

153 *Belfast Literary Society, 1801–1901*, p. 178.

154 'Obituary' in *The Dublin Christian Instructor, and Repertory of Education*, Vol. IV (1821) pp 242–43.

155 D'ALTON and O'FLANAGAN, *History of Dundalk*, p. 345.

156 McEWAN, W.D.H., *Funeral Address delivered on Sunday the 29th April, 1821, at the Grave of the late Rev. W. Neilson, D.D., M.R.I.A* ... (Belfast 1821) p. 10.

157 NELSON, J., 'Memoir of William Neilson', p. 58.

158 ibid., pp 58–59.

159 WOODS, T.S., 'History of Kilmore Presbyterian Church', in *Down Recorder*, 29 August 1885.

160 MAGEE, *The Neilsons of Rademon and Down*, p. 64.

161 WALSH, Luke, FITZSIMMONS, John, et al., *The Home Mission Unmasked ... in a Series of Letters* (Belfast 1844) p. 146.

162 NELSON, 'Memoir of William Neilson', p. 57.

163 SEERY, James, in 'Dr. Neilson's Irish Grammar' in *Bulletin of the Presbyterian Historical Society of Ireland*, Vol. 20 (March 1991) p. 5.

164 ROBB, Colin Johnston, *Irish News*, 9 January 1946.

165 *Belfast News Letter*, 1 May 1821.

166 MAGEE, op. cit., p. 68.

167 REID, op. cit., Vol. 3, p. 564.

168 McCONNELL, *Fasti*, p. 225.

169 CAMPBELL, John, *A Short History of the Non-Subscribing Presbyterian Church of Ireland* (Belfast 1914) pp 61–62.

170 D'ALTON and O'FLANAGAN, *The History of Dundalk*, p. 312.

171 'M.J.F.'[M.J.FULLEN] (Compiler), *A Digest of the Historical Account of the Diocese of Down and Connor by Rt Rev. Monsignor James O'Laverty MRIA, Having regard only to the Priests of Down and Connor between the years 1595–1895* (Belfast 1945) p. 161.

172 MAGEE, op. cit., p. 68.

173 *Belfast News Letter*, 8 May 1821. Obituary.

174 MULLIGAN, John F., *A Ramble Through Dromore* (Banbridge 1886) p. 25.

175 *Belfast News Letter*, 1 September 1910. Obituary, Joseph Nelson.

176 *Down Recorder*, 31 January 1891. Obituary, S.C. Nelson.

177 ibid.

178 ibid.

179 'M.J.F.', op. cit., pp 171, 193.

180 *Down Recorder*, 16 December 1899. Obituary, Professor Hodges.

181 ibid., 31 January 1891.

182 ibid.

183 ALLISON, R.Sidney, *The Seeds of Time: being a Short History of the Belfast General and Royal Hospital, 1850–1903* (Belfast 1972) p. 132.

184 ibid., p. 133.

185 *D.N.B.*, Vol. 18, p. 1,288.

186 *Irish Unitarian Magazine* (1846) p. 134.

187 DOOLIN, William, *Wayfarers in Medicine* (London 1949) p. 258.

188 WEBB, Alfred, *A Compendium of Irish Biography* (Dublin 1878) p. 502.

189 MORTON, Leslie T., *A Medical Bibliography* (London 1983) p. 539.

190 BURTCHAELL, G.D. and SADLEIR, T.U., *Alumni Dublinenses* (Dublin 1935) p. 785.

191 STOKES, Whitley (ed.)] *An Soisgéal Do Réir Lúcais, agus Gniovarha Na Neasbal. The Gospel According to St Luke, And The Acts of the Apostles* (Dublin 1799).

192 STOKES, Whitley, *Projects for re-establishing the internal peace and tranquility of Ireland* (Dublin 1799).

193 [STOKES, Whitley, (ed.)] *Na Ceithre Suisgéala Agus Gníomhartha na Neasbal: A Ngaoidheilg Agus A Mbéarla. The Four Gospels and Acts of the Apostles in Irish and in English* (Dublin 1806) 2 Vols.

194 [CONNELLAN, Thaddeus] *An English-Irish Dictionary, intended for the Use of Schools containing upwards of eight thousand English words with their corresponding explanation in Irish* (Dublin 1814).

195 STOKES, *Sir William, William Stokes: His Life and Work* (London 1898) p. 24, footnotes.

196 ANDERSON, op. cit., pp 211–13.

197 [STOKES, Whitley] *Seanráite Sholaimh A Ghaoidheilge Agus Mbéarla* (1815).

198 MORTON, op. cit., pp 271, 285, 358.

199 Manuscripts in Trinity College, Dublin. MSS. No. 4, 2–3.

200 Ó CASAIDE, op. cit., pp 15–17.

201 ibid., p.17.

202 ibid., p.18.

203 Ó SNODAIGH, op. cit., p. 15.

204 MAC CON MIDHE, Pádraig, 'Gaeilge an Dúin, II' in *An tUltach* (December 1968) p. 7.

205 BAILIE, et al., op. cit., p. 679.

206 McCONNELL, *Fasti*, p. 290.

207 BAILIE, et al., op. cit., p. 764.

208 Ó SNODAIGH, op. cit., p. 21.

CHAPTER IV

1 Ó BUACHALLA, *I mBéal Feirste ...*, p. 51.

2 STOTHERS, op. cit., p. 76.

3 *Records of the General Synod ...* Vol. 3, p. 489.

4 IRWIN, *Presbyterianism in Dublin, the South and West*, p. 100.

5 STOTHERS, op. cit., p. 78.

6 BOWEN, Desmond, *The Protestant Crusade in Ireland, 1800–1870* (Dublin 1978) p. 34.

7 STOTHERS, op. cit., p. 78.

8 BAILIE, et al., op. cit., pp 480–481.

9 BOWEN, op. cit., p. 220.

10 ibid., p. 260.

11 *Orthodox Presbyterian*, Vol. 2 (Oct. 1830) pp 15–16.

12 STOTHERS, op. cit., p. 80.

13 ibid., p. 79.

14 *Report of the Presbyterian Missionary Society in connection with the Synod at Cookstown, June 1833*, p. 8.

15 *Records of the General Synod ...* June 1833, p. 47.

16 *Report of the Special Synod at Dublin*, 1833, p. 67.

17 *Resolutions of the Special Synod at Dublin*, Sept. 1833, p. 2.

18 *Third Report of the Presbyterian Missionary Society*, 1834, p. 5.

19 ibid., p. 6.

20 *Minutes of the General Synod of Ulster at Derry*, 1834, p. 43.

21   ibid., *Appendix*, p. 50.

22   *Report of the Home Mission for 1835*, p. 1.

23   CONNELLAN, Thaddaeus, *An Prímér Gaoidheilge lé na bhrígh a Saicsbhéarla. The Irish-English Primer to the Irish Language* (London 1825).

24   *Report of the Home Mission for 1835*, pp 10–11.

25   ibid., p. 11.

26   *Report of the Home Mission for 1836*, p. 7.

27   BOYLAN, *A Dictionary of Irish Biography*, p. 17.

28   MASON, *The Life of William Bedell, D.D.* p. 377.

29   STOTHERS, op. cit., p. 29.

30   BOYLAN, op. cit., p.17.

31   STOTHERS, op. cit., p.29.

32   ibid., p. 141.

33   ibid., p. 124.

34   ibid., p. 125.

35   ANDERSON, Hugh, *The Life and Letters of Christopher Anderson* (Edinburgh 1854).

36   ANDERSON, Christopher, *Memorial on behalf of the Native Irish, with a view to their improvement in moral and religious knowledge through the medium of their own language* (1815).

37   ANDERSON, Hugh, op. cit., p. 137.

38   ANDERSON, Christopher, *Diffusion of the Scriptures in the Celtic or Iberian Dialects* (Edinburgh Bible Society, 1819).

39   ANDERSON, Christopher, *Historical Sketches of the ancient native Irish and their descendants* (Edinburgh 1828). A second edition (enlarged) appeared in 1830; the third edition was published in 1846 by Pickering of London – in this the title was changed to *The Native Irish and their Descendants*.

40   ANDERSON, Christopher (translator), *Gluaseachd an Oilithrigh no Turas an Chriosduighe o'n t-Saoghal so chum an t-Saoghal le teacht fa amhlughadh aisling. Aistrithghe o mBearla Eoin Bhunian*. Part I (Dublin 1837).

41   BOWEN, *Protestant Crusade*, p. 225

42   *The Fifth Report of the Irish Society for promoting the Education of the Native Irish, through the Medium of their Own Language* (Dublin 1823) p. 2.

43   [ANON.] *A Brief View of the London Hibernian Society, for Establishing Schools, and Circulating the Holy Scriptures in Ireland* (London 1837) p. 12.

44   ANDERSON, Hugh, op. cit., p. 127.

45   CRONE, John S., *A Concise Dictionary of Irish Biography* (Dublin 1937) p. 152.

46   *Thirty-First Report of the Irish Society, Established 1816, for Promoting the Scriptural Education and Religious Instruction of the Native Irish, Through the Medium of their Own Language* (Dublin 1849) p. 29.

47   MAGEE, Hamilton, *Fifty Years in the Irish Missions* (Belfast n.d. [c. 1899]) p. 20.

48   SCOTT, Hew, *Fasti Ecclesiae Scoticanae* (Edinburgh 1920) Vol. III, p. 437.

49   MacINNES, John, 'Caraid nan Gaidheal', in THOMSON,

Derick. S. (ed.), *The Companion to Gaelic Scotland* (Oxford 1983) p. 35.

50 MacINNES, John, op. cit., p. 35.

51 Ó CADHAIN, Máirtín, *Feasta* (February 1961) p. 12.

52 MacINNES, John, op. cit., p. 35.

53 *Records of the General Synod ...* 1834 p. 19.

54 STOTHERS, op. cit., pp 104–05.

55 BAILIE, et al., op. cit., p. 145.

56 MAGEE, Hamilton, op. cit., p. 50.

57 McCONNELL, *Fasti*, p. 252.

58 ibid., p. 188.

59 Anon., *On the Meeting House Steps: Two hundred years of Presbyterianism in Stewartstown, 1788–1988* (Church History Committee, 1988) p. 24.

60 STOTHERS, op. cit., p. 103.

61 MAGEE, Hamilton, op. cit., p. 22.

62 ALLEN, Robert, 'Extracts from the Journal of an Irish Scripture Reader', *Orthodox Presbyterian*, Series 2, Vol. 2 (Feb. 1839) p. 72.

63 MAGEE, Hamilton, op. cit., p. 22.

64 WALSH, Luke, et. al., *The Home Mission Unmasked*.

65 Ó BUACHALLA, *I mBéal Feirste ...*, p. 162.

66 MAGEE, Hamilton, op. cit., p. 24.

67 *On the Meeting House Steps ...*, p. 24.

68 DILL, Edward, *The Mystery Solved: or, Ireland's Miseries; The Grand Cause and Cure* (Edinburgh 1852) p. 285.

69 MAGEE, Hamilton, op. cit., p., 48.

70 BAILIE, et al., op. cit., p. 758.

71 *On the Meeting House Steps ...*, p. 18.

72 McCONNELL, *Fasti*, p. 188.

73 KILLEN, W.D., *Memoir of John Edgar* (Belfast 1869) p. 252.

74 STOTHERS, op. cit., p. 100.

75 McCONNELL, *Fasti*, p. 271.

76 *Orthodox Presbyterian*, Vol. VII (November 1835) p. 72.

77 BAILIE, et al., op. cit., p. 335.

78 HOLMES, R. Finlay, *Henry Cooke* (Belfast 1981) p. 1.

79 PORTER, J.L., *Life and Times of Henry Cooke, D.D., LL.D.* (Belfast 1875) pp 3, 5.

80 BARKLEY, John M., 'Henry Cooke – Man of his century; Preacher of Tory Politics' *Belfast Telegraph*, 12 December 1968, p. 10.

81 *Belfast News Letter*, 23 October 1832, Editorial.

82 *Orthodox Presbyterian*, Vol. VII (May 1836) pp 305–16.

83 PORTER, op. cit., pp 272–73.

84 *Report of the General Synod ...*, October 1838, pp 358–59.

85 CLARKE, R.S.J.(ed), *Gravestone Inscriptions, Belfast Vol. 3.* (U.H.F. 1986) p. 23.

86 *Orthodox Presbyterian*, Vol. VII (July 1836) pp 354–55.

87 'Report of the Committee of the Fisherwick-Place Auxiliary to the Synod of Ulster's Home Mission' in *Orthodox Presbyterian*, Vol. VII (August 1836) p. 386.

88 *Fifth Report of the Home Mission 1836*, pp 15–16.

89 *Sixth Report of the Home Mission 1837*, p. 8.

90 S.Ó.Mh., *Casán na Gaoidhilge. An Introduction to the Irish Language; compiled at the request of the Irish Teachers; under the patronage of the General Assembly in Ireland and dedicated to them as a tribute of esteem for their zeal in preserving and extending the knowledge of our beloved Mother-tongue* (Dublin 1841).

91 BECKETT, Colm, *Aodh Mac Domhnaill; Poet and Philosopher* (Dundalgan Press, 1987).

92 Ó BUACHALLA, *I mBéal Feirste ...*, p. 100.

93 FIELD, George, *An Index to the Places Mentioned in the Bible; intended as a Help to the Study of Sacred Geography, and compiled for the Use of the Fisherwick-Place Sabbath-School* (Belfast 1835).

94 *Orthodox Presbyterian*, Vol. VII (November 1835) p. 71.

95 Ó BUACHALLA, op. cit., p. 100.

96 Ó CASAIDE, op. cit., p. 66.

97 FIELD, George, *Casán na Gaoidhilge.*

98 ALASDRUIN, M.J., *Cláirseach Naomhtha na hÉireann* (Dublin 1835).

99 *Fifth Report of the Home Mission of the Synod of Ulster*, 1836.

100 ALASDRUIN, M.J. (translator), *Cara an Pheacaidhe*. From *The Sinner's Friend* (Maidstone 1837).

101 STOTHERS, op. cit., p. 151.

102 BARKLEY, John M., *Fasti of the General Assembley, 1840–1870, Part I* (Presbyterian Historical Society, 1986) p. 56.

103 ibid., p. 31.

104 STOTHERS, op. cit., p. 107.

105 ibid.

106 BARKLEY, *Fasti.*, Part I, p. 31.

107 IRWIN, *Presbyterianism in Dublin, the South and West*, p. 211.

108 McCONNELL, *Fasti*, p. 258.

109 *The Christian Freeman*, Vol. III (1835) pp 34–35.

110 LATIMER, W.T. 'Birr Reformed Church' *Christian Banner*, Vol. 19, No. 1 (March 1891) pp 55–56.

111 *Orthodox Presbyterian* (1839) p. 284.

112 BAILIE, et al., op. cit.

113 IRWIN, *Presbyterianism in Dublin, the South and West* pp 117, 223.

114 Stothers, op. cit., p. 924.

115 [ANON.] 'The Rev. William Crotty of Birr Presbyterian Church' in *Orthodox Presbyterian*, New Series, Vol. 2, No. 19 (July 1839) pp 251–52.

116 BOWEN, *Protestant Crusade*, pp 150–52.

117 CROTTY, Michael, *A Narrative of the Reformation at Birr* (London 1847).

118 Ó CUIV, Brian 'Irish in the Modern World', in Ó CUIV, Brian (ed.), A *View of the Irish Language* (Dublin 1969).

119 RODGERS, Robert J. 'Reformation at Birr' in *The Bulletin of The Presbyterian Historical Society of Ireland*, No. 2 (January 1972) pp 5–8.

120 SIMPSON, Jonathon, *Annals of my Life, Labours and Travels* (Belfast 1895) p. 299.

121 STOTHERS, op. cit., p. 90.

122 *Missionary Herald*, 1 September 1856, p. 124.

123 ibid., p. 123.

124 W.D.K. (ed.), *Select Works of John Edgar, D.D. LL.D* (Belfast 1868) p. 458.

125 ibid., p. iii.

126 KILLEN, *Memoir of John Edgar*, p. 5.

127 STEWART, David, *The Seceders in Ireland with Annals of their Congregations* (Presbyterian Historical Society, 1950) p. 218.

128 KILLEN, op. cit., p. 165.

129 ibid., pp 221–22.

130 EDGAR, John, 'A Cry from Connaught' in W.D.K. (ed.), *Select Works of John Edgar*, pp 482–83.

131 EDGAR, John, 'Ireland's Mission

Field' in ibid., 3 p. 554.

132 KILLEN, *Memoir of John Edgar*, p. 148.

133 STOTHERS, op. cit., p. 105.

134 BARKLEY, *Fasti*, p. 56, No. 413.

135 STOTHERS, op. cit., p.105.

136 ibid., p. 106.

137 IRWIN, *Presbyterianism in Dublin, the South and West*, p. 249.

138 McMANUS, Rev. Henry, *Sketches of the Irish Highlands: Descriptive, Social and Religious* (London 1863).

139 MAGEE, Hamilton, *Fifty Years in the Irish Mission*, p. 139.

140 BELMORE, Earl of, 'Gleanings for former Fermanagh Articles', *Ulster Journal of Achaeology*, Vol. III (1897) p. 218.

141 STOTHERS, op. cit., p. 107.

142 BARKLEY, *Fasti*, Part I, p. 25.

143 Ó CASAIDE, op. cit., p. 50, footnote.

144 STOTHERS, op. cit., p. 111.

145 BAILIE, et al., op. cit., p. 299.

146 BARKLEY, *Fasti*, p. 25.

147 BAILIE, et al., op. cit., p. 537.

148 *On the Meeting House Steps..*, pp 24–25.

149 KILLEN, *Memoir of John Edgar*, p. 200.

150 MAGEE, Hamilton, op. cit., p. 28.

151 BARKLEY, *Fasti*, p. 27.

152 STOTHERS, op. cit., pp 107–110.

153 SIMPSON, T.J., 'History of the Home Mission' in HOLMES, R.F.G. and KNOX, R.B., *The General Assembly of the Presbyterian Church in Ireland, 1840–1990* (1990) p. 67.

154 DILL, *Ireland's Miseries*, p. 63.

155 KILLEN, History of Congregations of the Presbyterian Church in Ireland and Biographical Notices of Eminent Presbyterian Ministers and Laymen (Belfast 1886), p. 246.

156 SIMPSON, *Life, Labours and Travels*, p. 301.

157 McCONNELL, *Fasti*, p. 262.

158 IRWIN, op. cit., p. 172.

159 STOTHERS, op cit., p. 100.

160 *Fifth Report of the Home Mission of the Synod of Ulster*, 1836, p. 3.

161 BARKLEY, *Fasti*, p. 24.

162 STOTHERS, op. cit., p. 112.

163 BAILIE, et al., op. cit., p. 45.

164 STOTHERS, op. cit., p. 112.

165 MAGEE, Hamilton, op. cit., p. 34.

166 ARMSTRONG, Thomas, *My Life in Connaught* (London 1906) p. 9.

167 IRWIN, *Presbyterianism in Dublin, the South and West*, p. 181.

168 BAILIE, et al, op. cit., p. 44.

169 STOTHERS, op. cit., p. 112.

170 BARKLEY, *Fasti*, Part I, p. 24.

171 ibid, p. 48.

172 BAILIE, et al., op. cit., p. 407.

173 IRWIN, *Presbyterianism in Dublin, the South and West*, p. 186.

174 MAGEE, Hamilton, op. cit., p. 89.

175 IRWIN, *Presbyterianism in Dublin, the South and West*, op. cit., p. 187.

176 ibid. p. 210.

177 STOTHERS, op. cit., p. 111.

178 BARKLEY, *Fasti*, Part I, p. 47.

179 ARMSTRONG, Thomas, op. cit., p. 136.

180 BAILIE, et al., op. cit., p. 675.

181 STOTHERS, op. cit., p. 112.

182 IRWIN, *Presbyterianism in Dublin, the South and West*, pp 191–92.

183 BAILIE, et al, op. cit., p. 675.

184 STOTHERS, op. cit., p. 110.

185 ibid., p. 111.

186 IRWIN, op. cit., p. 229.

187 BARKLEY, *Fasti*, Part I, p. 58.

188 MAGEE, Hamilton, op. cit.

189 STOTHERS, op. cit., p. 111.

CHAPTER IVB

190 WALSH, et. al., *The Home Mission Unmasked ...* .

191 ibid., pp 9–10.

192 ibid., pp 11–12.

193 ibid., p. 13.

194 ibid., pp 17–18.

195 ibid, pp 18–20.

196 ibid., pp 25–31

197 ibid., pp 32–34.

198 ibid., pp 35–37.

199 ibid., pp 37–42.

200 ibid., pp 53–63.

201 ibid.

202 SIMPSON, Life, Labours and Travels, p. 256.

203 MacSWEENEY, *Conor, Songs of the Irish, Issue No. 7* (Dublin, September 1843) p. 55.

204 *Newry Commercial Telegraph*, Tuesday 24 March 1846. County of Antrim Assizes. 'Extraordinary Case – A Priest's Curse. Charles McLoughlin v. Rev. Luke Walsh'.

205 O'LAVERTY, J., *An Historical Account of the Diocese of Down and Connor* (Dublin 1887) Vol. 4, pp 500–16.

206 Ó BUACHALLA, *I mBéal Feirste ...*, p. 162.

207. STOTHERS, op. cit., p. 120.

208 FITZSIMONS, Dr J., 'The Official Presbyterian Irish Language Policy in the Eighteenth and Nineteenth Centuries' in *Seanchas Dhroim Mór: Journal of the Dromore Historical Society* (1989) pp 10–13. This appears to be a reprinting of a paper which appeared in the *Irish Ecclesiastical Record*, Vol. 72 (1949) pp 255–64.

CHAPTER IVC

1 Ó BUACHALLA, *I mBéal Feirste ...*, p. 91.

2 CONNELLAN, Thaddaeus, *Litir an Ríogh: The King's Letter, translated into Irish; with a Grammatical Introduction to the Irish Language, and Reading Lessons: for the Use of His Majesty's subjects* (printed by R. Watts, London, 1825) p. v.

3 CONNELLAN, Thaddaeus, *An Teagascóir: The Irish-English Spelling Book. Intended to Assist the Native Irish in Learning English through the medium of the Irish Language* (printed by R. Watts, London, 1825), p. v.

4 O'DONAGHUE, David J., *The Poets of Ireland: A Biographical Dictionary* (London 1892–3) p. 94.

5 BRADY and CLEEVE op. cit., p. 98.

6 BRYCE, Reuben John, *Sketch of a Plan for a System of National Education for Ireland* (London 1828) p. 46.

7 Ó BUACHALLA, *I mBéal Feirste ...*, p. 72.

8 ibid., p. 75.

9 ANDERSON, Christopher, *Memorial in Behalf of the Native Irish.*

10 *The Fifth Report of the Irish Society, for Promoting the education of the Native Irish, through the Medium of their own language* (Dublin 1823) p. 2.

11 ANDERSON, Christopher, *Historical Sketches of the ancient native Irish ...*

12 ibid., 3rd Edition (London 1846).

13 Ó SNODAIGH, op. cit., p. 25.

14 EDGEWORTH, Maria, *Forgive and Forget, a Tale; and Rosanna,* translated into Irish for the Ulster Gaelic Society, by Thomas Feenachty, Teacher of Irish in Belfast. Printed Belfast; *Maith agus Dearmad, Sgéul beag; Rosanna, air na d-tairruing go fìrinneach ... go Gaoidheilg ... fa thearmonn na Cuideachta Gaoidheilge Uladh ... le Tomás Ó Fiannachtaigh* (Dublin 1833).

15 Ó BUACHALLLA, *I mBéal Feirste* ..., p. 71.

16 ibid., p. 92.

17 Ó CASAIDE, op. cit., p. 48.

18 FERGUSON, Lady, *Sir Samuel Ferguson in the Ireland of his Day* (Edinburgh 1896) Vol. I, p. 42.

19 Ó BUACHALLLA, *I mBéal Feirste* ..., p. 91.

20 [ANON.] IN MEMORIAM, Robert S. MacAdam, in *Ulster Journal of Archaeology,* Vol. I (1895) p. 152.

21 CLARKE, R.S.J., *Gravestone Inscriptions Vol. 2* (Ulster-Scot Historical Society, Belfast 1968) pp 93–94.

22 BIGGER, Francis Joseph, 'Memoir of Robert Shipboy MacAdam', in *Centenary Volume 1821–1921. The Belfast Natural and Philosophical Society* (Belfast 1924) pp 89–90.

23 FISHER, J.R. and ROBB, J.H., *Centenary Volume 1810–1910, The Royal Belfast Academical Institution* (Belfast 1913) p. 246.

24 Ó BUACHALLA, *I mBéal Feirste* ..., p. 70.

25 YOUNG, R.M., 'Memoir of Robert S. MacAdam' in *Belfast Literary Society, 1801–1901* (Belfast 1902) p. 100.

26 ANDERSON, *Historical Sketches of the Native Irish* ... (Edinburgh 1830) p. 222.

27 Ó BUACHALLA, *I mBéal Feirste* ..., p. 84.

28 Ó BUACHALLA, *Clár na Lámhscríbhinní Gaeilge ...* .

29 BRYCE, *Plan for a System of National Education,* p. 46.

30 Ó BUACHALLA, *I mBéal Feirste* ..., p. 81.

31 ibid., p. 82.

32 ibid., p. 96.

33 ibid., p. 83.

34 YOUNG, R. M., *Old Belfast,* pp 199–247.

35 Ó BUACHALLA, *I mBéal Feirste* ..., p. 84.

36 ibid., p. 88.

37 ibid., p. 174.

38 PATTERSON, R. Lloyd, 'Belfast Natural History and Philosophical Society' in *Belfast News Letter,* 9 January 1895, p. 3.

39 Ó BUACHALLA, *I mBéal Feirste* ..., p. 71.

40 [MacADAM, R.S.], *An Introduction to the Irish Language, intended for the Use of the Irish Classes in the Royal Belfast Academical Institution* (Belfast 1835).

41 Letter dated 10 January 1849, being MS 24 E 20 p. 81 in the Royal Irish Academy, quoted in DUFFY, Sean, *Nicholas O'Kearney. The Last of the Bards of Louth* (Éigse Oirialla 1989) p. 69.

42 MORRIS, 'Two Belfast Gaels', pp 3–6.

43 Ó MUIRGHEASA, Énrí, *Sean-Fhocla Uladh* (1907).

44 MacADAM. R.S., 'Is the Irish Language spoken in Africa?' in

Ulster Journal of Archaeology, Vol. 7 (1859) pp 195–200.

45 WATSON, Joe, 'The Belfast Protestant Heroes of the Irish Language Struggle' in *Fortnight*, No. 216, 18–31 March 1985, pp 19–20.

46 Mac PÓILIN Aodán, *The Protestant Gaelic tradition* (Iontaobhas ULTACH [nd. 1991]).

47 BECKETT, Colm, *Fealsúnacht Aodha Mhic Dhomhnaill* (Dublin 1967).

48 BECKETT, *Aodh Mac Domhnaill*, p. 21.

49 MORRIS, Henry, 'Two Belfast Gaels', p. 5.

50 Ó BUACHALLA, *I mBéal Feirste* ..., p. 81, footnote.

51 O'DONOVAN, John, *A Grammar of the Irish Language* (Dublin 1845) pp 451–53.

52 Ó BUACHALLA, *I mBéal Feirste* ..., p. 178.

53 de PAOR, Annraoi, 'Ceannródaí Gaeilge ... agus Teicneolaíochta' in *Comhar* Vol. 49, Number 1 (January 1990) pp 20–25.

54 YOUNG, *Old Belfast*, p. 282.

55 de PAOR, op. cit., p. 21.

56 ibid., p. 20.

57 PATTERSON, R. Lloyd, *Belfast News Letter*, 9 Jan. 1895.

58 McNEILLY, N. (ed.), *Selections from 150 years of Proceedings, 1831–1981* (Belfast Natural and Philosophical Society, Belfast 1981) p. 12.

59 BIGGER, 'Memoir of Robert Shipboy MacAdam', p. 90.

60 *Belfast Literary Society, 1801–1901*, p. 172.

61 Ó BUACHALLA, *I mBéal Feirste* ..., p. 49.

62 Mac PÓILIN, op. cit.

63 Ó BUACHALLA, *I mBéal Feirste* ..., p. 215.

64 KILLEN, John, *A History of the Linen Hall Library, 1788–1988* (Belfast 1990) p. 188.

65 BIGGER, F.J., 'Memoir of James MacAdam' in *Centenary Volume, 1821–1921, BNHPS* (1924) p. 89.

66 MOODY, T.W. and BECKETT, J.C., *Queen's University, Belfast 1845–1949: The History of a University* (London 1959) Vol. I, p. 122.

67 IN MEMORIAM, 'Robert S. MacAdam'.

68 YOUNG, *Old Belfast*, p. 255.

69 Personal communication from J.N.H. Nesbitt, Ulster Museum. Letter dated 6 Jan. 1984

70 Death Notice for R.S. MacAdam, in *Belfast News Letter*, 5 Jan. 1895.

71 BRYCE, R.J., *National Education for Ireland* ..., p. 46.

72 EDGEWORTH, Maria, *Forgive and Forget*, etc.

73 ATKINSON, Norman, *Irish Education: A History of education institutions* (Dublin 1969) p. 81.

74 MOODY and BECKETT, *Queen's, Belfast*, p. 1xvi.

75 STEWART, A.T.Q., B*elfast Royal Academy, the First Century, 1785–1885* (Belfast 1985) p. 53.

76 *TESTIMONIALS of R. J. Bryce, L.LLD, Principal of the Belfast Academy, candidate for the Professorship of Education in the University of Edinburgh* (Belfast 1875) p. 61.

77 EDGWORTH, MARIA, *Forgive and Forget*, etc.

78 STEWART, A.T.G., op. cit., p. 46.

79 MULLIN, *Presbytery of Coleraine*, p. 112.

80   BAILIE, et al., op. cit., p. 549.

81   STEWART, *The Seceders in Ireland*, p. 230.

82   SIMPSON, *Life, Labours and Travels*, pp 13–14.

83   MAWHINNEY, Graham and DUNLOP, Eull (ed.), *The Autobiography of Thomas Witherow 1824–1890* (Ballinascreen Historical Society, Draperstown 1990) p. 23.

84   ibid., p. 25.

85   MULLIN, Rev. T.H., *Aghadowey ...*, p. 102.

86   STEWART, A.T.Q., op. cit., pp 48–49.

87   Personal communication from Derek Dow, Archivist, Greater Glasgow Health Board, 17 Jan. 1984.

88   *Matriculation Albums of the University of Glasgow*.

89   *Testimonials of R.J. Bryce* (1875) p. 51.

90   CROZIER, *Life of the Rev. Henry Montgomery*, p. 78.

91   *Testimonials of R.J. Bryce* (1838) p. 39.

92   BARKLEY, *Short History*, p. 46.

93   HOLMES, *Henry Cooke*, pp 64, 66.

94   STEWART, David, op. cit., p. 396.

95   Ó BUACHALLA, *I mBéal Feirste ...*, p. 72.

96   STEWART, A.T.Q., op. cit., p. 73.

97   ibid., pp 73–74.

98   ROWAN, P. & B., *The Eighteenth Century: a Catalogue of Books and Manuscripts..relating to Ireland*, No. 31., Item 399 (n.d.).

99   VALLENCEY, Charles, *A Grammar of the Iberno-Celtic or Irish Language* (Dublin 1782) 2nd ed.

100 VANE, *Memoirs and Correspondence of Viscount Castlereagh ...*, Vol. 1, p. 180.

101 STOTHERS, op. cit., p. 71.

102 BRYCE, *Sketch of a Plan for a System of National Education for Ireland* (London 1828).

103 Personal communication from Derek Dow. Letter dated 17 Jan. 1984.

104 *Testimonials of R.J. Bryce* (Belfast 1875). Letters from Maria Edgeworth, pp 60–62.

105 LE FANU, Emma L., *Life of Dr Orpen* (London 1860) pp 60–61.

106 ORPEN, C.E.H., *Errors of the Irish Bible* (Dublin 1833).

107 ORPEN, C.E.H., *The Claim of millions of our fellow-countrymen of present and future generations to be taught in their own and only language; The Irish. Addressed to the Upper Classes in Ireland and Great Britain* (Dublin 1821).

108 *Testimonials of R.J. Bryce* (1838) p. 20.

109 SIBBETT, R.M., *For Christ and Crown: The Story of a Mission* (Belfast 1926) p. 72.

110 BRYCE, R.J., *The Irish Colleges'Bill, examined in its bearings on the educational, religious, and financial interest of the country, in three letters to Thomas Wyse, M.P.* (Dublin 1845).

111 MacEÓINÍN, Uinseann, 'An Dr Mac Éil agus Coláistí na Bainríona' in *Galvia: Journal of the Archaeological and Historical Society of Galway*, Vol. 9 (1962) pp 22–23.

112 STEWART, A.T.Q., *Belfast Royal Academy*, p. 56.

113 YOUNG, R.M., 'Memorial of the Rev. Reuben John Bryce, LL.D.' in *Belfast Literary Society, 1801–1901*, p. 135.

114 ibid., p. 158.

115 PRENTER, Samuel, *Life and Labours of the Rev. William Johnston, D.D.* (London 1895).

116 STEWART, A.T.Q., op. cit., p. 46.

117 MULLIN, Julia E., *The Presbytery of Coleraine*, p. 110.

118 SMALL, Robert, *History of the Congregations of the United Presbyterian Church from 1733 to 1900* (Edinburgh 1904) Vol. 2, p. 475.

119 ALEXANDER, Elinor (ed.), *Primate Alexander, Archbishop of Armagh: A Memoir* (London 1913) p. 37.

120 ANON., *Faith versus Regium Donum. Notices of the late Rev. James Bryce of Killaid of the grounds of his opposition to the Royal Bounty.* (Alex. Mayne, Belfast 1864).

121 MULLIN, Julia E., op. cit., p. 110.

122 MULLIN, T.H., *Aghadowey ...*, p. 205.

123 SHEARMAN, Hugh, *Belfast Royal Academy, 1785–1935* (Belfast 1835) p. 17.

124 BYRNE, Art and McMAHON, Sean, *Great Northerners* (Swords 1991) p. 24.

125 UA DUINNÍN, Pádraig, 'An Bríseach agus a Threabh' in *The Leader*, 6 October 1906, p. 101.

126 UA DUINNÍN, Pádraig, 'Leabhar Ó Láimh an Bhrísigh' in *The Leader*, 11 February 1911, p. 634.

127 EDITOR, *Celtia* (March 1907) p. 33.

128 LATIMER, W.T., *Ulster Biographies, relating chiefly to the Rebellion of 1798* (Belfast 1897) pp 93, 105.

129 DUFFY, Charles Gavan, *My Life in Two Hemispheres* (London 1898) Vol. 1, p. 203.

130 HOLMES, *Henry Cooke*, p. 41.

131 LATIMER, op. cit. p. 93.

132 W.T.L. (W.T. Latimer), 'James McKnight, LL.D.' in *Brief Biographies of Irish Presbyterians. Eighth Annual Report of the Presbyterian Historical Society of Ireland, 1914–1915* (Published 1915) p. 13.

133 DUFFY, op. cit., Vol. 1, p. 204.

134 ADAMS, J.R.R., 'The Printing of the Montgomery Manuscripts, 1785–1869' in *Linen Hall Review* Vol. 9 (Spring 1992) p. 15.

135 *News Letter, Souvenir Edition. Anniversary Supplemen 1737–1987*, 4 September, 1979, p. 112.

136 REID, John, *Bibliotheca Scoto-Celtica; or, An account of all the books which have been printed in the Gaelic language, with bibliographical and biographical notices* (Glasgow 1832).

137 *Belfast News Letter*, 23 October 1832. Editorial.

138 DUFFY, op. cit., Vol.1, pp 204–05.

139 LATIMER, op. cit., p. 105.

140 SEGNARY, Proinsias Paul, *Eagna Fhirinneach; No, Smaointighthe do gach La do'n tSeachtain, air na Sgriobhadh ann Iodallais. Air n'athrughadh o Bhearla go Gaoighilge, le Seaghan Ó Connuill* (1813).

141 Ó NEILL, Séamus, 'James McKnight' *Irish Times*, 7 May 1976.

142 Ó CASAIDE, op. cit., p. 47.

143 SIMMS, Samuel, 'Henry R. Montgomery' in McNeilly, N. (ed.), *Selection from 150 Years of Proceedings of the Belfast Natural History and Philosophical Society* (Belfast 1981) p. 220.

144 MONTGOMERY, Henry
    Riddell, *Specimens of the Early
    Native Poetry of Ireland, in English
    Metrical Translations* (Hodges
    Figgis, 1892).

145 Ó CASAIDE, op. cit., p. 48.

146 [MONTGOMERY, Henry R.] *An
    Essay Towards Investigating the
    Causes that have Retarded the Progress
    of Literature in Ireland, and the
    Most Efficient Means of Promoting
    its advancement* (Belfast 1840).

147 ibid., p. 12.

148 Ó SNODAIGH, op. cit., p. 23.

149 HEWITT, John (ed.), *Art in
    Ulster 1557–1957; with biographies
    of the artists by Theo. Snoddy*
    (Blackstaff Press, Belfast 1991)
    p. 158.

150 FERGUSON, Lady, *Sir Samuel
    Ferguson*, Vol.I, p. 3.

151 PORTER, Henry Cooke, p. 25.

152 FISHER and ROBB, *Royal Belfast
    Academical Institution*, pp 169–170.

153 SHEARMAN, Hugh, op. cit., p.38.

154 BLACK, R.D. Collison, *Centenary
    Volume of the Statistical and Social
    Inquiry Society of Ireland,
    1847–1947*(1947) pp 68–70.

155 FERGUSON, Lady, op. cit.,
    Vol. I, pp 36, 42.

156 ibid., Vol. I, p. 39.

157 ADAMSON, Ian, *The Ulster
    People: Ancient, Medieval and
    Modern* (Bangor 1991) p. 39.

158 BROWN, Malcolm, *Sir Samuel
    Ferguson* (Lewisburg 1973) p. 1.

159 Members of the Dominican Order
    (eds), *The Veritas Book of Poetry.
    Book IV.* (Dublin, ND [post
    1918]) p. 116.

160 FERGUSON, Lady M.C.,
    'Introduction', in *Lays of the Red
    Branch* (London 1897) p. XVIII.

161 HODDER, William, 'Ferguson
    his literary sources' in BROWN,
    Terence and HAYLEY, Barbara
    (eds), *Samuel Ferguson: a
    Centenary Tribute* (Dublin 1987).

162 HUME, David, 'Remembering
    Ferguson and our Culture' in *New
    Ulster: Journal of the Ulster Society*,
    Issue 2 (1986) pp 11–12.

163 Ó DÚILL, Gréagóir, 'Samuel
    Ferguson, An Stát agus an Léann
    Dúchais' in *Studia Hibernica*,
    No. 19 (1979) p. 114.

164 BECKETT, J.C., 'The Anglo-
    Irish' in LOUGHREY, Patrick (ed.),
    The People of Ireland (Belfast 1989).

165 BELL, Margaret, *A History of St
    John's Church, Donegore* (Antrim
    1988) p. 47.

166 DRUMMOND, W.H., 'Biography
    of William Hamilton Drummond'
    in *Belfast Literary Society*,
    1801–1901, pp 35–39.

167 ALLISON, *The Seeds of Time*,
    pp 78–79.

168 MERRICK and CLARKE, *New
    Burying Ground*, pp 199–200.

169 MILLIN, S. Shannon, *History of
    the Second Congregation*, p. 42.

170 READ, Charles A., *The Cabinet of
    Irish Literature* (London 1902)
    Vol. II, p. 283.

171 *D.N.B.*, Biography of William
    Hamilton Drummond.

172 BENN, George, *A History of the
    Town of Belfast, 1799–1810*
    (London 1880) Vol. II, p. 231.

173 MILLIN, S. Shannon, *Sidelights
    on Belfast History*, p. 138.

174 IRWIN, *Presbyterianism in Dublin,
    the South and West*, p. 323.

175 DRUMMOND, William
    Hamilton, *Ancient Irish Minstrelsy*
    (Dublin 1852).

176 Ossianic Society, *Prospectus and Annual Report for the year 1855*.

177 BARRON, Philip (ed.), *Ancient Ireland*, No. II, 10 January 1835.

178 DRUMMOND, *The Giant's Causeway*.

179 HARDIMAN, James, *Irish Minstrelsy, or Bardic Remains of Ireland; with English Poetical Translations* (London 1831).

180 MONTGOMERY, *Specimens of the Early Native Poetry of Ireland*.

181 WALSH, Paul, *Gleanings from Irish manuscripts* (Dublin 1918) p. 3.

182 *Northern Whig*, October 1865. Obituary.

183 DRUMMOND, 'Biography of the Rev. William Hamilton Drummond', pp 37–39.

184 A.M.P., 'Biography of The Rev. John Scott Porter' in *Belfast Literary Society, 1801–1901*, pp 91–97.

185 Ó CASAIDE, op. cit., pp 68–69.

186 BARKLEY, *Short History*, p. 24.

CHAPTER V

1 MEYER, Kuno, 'A School of Irish Research' in Celtia (May–June 1903). Reprinted in Ó LÚING, S., *Kuno Meyer 1858–1919: A Biography* (Dublin 1991) p. 243.

2 CARSUEL, Seon, *Foirm na n-Urrnuidheadh* (Dún Éideann 1567). (*Carswell's translation of Knox's Book of Common Order*). New Edition: THOMSON, R. L. and MATHESON, Angus (eds), (Scottish Gaelic Texts Society, Edinburgh 1970).

3 BEST, R.I., *Bibliography of Irish Philology and of Printed Irish Literature* (Dublin 1913) pp 244–45.

4 Ó GLAISNE, Risteard, 'Léann agus Diagacht Protastúnach in Éirinn, 1500–1700', in MAC CONMARA, Mairtín, *An Léann Eaglasta in Éirinn, 1200–1900* (Dublin 1988).

5 THOMSON, *The Companion to Gaelic Scotland*, p. 37.

6 *Records of the General Synod of Ulster*, Vol. I, p. 403.

7 ibid., Vol. I, p. 422.

8 ibid., Vol. I, p. 498.

9 HUTCHINSON, Francis (Comp.), *The Church Catechism in Irish* (Printer, James Blow, Belfast 1722).

10 McGUINNE, *Irish Type Design*, p. 166.

11 NELSON, *Charles, Shamrock ...*, pp 40–44.

12 STOTHERS, op. cit., p. 60.

13 *Bolg an Tsolair: or, Gaelic Magazine. Containing Laoi na Sealge: or, The Famous Fenian Poem, called The Chase; with a collection of Choice Irish Songs, translated by Miss Brooke. To which is prefixed, an Abridgement of Irish Grammar; with a vocabulary and familiar dialogues* (Printed at the Northern Star Office, Belfast 1795) [No. 1].

14 STOTHERS, op. cit., p. 62.

15 NEILSON, *An Introduction to the Irish Language* (Dublin 1808). Second Edition (Achill,1843). Third Edition (ULTACH Trust, Belfast 1990).

16 [NEILSON, Rev. William], *Ceud Leabhar na Gaoidheilge* (Shacklewell 1810).

17 EDGEWORTH, Maria, *Forgive and Forget*, etc.

18 [MacADAM, Robert] *An Introduction to the Irish language ...*, p. 54.

19 McLEOD, Norman, D.D.
    Minister of St. Columba's Parish,
    Glasgow, *PSALMA DHAIBHÍ,
    Rígh Israel.* (A Londuin: ar na chur
    na gclo re Richard Watts 1836).
    The Psalms of David in the Irish
    Language. Now for the first time
    rendered into metre.

20 [TONNA] Charlotte Elizabeth,
    'Review of: The Psalms of David
    in the Irish Language' in *The
    Christian Lady's Magazine* Vol. 6
    (December 1836) pp 559–62.

21 *Bolg a t-Solair an ceud rann.
    Clódh-bhuailte a mBéul-fears'de a
    gCondae Aontrim* (1837).

22 *Bolg a t-Solair an dara rann.
    Clódh-bhuailte a mBéul-fears'de a
    gCondae Aontrim* (1837).

23 Anon, 'Review of: Bolg a T-solair
    an ceud rann. Bolg a T-solair an
    dara roinn. The Provision-bag,
    parts 1 and 2' in *The Orthodox
    Presbyterian*, Vol. 8 (September
    1837) p. 419.

24 MacLEOID, Tormoid, *Leabhar
    nan Cnoc; Comh-chruinneachadh
    do nithibh Sean agus Nuadh; airson
    Oilean agus Leas nan Gaidheal*
    (Greenock 1834) pp 96, 115, 155.

25 BOWEN, *The Protestant Crusade*,
    p. 225.

26 Anon, Review of: Bolg a T-solair
    ..., op. cit., p. 420.

27 [FIELD, George], *An teagasg
    Criosduigh do reir ceisd agus
    freagradh air na tharruing go
    bunadhusach as Briathair shóilleir
    De agus air na chraobhsgaoileadh
    chun leas spiriodalta a thabhairt do
    dhaoinibh hÉirinn. Christian
    Instruction, in question and answer,
    carefully drawn from the pure word
    of God, and enlarged upon, for the
    spiritual instruction of the people of
    Ireland, etc.* (The Shorter
    Catechism in Irish 1837).

28 Anon, 'Review of: An teagasg
    Criosduigh ... ' in *The Orthodox
    Presbyterian*, Vol. 8 (June 1837)
    pp 323–24.

29 Ladies' Gaelic Society, Leabhar na
    m-Ban Uasal Uladh-an chéad
    mhiniuagh *Sé spiorad Dé Ughdar
    na Sgriobtúir (The spirit of God is
    the Author of the Scriptures). A Tract
    published under the sanction of the
    Ladies' Gaelic Society.* Reviewed in
    Orthodox Presbyterian, New series,
    Vol. I (July 1838) pp 248–49.

30 Ladies' Gaelic Society, *An Irish
    Primer compiled and published
    under the Patronage of the Ladies'
    Gaelic Society* (Belfast 1838)

31 Ó CASAIDE, op. cit., p. 51.

32 McGUINNE, *Irish Type Design*,
    p. 93.

33 S. Ó Mh., *Casán na Gaoidhilge.*

34 Ó BUACHALLA, *I mBéal Feirste
    ...*, p. 92.

35 STOTHERS, op. cit., p. 115.

36 ALASDRUIN, *Cara an Pheacaidhe.*

37 MacMANUS, *Sketches of the Irish
    Highlands ...*, p. 70.

38 ALASDRUIN, *Cláirseach
    Naomhtha na hÉireann.*

CHAPTER VI

1   DALY, Dominic, *The Young
    Douglas Hyde* (Dublin 1974) p. 164.

2   Mac AODHA, Breandán S., 'Was
    this a Social Revolution?' in
    Ó TUAMA, Seán, *The Gaelic
    League Idea* (Cork 1972) p. 20.

3   BLANEY, Roger, 'Dr John St
    Clair Boyd (1858–1918)' in *Ulster
    Local Studies* Vol. 9, No. 18
    (Summer 1984) p. 20.

4   *The Gaelic Journal* Vol. VI, No. 8 (1 December 1895) p. 142.

5   BARKLEY, *Fasti*, p. 29

6   DUNLOP, Eull, *Buick's Aghoghill* (Mid-Antrim Historical Group, 1987).

7   DUNLOP, Eull, 'Rev. Frederick Buick: the last of the Surviving Fathers' in *Bulletin of the Presbyterian Historical Society of Ireland*, Vol. 19 (January 1990) pp 31–33.

8   *Journal of the Royal Society of Antiquaries of Ireland*, Vol. 31 (1901).

9   ADAMS, G.B., 'The Last Language Census in Northern Ireland' in ADAMS, G.B.(ed.), *Ulster Dialects: an Introductory Symposium* (Holywood 1964) p. 139.

10 *Annual Report and Proceedings of the Belfast Naturalists' Field Club*, 1896, 1897, 1898

11 *The Gaelic Journal*, Vol. 7 (May 1896) p. 1.

12 *Irish News*, 24 October 1905.

13 ibid., 26 October 1905.

14 MacMINN, Richard, 'Presbyterianism and Politics in Ulster, 1871–1906' in *Studia Hibernica*, No. 21 (1981) pp 127–146.

15 ABERDEEN, Lord and Lady, *We Twa* (1925), Vol. 2., p. 173.

16 Ibid., Vol. 1, p. 219.

17 *Who's Who 1900* (London 1900) p. 115.

18 DAY, Anna, *Turn of the Tide: The Story of the Peamont* (Dublin) p. 11.

19 *We Twa*, Vol. 2, p. 180.

20 Ibid., p. 181.

21 Editor, *Celtia*, Vol.7 (January 1907) p. 18.

22 JORDAN, Alison, *Margaret Byers* (Institute of Irish Studies, Belfast 1990)

23 MOODY and BECKETT, *Queen's, Belfast ...* . p. 374.

24 Ibid., p. 419.

25 McCURRY, S.S., *The Ballads of Ballytumelty. Revised and enlarged. With an Introduction on the Ulster Dialect by Sir John Byers*, M.A., M.D. (Belfast [c.1918]).

26 BYERS, John, *The Characteristics of the Ulsterman* (Belfast [c.1920]).

27 PEPPER, John, *What a Thing to say* (Belfast 1977).

28 *Irish Book Lover . The Ferguson Centenary*, Vol. I (April 1910) p. 113.

29 Census return for Dougan Family, Croft Rd in 1901. PROI.

30 BAILIE, et al., op. cit., pp 6, 10.

31 MOODY and BECKETT, *Queen's, Belfast ...* . pp 292, 378–79, 514, 599.

32 HEWITT, *Art in Ulster*, p. 161.

33 HAMILTON, *History of the Irish Presbyterian Church*.

34 BARKLEY, *Fasti*, Part I, p. 42.

35 *Thom's Irish Who's Who for 1923*, p. 102.

36 BAILIE, et al., op. cit., p. 225.

37 *Celtia. A Pan-Celtic Magazine*, Vol. VIII, No. 3 (March 1908) p. 39.

38 MOODY and BECKETT, *Queen's, Belfast ...* ., pp 370–71.

39 FISHER, and ROBB, *Royal Belfast Academical Instituition*, pp 183–84.

40 MERRICK and CLARKE, ... *New Burying Ground*, pp 119–20.

41 MARTIN, F.X. and BYRNE, F.J. (eds), *The Scholarly Revolutionary: Eoin MacNeill, 1867–1945, and the making of the New Ireland* (Shannon 1973) pp 322–23.

42   *Northern Whig*, 19 February 1958.
43   MILLIGAN, C.F., *My Bangor*
     (Bangor 1975) p. 52.
44   MOODY and BECKETT,
     Queen's, Belfast ... ., p. 564.
45   Personal communication from
     Colán MacArthur, his son, dated
     29 October 1982.
46   *Belfast Feis, Prospectus, St Mary's
     Hall*, 11–12 December 1902.
47   Personal communication from Ian
     MacArthur, his son, dated 6
     November 1982.
48   MOODY, and BECKETT,
     Queen's, Belfast ... ., p. 582.
49   Mac ARTÚIR, Uilliam,
     'Teachtaireacht ón Ridire Uilliam
     Mac Artúir' in Mac AIRT, Seán (ed.),
     Fearsaid (Cumann Gaelach Queen's
     University, Belfast 1956) p. 7.
50   MOODY and BECKETT,
     Queen's, Belfast ... ., p. 582.
51   Queen's College, Belfast, *The Book
     of The Fête, 29 May–1 June*
     (Belfast 1907) p. 108.
52   Personal communication from Dr
     Dickson's daughter, Miss Barbara
     Dickson, 20 April 1983.
53   *Book of the Fête*, p. 108.
54   Mac AIRT, Seán, *Fearsaid*, op. cit.
     p. 11.
55   *D.N.B.*, Biography of William
     Porter MacArthur.
56   Personal communication from
     Colán MacArthur.
57   ibid.
58   MOODY and BECKETT,
     Queen's, Belfast ... ., p. 648.
59   MacARTHUR, Sir William Porter,
     'Medical History of the Famine' in
     EDWARDS, R.D. and WILLIAMS,
     T.D. (eds), *The Great Famine:
     Studies in Irish History, 1845–52*
     (Dublin 1956) pp 263–315.

60   Personal communication from
     Colán MacArthur 27 February, 1986.
61   WEAVER, John and FROGGATT,
     Sir Peter, *The Wild Geese. Supplement
     to the Ulster Medical Journal*
     (August 1987) pp S35–S36.
62   *D.N.B.*, op. cit.
63   Nuffield Provincial Hospitals
     Trust, *Survey of the Hospital
     Services of Northern Ireland* [n.d.].
64   *Hospital News (A journal of the
     Northern Ireland Hospitals
     Authority)* Vol. 6, No. 3
     (September 1964) p. 68.
65   Mac AIRT, Seán, *Fearsaid*, op. cit.
66   *North Down Spectator*, 27 October
     1956.
67   CLARKE, R.S.J. (ed.) *Gravestone
     Inscriptions, Balmoral Cemetery,
     Belfast, Vol. 3* (Ulster Historical
     Foundation, 1968) p. 131.
68   Personal communication from the
     daughter of Charles Dickson,
     Barbara, dated 20 April 1983.
69   *The Medical Who's Who, 1914*
     (London 1914) p. 172.
70   CLARKE, R.S.J., *Gravestone
     Inscriptions, Co. Down. Vol. 19*
     (Ulster Historical Foundation,
     Belfast 1983) p. 124.
71   Ibid.
72   DICKSON, Charles, *The Wexford
     Rising in 1798* (Tralee 1955) p. 1.
73   FISHER and ROBB, *Royal Belfast
     Academical Institution*, p. 316.
74   Personal communication from
     Barbara Dickson, cf 68.
75   *We Twa*, Vol.2, picture facing p. 279.
76   Personal communication from
     Barbara Dickson, cf 68.
77   Mac AIRT, Seán, 'An Cumann
     Gaelach, 1906–1956' in *Fearsaid*
     (Belfast 1956) p. 11.
78   Ó SNODAIGH, op. cit., p. 29.

79 *The Medical Who's Who, 1925* (London 1925) p. 165.

80 DICKSON, Charles, 'On Enteric Fever and Typhoid Carriers' in *Journal of the Royal Sanitary Institute* (1911).

81 BRADY and CLEEVE, op. cit., p. 60.

82 POWELL, Malachy, 'Admission of Dr Charles Dickson to Honorary Fellowship of the Royal Academy of Medicine in Ireland' in *Irish Journal of Medical Science*, Vol. 142 (1973) pp 3–5.

83 Death of Dr Charles Dickson, *Irish Times*, 2/3 January 1978.

84 Personal communication from Barbara Dickson, cf 68.

85 DICKSON, Charles, *The Life of Michael Dwyer* (Dublin 1944).

86 DICKSON, *The Wexford Rising ...*, op. cit.

87 DICKSON, Charles, *Revolt in the North, Antrim and Down in 1798* (Dublin 1960).

88 POWELL, op. cit.

89 Ó HAGÁIN, P., 'John Mitchel', a letter in *Treoir, the Journal of Comhaltas Ceoltóirí Éireann*, Vol. 20 (1988) p. 42.

90 TOWERS, Robert P., 'Obituary: Dr Charles Dickson' in *Irish Journal of Medical Science*, Vol. 147 (1978) pp 45–46.

91 BREATHNACH, Diarmuid and NÍ MHURCHÚ, Máire, *Beathaisnéis a Dó, 1882–1982* (Dublin 1990) p. 115.

92 PINE, L.G. (ed.), *Burke's Landed Gentry of Ireland* (London 1958) p. 155.

93 D'ARCY, Charles Frederick, *The Adventures of a Bishop* (London 1934) p. 110.

94 KILLEN, W.D., *History of*
Congregations, pp 284–87.

95 KILLEN, *Reminiscences of a long Life*, p. 4.

96 BREATHNACH and NÍ MHURCHÚ, op. cit., p. 116.

97 NÍ ÓGÁIN, Róis, *Duanaire Gaedhilge, Vol. I; Cnuasacht de na Sean-Amhránaibh is áilne agus is mó clú* (Dublin 1921).

98 NÍ ÓGÁIN, Róis, *Duanaire Gaedhilge, Vol. II; Amhráin agus Dánta do scríobh Filidhe do mhair idir 1600 agus 1800* (Dublin 1924).

99 NÍ ÓGÁIN, Róis, *Duanaire Gaedhilge, Vol. III; Dánta Staireamhla, Dánta Diadha, Laoidhthe Fiannaidheachta, Trí Truagha na Sgéalaidheachta, agus eile* (Educational Company of Ireland, Dublin 1930)

100 BREATHNACH and NÍ MHURCHÚ, op. cit., p. 116.

101 *Irish Book Lover*, March–April 1930.

102 *An tUltach*, April 1930.

103 BREATHNACH and NÍ MHURCHÚ, op. cit., p.116

104 YOUNG, Rose M., 'Irish in Rathlin' in *Irisleabhar na Gaedhilge (The Gaelic Journal)* Vol. 6 (Dec. 1895) pp 139–40.

105 NÍ ÓGÁIN, Róis, 'Irish Piety as shown in Greetings, Phrases and occasional Prayers' in *The Gaelic Churchman*, Vol. I (Nov. 1919) pp 7–9.

106 McCANN, Jack, 'Margaret Dobbs' in *The Glynns: Journal of the Glens of Antrim Historical Society*, Vol. 11 (1983) p. 43.

107 *Northern Whig*, 23 June 1921.

108 HANKINSON, C.F.J. (ed.), *Debrett's Peerage, Baronetage, Knightage, and Companionage* (London 1952) p. 2042.

109 *Who's Who 1938* (London 1938) p. 3735.

110 BYRNE and McMAHON, *Great Northerners.*

111 SCOTT, Patrick, 'Robert Lynd: Eloquent Listener', *Irish Times* 23 April, 1979, p. 13.

112 FITZGERALD, Garret, *All in a Life; An Autobiography* (Dublin 1991) p. 3.

113 ARNOLD, J.C., *R.M. Jones of Inst: A Memoir* (Belfast 1952) p. 31.

114 [COMBE, H.T.] *The Dowry of the Past: The Story of Berry Street Presbyterian Church* (Belfast 1969).

115 'Speech of R.J. Lynd' in *The Cooke Centenary. Commemorative Addresses illustrative of the life of Rev. Henry Cooke D.D., L.LD.* (Belfast 1888).

116 BRIAN DONN, 'The Sentiment of Ireland' in *Guth na nGaedheal* (March 1906) pp 5–7.

117 UA FHLOINN, Riobárd, 'A Plea for Extremists ...' in *Uladh: A Literary and Critical Magazine.* Lughnasa Number (September 1905).

118 LYND, Robert, 'The Driver' in *Selected Essays* (London 1923) p. 79.

119 LYND, Robert, *Ireland a Nation* (New York 1920) p. 187.

120 LYND, Robert, *Home Life in Ireland* (London 1910) pp IX–X.

121 ibid., p. 92.

122 ibid., pp 106–07.

123 ibid., p. 137.

124 ibid., pp 180–81.

125 ibid., p. 313.

126 SCOTT, 'Robert Lynd', op. cit.

127 McMAHON, Sean (ed.), *Galway of the Races: Selected Essays: Robert Lynd* (Dublin 1990) p. 42.

128 Ó DROIGHNEÁIN, Muiris,

'Letter' in *An tUltach*, Vol. 36, Number 11 (Nov. 1959) p. 9

129 Ó DUIBHÍN, Ciarán, 'Aoidhmín Mac Gréagóir, 1884–1950 in *An tUltach*, Vol. 71, Number 3 (Mar. 1994).

130 *Medical Directory for 1875.* Courtesy of Mr Michael Bott, Keeper of Archives, University of Reading.

131 ibid., 1881

132 ibid., 1883–1888.

133 Ó DUIBHÍN, op. cit.

134 *An Claidheamh Solais*, Vol. II (17 March 1900) p. 9, Vol. II (14 July 1900) pp 280–81.

135 Census Return, P.R.O.I., dated 31 March 1901.

136 *Belfast News Letter*, 3 March 1903. Obituary, Mrs McMillan.

137 Will Book 1903, P.R.O.N.I. Probate of Will of Emily Miriam Louisa McMillan.

138 Census Return, 1911, P.R.O.I.

139 Mac GRÍOGÓIR, Aodhmáin and Mac CATHMHAOIL, Seaghan, *Fréamhacha na hÉireann* (Dublin 1906).

140 Mac GRÉAGÓIR, Aoidhmín, *Sgéaltan X Rachreann* (Dublin 1910).

141 O'RAHILLY, op. cit., p. 191.

142 HOLMER, Nils M., *The Irish Language in Rathlin Island, Co. Antrim* (Royal Irish Academy, 1942) p. 132.

143 Mac GIOLLA DOMHNAIGH, Gearóid and STOCKMAN, Gearóid, (eds), *Athchló Uladh* (Belfast 1991).

144 DOWNEY, Gerard and STOCKMAN, Gerard, 'From Rathlin and the Antrim Glens: Gaelic Folktales in Translation' in

Ulster Folklife, Vol. 37 (1991) pp 71–96.

145 Ó DUIBHÍN, op. cit.

146 DINNEEN, Patrick S., *Foclóir Gaedhilge agus Béarla: An Irish-English Dictionary* (Irish Texts Society, Dublin 1927) pp xiii, xxiii.

147 Personal communication, from Tomás Ó hÉanáinn, dated August 1984.

148 UA CNAIMHSÍ, Pádraig, 'Seosamh Mac Grianna agus Polaitíocht na Linne Sin' in *An tUltach*, Vol. 69 (July 1992) p. 11.

149 CÚ ULADH, *Ciall na Sean-Ráidhte* (Coiste Ceanntair Bhéal Feirste, Belfast 1914).

150 de BLAGHD, Earnán, *Trasna na Bóinne (Over the Boyne)* (Dublin 1957) p. 16.

151 ibid, p. 17.

152 BOYLAN, *A Dictionary of Irish Biography*, p. 25.

153 BYRNE and MacMAHON, *Great Northerners*, p.12.

154 Mac ANNA, Tomás 'The Spirit that was Blythe', *Irish Times*, 24 January, 1990.

155 de BLAGHD, Earnán, Vol. 1: *Trasna na Bóinne* (1957); Vol. 2: *Slán le hUltaibh* (1970); Vol. 3: *Gaeil A Muscailt* (1973) (Sáirséal agus Dill, Dublin).

156 de BLAGHD, Earnán, *Briseadh na Teorann* (Dublin 1955) p. 7.

157 *WHO'S WHO ... IN IRELAND* (London 1973) p. 28

158 *Prospectus of the The Gaelic Fellowship (City Y.M.C.A.).*

159 PASKER, John, Letter in *The Church of Ireland Gazette*, 31 January, 1947.

160 DORNAN, W.E., *One Hundred Eventful Years, 1850–1950: An*

Outline History of the City of Belfast Y.M.C.A. (1950) p. 81.

161 Mac CON MIDHE, Pádraig, 'Gael Eile Imithe (Another Gael Gone)' in *An tUltach*, Vol. 42, No. 11 (November 1965) p. 13.

162 ibid.

163 *Inniu*, 2 October 1965. Obituary, Sean Pasker.

164 Ó GLAISNE, Risteárd, 'Seán Pasker' in *Feasta*, Vol. 36 (January 1983) p. 4.

165 ibid., p.8.

166 NÍ BHRIAIN, Eibhlín, 'Tuarascáil' *Irish Times*, 2 February 1983.

167 BAILIE, et al., op. cit., p. 740.

168 CANDIDA, 'An Irishwoman's Diary' *Irish Times*, 24 March 1980, p. 9.

169 *Department of Health and Social Services: Registrar General Northern Ireland. The Northern Ireland Census 1991: Summary Report* (H.M.S.O. 1992) p. 159.

170 'Protestant and Gaelic'. Television film shown on BBC 2, 2 February 1990.

171 ADAMSON, Ian (ed.), *The Battle of Moira: being the Epic Poem 'Congal' by Samuel Ferguson* (Printed by the *Newtownards Chronicle*, 1980).

172 McCAUGHEY, Terence P., *Irish Times*, 12 February 1981.

173 McGIMPSEY, Christopher, 'Tuarascáil', *Irish Times*, 21 October 1992, p. 15.

174 ibid.

175 'Tuarascáil', *Irish Times*, 20 May 1990.

176 Constitutional Case, *Irish Times*, 20 May 1990,

177 *Inniu*, 8 November 1974. He gave a talk to the Advertising and

Public Relations Circle on Unionists
and the Irish language, etc.
178 *Sunday Press*, 6 April 1980.
179 Mac ARTHUR, Colán,
Dunfanaghy Congregation (1978)
p. 49.
180 STOTHERS, op. cit., p. 132.
181 ibid., pp 5, 134.
182 ULTACH Trust. *First Annual
Report* (Belfast 1991) p. 19.
183 STRINGER, Peter and
ROBINSON, Gillian (eds), *Social
Attitudes in Northern Ireland*
(1991) p. 18.

APPENDIX
1 *The Northern Ireland Census 1991:
Summary Report. Department of
Health and Social Services Registrar
General* (Her Majesty's Stationery
Office, Belfast 1992) p. 159.
2 Letter dated 25 Feb. 1992 to
DENI from Séamus de Napier,
Chairman, The European Bureau
for Lesser Used Languages (NI
Subcommittee).

3 Ulster Marketing Surveys Limited.
Irish Language – Potential for
Educational Programmes. Omnibus
Survey, carried out for Ulster
Television Limited, May 1985.
4 SWEENEY, Kevin 'The Irish
Language in Northern Ireland
1987', *Policy, Planning and
Research Unit, Occasional Paper
No. 17* (August 1988).
5 Personal Communication from
Dolores Mhic Geidigh, BBC
Radio Foyle, 8 June 1989.
6 *Irish Times* 'Tuarascáil', 16
October 1991, p. 9.
7 ADAMSON, Ian, *The Identity of
Ulster: the Land the Language and
the People* (Belfast 1982) p. 81.
8 *The Northern Ireland Census 1991:
Irish Language Report. Department
of Health and Social Services*.
Registrar General (H.M.S.O.,
Belfast 1993).

INDEX